HOW THE VOTE WAS WON
And Other Suffragette Plays

DALE SPENDER is an Australian writer and researcher who has lived and worked in London for the last ten years. Educated on a curriculum of 'womanless history' she was convinced that women had no past and has never fully recovered from her astonishment at discovering that women have indeed a glorious past but that it has been suppressed. She now devotes much of her energy to recovering and publicising that past.

She is the author of *Man Made Language* (Routledge and Kegan Paul, 1980), *Invisible Women* (Writers' and Readers', 1982), *Women of Ideas and What Men Have Done to Them*, (Routledge and Kegan Paul, 1982), *There's Always Been a Women's Movement* (Pandora Press, 1983), *For the Record* (The Women's Press, 1985). She is editor of *Learning to Lose* with Elizabeth Sarah (The Women's Press, 1980), *Men's Studies Modified* (Pergamon Press, 1981), *Feminist Theorists* (The Women's Press, 1983) and *Time and Tide Wait for No Man* (Pandora Press, 1984). She also edits *Women's Studies International Forum*.

With her sister, Lynne Spender, she has written *Scribbling Sisters* (Hale and Iremonger, 1984) and forthcoming is *Mothers of the Novel* (Routledge and Kegan Paul), and with Sally Cline, *Reflecting Men* (Andre Deutsch).

She has an abiding interest in the theatre, and once wanted to go on the stage. Her great regret is that she cannot perform in any of these suffrage plays.

CAROLE HAYMAN is a graduate of Leeds University and Bristol Old Vic Theatre School. She is an actress and director with a long track record in innovative work. After a year at the Bristol Old Vic Theatre she joined the Traverse Theatre Workshop in Edinburgh, a company specialising in the work of new writers. She did plays by Howard Brenton, John Spurling, Snoo Wilson, David Edgar and Stanley Eveling. In 1974 she was a founder member of Joint Stock Theatre Company and began appearing in plays at the Royal Court Theatre. In ten years she has played in over twenty productions there, including *As Time Goes By* (Mustapha Matura), *Magnificence* (Howard Brenton), *Light Shining in Buckinghamshire* (Caryl Churchill), *Wheelchair Willie* (Alan Brown), *Cloud Nine* (Caryl Churchill), *Sugar and Spice* (Nigel Williams) and most recently *Top Girls* (Caryl Churchill), for which she won an Obie. She also claims to be on the cover of more Methuen Playscripts than anyone she knows. In 1980 she began directing and was responsible for bringing to the Royal Court the work of Sarah Daniels (*Ripen Our Darkness*, 1980) and Sue Townsend (*Bazaar and Rummage*, 1982). She has also directed at the Soho Poly Theatre and in 1984 was the first woman to direct a play for Joint Stock Theatre Company. *The Great Celestial Cow* was researched by herself and the company and written by Sue Townsend.

Carole is currently commissioned to write a series for Yorkshire Television and has a new Joint Stock project in preparation.

Front cover photograph: BBC Hulton Picture Library

HOW THE VOTE WAS WON

And Other Suffragette Plays

HOW THE VOTE WAS WON
by
Cicely Hamilton and Christopher St John

VOTES FOR WOMEN
by
Elizabeth Robins

LADY GERALDINE'S SPEECH
by
Beatrice Harraden

A CHAT WITH MRS CHICKY
and
MISS APPLEYARD'S AWAKENING
by
Evelyn Glover

A WOMAN'S INFLUENCE
by
Gertrude Jennings

THE APPLE
by
Inez Bensusan

Researched by
Candida Lacey

Introduced by
Dale Spender

With notes for performance by
Carole Hayman

A Methuen Theatrefile
Methuen · London and New York

A METHUEN PAPERBACK

This volume first published in Great Britain in 1985
by Methuen London Ltd, 11 New Fetter Lane, London EC4P 4EE
and in the United States of America,
by Methuen Inc, 29 West 35th Street, New York, NY 10001

How the vote was won: and other suffragette plays
— (A Methuen theatrefile)
1. English drama — 20th century   2. Women —
Suffrage — Drama
I. Spender, Dale   II. Hayman, Carole
822'.912'080358   PR1272

ISBN 0-413-58380-5

Printed in Great Britain

CONTENTS

ACKNOWLEDGEMENTS

Without the detective skills of Candida Lacey, some of these plays could never have been reclaimed. For all her perseverence, perspicacity and patience, I would like to thank her enormously.

To David Doughan of the Fawcett Library, and to all those people who have worked to ensure that the Fawcett Library continues to preserve women's heritage, I owe much. Without their efforts I would not have known of the existence of these plays and I would have had much less chance of being able to locate them.

Jane Marcus, who has been a source of inspiration when it comes to Elizabeth Robins, deserves much praise, and I would like to thank Julie Holledge for her book *Innocent Flowers: Women in the Edwardian Theatre*, on which I have drawn for some of my information.

Mabel Smith who has carefully preserved the papers, publications and image of Elizabeth Robins merits many thanks, and I am grateful to her for her copy of *Votes for Women* and for her permission to reprint it; likewise I am grateful to Sir Leslie Bower for permission to reprint the work of Cicely Hamilton.

Every effort has been made to trace the copyright holders of the plays reprinted here, but sometimes that has not proved possible.

Dale Spender, January 1985.

INTRODUCTION

When last century some women decided that they wanted the vote, they found themselves in quite a predicament. For the only way women could get the vote was by persuading the all-male Members of Parliament to give it to them. One difficulty was that there was no reason that the Members of Parliament should take any notice of people who did *not* have the vote. Such men may have been readily responsive to their constituents who *could* vote – and who could vote for or against them at the next election – but they had no need to listen to the women who had no political influence.

This was the problem the women faced when they began their campaign for women's suffrage; while they had no vote they were of no account in political circles and while they were of no account in political circles there was no way they could win the vote. And if this wasn't a big enough obstacle, they also had to deal with many Members of Parliament who were outrightly opposed to women's suffrage. There were men in Parliament who saw the vote as a symbol of power and privilege which rightfully belonged exclusively to the male sex and who were adamant that they would never be so foolish as to vote away their own supremacy – by granting the vote to women!

So the women were not at all sure as to how they should proceed. How could they *persuade* men to take notice of them and to give up their male power? The only sensible strategy that suggested itself to the women was a 'policy of good behaviour'. If they were to prove themselves worthy of the vote – so reasoned the campaigners for women's suffrage – if they were to show that they were reasonable and responsible human beings, then surely men would be obliged to concede that there were no good grounds for denying women the vote. And when there was no argument *against* giving women the vote, why then it would be granted.

For more than thirty years women adopted the policy of good behaviour. From 1866 when women organised the first petition for women's suffrage (which John Stuart Mill presented to Parliament: for of course the women were not allowed to do so), women worked to prove that they were fit persons to exercise the vote. They used every existing consitutional means to promote their 'cause'. They formed suffrage societies, held meetings, wrote to Members of Parliament, organised floods of telegrams to protest at behaviour in the House (or occasionally to congratulate Members on their support). They embarked on an educational programme designed to convince the whole society that the world could be a better place if women and men were to have equal citizenship. And above all, they were good!

The women were determined that not a breath of scandal should touch their suffrage societies. They insisted that there be no acts of unwomanly or unlady-like behaviour, no indecorous comments or deeds which could be used against them. Even when they were misled by politicians – who repeatedly promised to consider women's suffrage during the elections but who never mentioned it once they succeeded in entering the House – even when they were angry, frustrated and bitter about the way they were being treated, the women still maintained their stance of good behaviour and addressed men in the most respectful and politest of terms. For they genuinely believed that an unblemished record as decent and proper women was their strongest claim for the franchise.

But the policy did not work. At the end of the nineteenth century women were no closer to getting the vote than they had been when they first raised the issue. On the contrary, the passing of more than thirty years had allowed the opposition to women's suffrage to become well organised and there was almost a ritual of ridicule in Parliament whenever 'the ladies' were mentioned. Women were still without any political influence and nowhere was this more apparent than on the floor of the House where women were invariably treated as a joke. And to make matters worse, all those many years of 'good behaviour' were often mocked.

More than one generation of women had put their energy into peaceful and polite persuasion only to become figures of fun in the press and in Parliament. It was partly because they had been so good that they could be accused of not being serious about suffrage. Men, it was pointed out, had been obliged to fight for the vote; men had staged demonstrations, even riots, and had made it clear how many of them wanted the vote and how far they were prepared to go to get it. Yet where were the women's protests and uprisings?

The policy of good behaviour had dictated that women should avoid publicity. Concerned to protect their womanly reputations, to avoid infamy and notoriety, women had conducted their campaigns most discreetly. But it was this very exemplary behaviour which now lay them open to the charge that they were not prepared to stand up and be counted. It was not even possible to say how many women wanted the vote – ran the argument against them – when women had behaved in such a retiring manner. And as there was no obvious *public* demand, declared many a clever politician, it would be nothing short of irresponsible to force the vote on women who may not desire it.

By the beginning of the twentieth century, however, yet another generation of young women had joined the ranks of the campaigners for women's suffrage. And when they came to sum up the situation they concluded – not unsurprisingly – that the policy of good behaviour hadn't worked. It had got them nowhere and was being used against them. The suffrage movement had become bogged down in their view, and needed new life. Not for them the practice of polite and deferential requests; not for them patience and restraint. For not only had the policy of the past been a futile one they insisted, it had also been demeaning. It allowed men to sneer and jeer at women – and then ignore the case, anyway. They wanted VOTES FOR WOMEN and they wanted them NOW! And they too were prepared to fight for what they wanted.

It was no good being good argued the new strategists Christabel Pankhurst and Teresa Billington. Why should men give women the vote while women were being so polite, patient, reasonable – and good? Everything was going so smoothly for men that they had no incentive to change their minds. But what would be the response of the men if women started making trouble, if women made so much trouble that it was easier to give them the vote than it was to withhold it?

This was the political logic behind the new suffrage society, the Women's Social and Political Union (formed in Manchester in October 1903). Not *good* conduct, but *bad* conduct became the order of the day with this new movement. Women were encouraged to stop being womanly, to stop shunning publicity, to stop being respectful and reasonable to the politicians. Instead, women were to make nuisances of themselves, to ask awkward questions at political meetings, to list the lies that they had been fed and to generally start making fun of political figures who had for so long been making fun of women and their demand for the vote.

Some of the older members of the suffrage societies were horrified at this new trend. When in 1905 Christabel Pankhurst and Annie Kenney asked questions at a political meeting and ended up in prison as a result – and it was front page news in all the papers

– there were cries that these two were a disgrace to their sex and that they had put the cause back fifty years. Millicent Garrett Fawcett (whose credentials were impeccable – she had been a leader of the constitutional movement since she had helped with that first petition in 1866) was not quite so quick to pass judgement. These new women (later to be termed the 'suffragettes' to distinguish them from the better behaved 'suffragists') had done more in a day to put women's suffrage on the public agenda, she said, than the consitutionalists had done in a decade. And although she did not join the suffragettes in their 'outrageous' acts, she continued to concede their value in making society, politicians included, sit up and take notice of the demand – VOTES FOR WOMEN – NOW!

Women *were* gaining political influence, and at the same time were helping to construct the public demand. With such visibility – and audibility – it was becoming increasingly difficult for the women to be ignored.

The new strategy of troublemaking, however, still had its critics, even among some of the most ardent supporters of suffrage, partly because it amounted to a declaration of war. The 'gloves were off' and men were 'fair game' and the suffragettes were held responsible for ushering in an era of 'sex antagonism' with women on one side and men on the other. Then, as now, many people were uncomfortable with the idea of a sex war and rather than criticise men for protecting their power and privilege, they were ready to blame the suffragettes for promoting division between the sexes. Unfortunately, the debate sometimes reached the stage where it was not whether women's suffrage was right or wrong that was the issue, but whether the suffragettes were right or wrong.

Yet the suffragettes were by no means the harridans that history has often painted them. True, they were impatient, but who wouldn't have been after all those years? True, they did cause a lot of trouble, but they were taunted to action by some of the most respected political figures of the day. And there was little likelihood that they would abandon their tactics because they were criticised – for it was obvious that their new policy was working.

Looking back on their exploits one thing that stands out is their immense energy, vitality, enthusiasm, high spirits. This does not mean they were not serious about women's rights – they were deadly serious as their sufferings on hunger strike indicated – but it was an exhilarating and joyous struggle in which they were engaged. They felt that there was 'the spirit of a new age' in the air, and they saw themselves as its representatives. They were serious enough to insist on woman-only societies, but at the same time they used their new-found political acumen to organise some of the most publicity-generating pranks.

For women who had been reared under the rigid constraints of late Victorian and Edwardian times it must have been liberating to take charge of their own lives and to embark on their programme of shocking activities. And all in the name of a good cause. These exuberant suffragettes 'arrived in all sorts of guises, and appeared in all sorts of places', wrote Ray Strachey, herself a campaigner for women's rights, but of a more constitutional mould. 'Now one would appear as a messenger boy. Once they chained themselves to the railing in Downing Street, and so gained time to make longish speeches before being hauled off to Bow Street; another was found chained to a statue in the lobby of the House of Commons, a thoroughly strategic position. They sprang out of organ lofts, they peered through roof windows, and leapt out of innocent looking furniture vans; they materialised on station platforms, they harangued the terrace of the House from the river, and whenever they were least expected, they were there.' (*The Cause*, 1928; p. 312).

They curtsied to the King and demanded the vote, they organised huge parades, processions and demonstrations, and they dug up the golf greens of England leaving behind the message, 'No Votes – No golf!'. They would do anything to get their message across and to have the world know that women wanted the vote and that it was unreasonable to deny them.

Of course, the vote was by no means all they wanted. It was but a symbol of equality, a starting point for raising the whole range of equality issues from equal pay to equal grounds for divorce, from equal work to an equal moral standard. And few were the women who were unaffected by these issues; whether it was a working-class woman who was required to work for lower wages than a man (and who was required to run a home as well) or a middle-class woman who was required to live in idleness and dependence, the demand for an end to *sex disability* swept through society and became one of the most talked-about topics. Women in every occupation – and women who wanted to enter *every* occupation – were caught up in the campaign for sex equality and the vote.

Actresses were no exception. They had numerous reasons for wanting sex equality. Not without cause they wanted a code of sexual conduct which was the same for both sexes, for why should they be branded as 'loose' and 'indecent' for going on the stage when no such condemnation applied to men? And they wanted equal pay. But more fundamentally they wanted then (as so many actresses want now) an equal chance to perform good parts in the theatre. There were so few plays with strong roles for women. Almost without exception the plays were written by men and when women did appear it was generally to support the men and in such narrow and stereotyped roles as dutiful wives that the actresses could find little challenge or satisfaction in playing such parts.

Part of the problem was the way in which the theatrical world was organised. Theatres were run by actor-managers who selected the plays for performance, and not surprisingly they made their decisions with a view to casting themselves centre-stage. So when the actresses protested that they were working in a male dominated profession, they had ample evidence to support their case. Men were responsible for deciding what was performed, they made their choices from plays written by men, and they generally selected plays in which the major parts were for men. Because there were fewer parts for women, and because they were invariably rigidly stereotyped, some of the greatest actresses of the time could find themselves in a real quandary when they were offered a 'big part', but one which portrayed a woman in one of the limited and negative roles of either the 'wicked woman' or 'virtue personified'. The actresses wanted not just more parts, but better parts, and the most sensible way of achieving these aims, was to have more women making the decisions in the theatre. For despite all the seeming independence of the women on the stage, it did not escape the attention of many of the actresses that they were as dependent on the decisions of men as were middle-class wives in the home. And as some of the most spirited women of the day had 'gone on the stage' precisely because they wished to be genuinely independent of men, it is understandable that they should have started to cause trouble in the theatre, as they did at political meetings.

Sometimes it was the same women who did both. Elizabeth Robins for example, was a member of the Women's Social and Political Union; she was also a leading actress and author and it was inconceivable to her that women should fight for equality in the political arena, and not at their work place. For years she had been frustrated by the male domination of the theatre – by the absence of opportunity for women playwrights, directors and actresses – and because she wanted a fair deal for women in the theatre she helped to start the Actresses' Franchise League.

In December 1908 the first public meeting of the Actresses' Franchise League was held in the Criterion Restaurant in London. It was a glittering affair with four hundred actresses present, including some of the stars such as Ellen Terry, Violet Vanbrugh, Eva Moore and Decima Moore, Evelyn Sharp and Cicely Hamilton. That so many women attended indicated that the actresses had already in large measure been 'converted to the cause' and many of them were members of the militant groups (the Women's Social and Political Union, and the Women's Freedom League) or of the constitutional group (the National Union of Women's Suffrage Societies). Because they did not want to be distracted by a debate over which group had the right 'tactics', the members of the League decided from the outset to support *all* suffrage societies and to use their professional skills to further the campaign for the enfranchisement of women. But this was only one of the aims of the League; another was to set the theatrical world in order and to make the theatre a better place for women.

While many of the actresses sympathised with and supported the militants it was not all that easy for them to engage in political agitation, *and* to appear nightly in the theatre. This was because so many militants were arrested and imprisoned and as, in the main, actresses were working women, they simply could not afford to miss the curtain up or to damage their prospects for future employment. Kitty Marion was one member of the League however, who was a militant (and who was repeatedly imprisoned) and who eventually had to give up her theatrical career, but not before she had done her share of agitation back stage where she protested vehemently about the use of the 'casting couch' means of obtaining employment.

If they couldn't break windows, dig up golf courses – or sail over the House of Commons in a balloon bearing the bold demand VOTES FOR WOMEN – there were many other things that the actresses could do to support 'the cause'. It was not uncommon at the time for a political meeting to include a performance item – a song, recitation or dance, presumably to break the monotony – and while there was absolutely no need to introduce such 'events' to hold the attention of women at suffrage meetings, when the actresses did begin to appear on the platforms and to recite, their efforts were much appreciated. Encouraged by their success and stimulated by the political atmosphere at meetings, parades and demonstrations, it was not long before some of the actresses began to think of bigger and better things.

Why not write and act speeches which were specifically suited to the occasion? Why not a character-sketch or a monologue that contained some of the arguments for the vote? Why not, indeed! And out of this need emerged a sort of one-woman political theatre. 'Entertainment' became part of the suffrage gatherings and was enormously popular – and effective. The actress, in costume and with stage props, could give a performance which ranged from a serious appeal for women's rights to an hilarious exposé of the 'Antis' (those who were anti-suffrage). Drama and political agitation were soon proceeding hand in hand.

From monologues it was not such a big step to duologues; and from duologues it was not such a big step to full-length plays.

As more and more suffrage societies requested appearances from members of the Actresses' Franchise League at their gatherings, the League decided to set up a special play department to meet the demand. In charge of the department was an Australian, Inez Bensusan, who was well qualified for the job. Not only had she been on the stage in Australia, she was also a writer – of short stories and suffrage articles – and she was completely committed to the development of women's theatre.

Inez Bensusan had problems to begin with. She needed plays for the actresses to perform – purpose-written suffrage plays which could achieve the dual aim of stimulating the supporters while winning over the opponents. She needed a full time company of actresses who could go on tour and be organised to get from one suffrage gathering to another. And she needed money. Yet she had none of these when she started. No suitable plays. No permanent actresses, only those who were willing to work for suffrage part time, on their days off. And she had no money. Still, despite all the obstacles, the play department was fuelled by enthusiasm and began to function, staging its first performances at a Votes for Women Exhibition at the Prince's Skating Rink in Knightsbridge in 1909. For a week while the Exhibition lasted, there were five performances a day of the eighteen different acts that had been prepared, and the audience was sufficiently pleased to contribute £369.19.6 to the coffers.

Women who had not previously written plays – partly because it was such a futile business with so little chance of them being performed in the actor-managers' theatres – were drafted in to write for the League. Novelists such as Beatrice Harraden were persuaded by Inez Bensusan to try their hand at suffrage theatre, and Gertrude Jennings, Madeline Lucette Ryley and Cicely Hamilton all made use of this new opportunity for women's theatre. And it was a play of Cicely Hamilton's – written with Chris St. John otherwise known as Christabel Marshall – which was the League's first smash hit *How the Vote Was Won*.

For women in the theatre, this was a glorious time. If they had been minimised in the mainstream theatre they had certainly not been demoralised for with the establishment of the Actresses' Franchise League they had created an alternative and inspirational drama of their own. And it was self-consciously women's drama, a drama which reflected their interests and which was built on their priorities as women. The affirmation and confidence they derived from writing, producing and staging their own popular propaganda plays around the country, not only helped to strengthen their resolve for the vote (and to do likewise for their audiences) but also fortified them to make their demands within mainstream theatre. In 1911, the women confronted the theatrical establishment, as one actress, Lena Ashwell, explained:

'At the time of the coronation of King George and Queen Mary a gala performance was arranged to take place at His Majesty's Theatre. The arrangements were advertised, a programme of plays in which all the leading actors of the day could take part with just two or three women needed to support them. I appealed to Sir Charles Wyndham that it would be a matter of discussion for the Manager's Association, out of courtesy, to include a play in which the women might appear. Nothing was done, however, so I composed a letter to Her Majesty, the Queen, expressing the regret of the actresses that we were excluded. I submitted a copy to Sir Charles with a note saying that, unless something was done, I should most certainly send the letter. Sir Charles told me that the association had decided to do nothing. The meeting had, indeed, broken up when he said that it would be as well for them to hear the letter which I was sending, and they all hastily sat down to review the situation. I was given twenty-four hours to get the approval of the actresses and find a suitable play in which they could appear. Both these obstacles were easily overcome as everyone wanted to be included and I had already produced *The Vision of Delight* by Ben Jonson for the benefit performance at the Kingsway and had had special music written for it. On that memorable night this little masque ended the programme.' (Lena Ashwell, *Myself a Player*, pp. 167-8; quoted in Julie Holledge, *Innocent Flowers: Women in the Edwardian Theatre*, Virago, 1981; p. 77).

It is extremely difficult to divorce art and politics in this context. For women for whom the politics of male domination restricted their opportunities to practise their art, as writers, directors and performers, it would not have been possible to separate the art from the politics. Nor would the distinction between the two have become clearer once women started to practise their art on the suffrage stage in a political setting of their own making. But because among some of those who pass judgement on what is good art –and what is not – there is a firm belief that art and politics do not mix, it is not uncommon to find the assessment that the women's political theatre of the first decades of the twentieth century was not good art.

I do not agree with this assessment; in fact I do not agree with the division between art and politics itself. Because the plays that the women produced were for propaganda purposes, they aren't by definition bad plays. To my mind, this period of political ferment helped to produce an exciting and entertaining drama which I can thoroughly enjoy and appreciate today. So many of the incidents dramatised are still relevant today (from plays about men not doing the housework – even when the women are in paid work – to plays about boys getting more than their fair share of resources and at the expense of girls) that they have not lost their appeal. They deserve to be read – and performed – in their own right, for the insights they continue to offer.

These plays have added dimensions as well. They are part of women's political and theatrical history. They are an expression of the policy of bad behaviour, for with their mockery, their elements of farce, and their blatant disrespect for men, they could never have been written during the nineteenth century when women were still trying to win men's approval for votes for women. These plays are part of that spirit of optimism, that faith in a new age, which was represented not just in the area of party-politics or the Actresses' Franchise League but also in the Artists' Franchise League and the Women Writers' Suffrage League. This was a time when women's creativity bloomed, when the first Women's Press was established and when there were scores of pamphlets, periodicals, articles and journals published by and about women. It was a time when feminist fiction (some written by Elizabeth Robins) and feminist non-fiction (such as Cicely Hamilton's *Marriage as a Trade*) was appearing with increased frequency, when Rebecca West was embarking on her journalistic career at *The Freewoman*, when Sylvia Pankhurst was putting her art at the service of the suffrage movement and Ethel Smyth was composing the stirring *March of the Women*. What was happening in the theatre had its parallels in the other branches of the arts, for this was an era when women flourished, when they broke with oppressive conventions and male dominance, took matters into their own hands and tried all manner of occupations. It is a period of women's history of which we should be rightfully proud.

Yet like so many other aspects of women's creative and cultural past, these plays have languished among the obscure and forgotten. The explanation for their neglect lies not within the plays themselves but in the fact that more than sixty years later the aim of sex equality still has not been achieved. The actor-managers may have gone but their successors are still men who continue to make selections from plays written mostly by men and with the best parts for men. So unusual is it for a woman playwright to find an opening on the mainstream stage that whenever one does appear she is generally hailed as the first of her kind. But since Aphra Behn took up her pen in the seventeenth century and wrote some of her propagandising feminist plays, women have proved that they can write drama, and good drama, and all that they require is an equal chance. The plays included here are part of that heritage of good women's writing, and part of the tradition of working for an equal chance.

Dale Spender, 1985

When I first began working as an actress, I appeared almost exclusively in plays by men. I had very little idea that there were any plays by women and nor, it seems, had the men who ran the theatres in which I worked. That was sixty years after the plays in this volume were written and performed. I am happy to say that I eventually saw the error of my ways (though it took ten years to undo entrenched ideas received through a thoroughly male education) but I can't say that the State of the Art has changed that much during my time in theatre. Today, of course, there are some plays written and performed by women, even a few are directed by women; a 1983 survey by the Conference of Women Theatre Directors and Administrators found that 11% of all plays being produced were by women and 12% were directed by them, not exactly a record to sit back on. Achieving a proper balance of female to male at work is clearly very hard. One has the impression of a very large brick wall standing impervious, whilst successive waves of small women run at it with their heads down; result, bleeding foreheads. The arbiters of taste in our society are still almost all male and that includes the people who put on plays. If monkeys ran theatres presumably they'd mount plays by other monkeys and monkey critics would prefer them to, let's say, plays by gnus . . .

As recently as 1984 I had a conversation with a well known writer friend in which she said jokingly, that she was considering writing her next play under a male pseudonym. She was curious to see if it would provoke the same patronising 'didn't she do well' type of review, as the rest of her work. We agreed that, whatever else, it would certainly be taken much more seriously and we had a good giggle over what the reaction would be, if, after stunning accolades, she revealed herself as a gnaughty gnu. She'd probably have to flee the country.

This conversation seems to me typical of womens' rueful acknowledgement of the state of play and also of the anarchy and humour that distinguishes their work. It's a volatile and unpretentious mix and it's a strong element in all the plays gathered here. They ruffle, provoke, instruct and amuse; in may ways they are the natural forerunners of some of the best plays of our time. I'm thinking of *Top Girls* by Caryl Churchill, *Ripen Our Darkness* by Sarah Daniels and *The Great Celestial Cow* by Sue Townsend, all notable for their wit, practical everyday content and challenging perspective. Though word of mouth has made these plays cult classics, none of them were well received in the press or won any glittering prizes. Obviously too gnu-like. Women in theatre are still fighting a tough battle for credibility, not least of all with their own sex. A member of the audience of *Top Girls* was heard to remark over the interval gin and tonic that the play was really very enjoyable and not boring at all, despite having no men in it. The speaker was a woman. Which all goes to show how far we have to go before the aims of the Actresses' Franchise League are achieved. These plays have much to offer as a starting point; they are funny, direct, simple and rousing. Their subject is as relevant today as it was in 1910; though we have the vote, we are still not equal. I hope they will be performed and their performance will encourage other women to seek out their own culture and not, like me, wait ten years to discover that they have one.

The beauty of all these plays is that they can be done very simply and cheaply. A minimum of set and costume, a few props, unfussy staging, will bring them swiftly to life. It might be good to try them without set and in modern dress to really bring the parallels home. The style they are written in would have been very familiar to Edwardian audiences brought up on melodrama, comedy of manners, and the cautionary tale. They expected to laugh, cry and be taught a moral they could chew on in the pub. The acting of the period tended to be rather hammy and sentimental, nowadays a more robust naturalism would be appropriate. I would recommend a light touch with characterisations and a resistance to hammering the message. The text takes care of the latter very adequately and the more truthful and 'real' the performances, the more the arguments will be felt. This shouldn't in any way restrict the fun of a play like *How The Vote Was Won* which calls for classic farce playing, or the drama of *Votes For Women* which has some very emotional scenes.

Carole Hayman, 1985

HOW THE VOTE WAS WON

HOW THE VOTE WAS WON
Cicely Hamilton and Christopher St John
(First produced at the Royalty Theatre, London, on 13 April, 1909)

This play began as a pamphlet, written by Cicely Hamilton, illustrated by C. Hedley-Charlton and published in 1908 by the Women Writers' Suffrage League (of which Cicely Hamilton was a member). The pamphlet was so successful and entertaining that its theatrical potential was quickly perceived and Cicely Hamilton found herself another collaborator, Christopher St John (Christabel Marshall), and the two of them soon wrote this lively play.
The vote, of course was a long way from being won, but some of the creative thinkers of the women's movement had clear ideas about how their goal could be achieved. The play opens with women everywhere going on strike and reporting to their nearest male relative to be supported. If men were going to argue that woman did not need the vote because they were 'looked after' by men, then women should take men at their word and insist on being looked after. Confronted with a houseful of female relatives who have all given up their jobs and come to be supported, the anti-suffrage hero, Horace Cole, (who earns £3.10.00 a week) soon realises the error of his ways and rushes from the house to join the throngs of similarly converted men who are marching on Parliament to demand that the government give votes to women – now!)

That Cicely Hamilton should have come up with an economic argument for women's suffrage was not all surprising; her best-selling book *Marriage as a Trade* was an analysis of women's economic exploitation and she had definite ideas about how this exploitation could be ended and how women could achieve economic and psychological independence. Nor was it surprising that Cicely Hamilton should try her hand at playwrighting; she had begun her own working life as an actress. *How the Vote Was Won* was not her first venture into the theatrical world. She had written plays from the 1890s onwards, although she did not always acknowledge them for, as she stated in her autobiography, *Life Errant* (1935), managers, 'warned me that it was advisable to conceal the sex of its author until after the notices were out, as plays which were known to be written by women were apt to get bad reviews' (p. 60). One of her later plays which she did acknowledge and which was a success was *Diana of Dobson's* which was performed at the Kingsway Theatre on 12 February, 1908.

Christopher St John was a very colourful figure. After coming down from Oxford she had worked as a secretary for Lady Randolph Churchill but she wanted to be a writer and went on to write novels. She also fell in love with Edith Craig (Ellen Terry's daughter) and it was Edith Craig (who made an enormous contribution to the theatre, particularly with her Pioneer Players) who produced *How the Vote Was Won*.

The first performance of the play was at the Royalty Theatre London on 13 April, 1909 and it was an immense success. But when it started to tour the country there were the usual difficulties because most of the original cast were committed elsewhere. Edith Craig had virtually to recast for every performance. Later however, the play had a run of its own with a permanent cast. The audience loved it; even the critics thought it was marvellous and rather than insist that propaganda and playwrighting do not mix, they took quite the opposite line;

> *The Times*: 'The audience were delighted. How could they help it? . . . The dénoument, conceived and carried out in the finest spirit of farce, reflects the highest credit on the authors.'

> *The Star*: 'Genuinely funny . . . the desolating effects of a general strike of women

workers, as observed in operation in the home of Horace Cole, clerk, of Brixton, are as significant as they are truly comic.'

The Stage: 'Beneath its fun there is a deal of propaganda which, however, rather engenders the wish that political questions could be made as lively and as pleasant in another place.'

Daily Graphic: 'It is an ingenious idea, and the play is full of clever lines. A crowded house was provoked to cheering and counter-demonstrations by the vigorous arguments.'

Pall Mall Gazette: 'The story is funny enough, but the way in which it is told is funnier still . . . The fact that it is so acutely controversial is not at all against it – is, in fact, a virtue rather than a defect, for the Theatre of Ideas is upon us. All that really matters is that it is clever and it is witty, and that it kept yesterday's audience brimming with excitement and in roars of laughter. It is in fact a long time since we have seen nearly so amusing a one-act play, and if some London manager does not snap it up for his theatre we shall be rather surprised.'

Dale Spender

Characters

HORACE COLE, *a clerk, about 30*
ETHEL, *his wife, 22*
AGATHA, *his sister*
MOLLY, *his niece*
MADAME CHRISTINE, *his distant relation*
MAUDIE SPARK, *his first cousin*
MISS LIZZIE WILKINS, *his aunt*
LILY, *his maid of all work*
GERALD WILLIAMS, *his neighbour*
WINIFRED, *Ethel's sister*

Note on Performance

This is a smashing one to begin with. A wonderfully witty cautionary tale with all the elements of a good farce. A classic one situation piece, it could be staged very simply with a table, some chairs and something to indicate fireplace and window; a fender perhaps, and a frame. If economics allow, the frame could have a painted window canvas. The doors could be offstage to save set making and the costumes could be token: Long skirts and tops with certain things featured, like Lily's hat and Winnie's badge. Full Edwardian dress isn't at all necessary unless you are going to build a complete set also. There is a wide cross section of enjoyable characters from bold Winnie to fluffy Ethel. Aunt Lizzie and Maudie Spark are gems and Horace could be played by a woman which would be a lot of fun and is the sort of theatrical treat audiences love. The irony of the ending will not be lost on any woman who still has her sense of humour. Months and months of careful strategy poured at the last minute into the weaker vessel who goes off declaring he thought of the idea in the first place!

Carole Hayman

Scene: *Sitting-room in* HORACE COLE'S *house at Brixton. The room is cheaply furnished in a genteel style. The window looks out on a row of little houses, all of the Cole patttern. The door (centre) leads into a narrow passage communicating at once with the front door. The fireplace (left) has a fancy mantel border, and over it is an overmantel, decorated with many photographs, and cheap ornaments. The sideboard (right), a small bookcase (right), a table (left centre up stage), and a comfortable armchair (centre by table), are the chief articles of furniture. The whole effect is modest, and quite unpleasing.*

Time: *Late afternoon on a spring day in any year in the future.*

When the curtain rises, MRS HORACE COLE *is sitting in the comfortable armchair (centre) putting a button on to her husband's coat. She is a pretty, fluffy little woman who could never be bad-tempered, but might be fretful. At this minute she is smiling indulgently, and rather irritatingly, at her sister* WINIFRED, *who is sitting by the fire (left) when the curtain rises, but gets up almost immediately to leave.* WINIFRED *is a tall and distinguished looking young woman with a cheerful, capable manner and an emphatic diction which betrays the public speaker. She wears the colours of the NWSPU.*

WINIFRED: Well, good-bye, Ethel. It's a pity you won't believe me. I wanted to let you and Horace down gently, or I shouldn't be here.

ETHEL: But you're always prophesying these dreadful things, Winnie, and nothing ever happens. Do you remember the day when you tried to invade the House of Commons from submarine boats? Oh, how Horace did laugh when he saw in the papers that you had all been landed on the Hovis wharf by mistake! 'By accident, on purpose!' Horace said. He couldn't stop laughing all the evening. 'What price your sister, Winifred?' he said. 'She asked for a vote, and they gave her bread.' He kept on – you can't think how funny he was about it!

WINIFRED: Oh, but I can! I know my dear brother-in-law's sense of humour is his strong point. Well, we must hope it will bear the strain that is going to be put on it today. (Of course, when his female relations invade his house – all with the same story, 'I've come to be supported' – he may think it excrutiatingly funny. One never knows.)

ETHEL: Winnie, you're teasing me. They would never do such a thing. They must know we have only one spare bedroom, and that's to be for a paying guest when we can afford to furnish it.

WINIFRED: The servants' bedroom will be empty. (Don't forget that all the domestic servants have joined the League and are going to strike, too.)

ETHEL: Not ours, Winnie. Martha is simply devoted to me, and poor little Lily *couldn't* leave. She has no home to go to. She would have to go to the workhouse.

WINIFRED: Exactly where she will go. (All those women who have no male relatives, or are refused help by those they have, have instructions to go to the relieving officer. The number of female paupers who will pour through the workhouse gates tonight all over England will frighten the Guardians into blue fits.)

ETHEL: Horace says you'll never *frighten* the Government into giving you the vote. He says every broken window is a fresh nail in the coffin of women's suffrage. It's quite true. Englishmen can't be bullied.

WINIFRED: No, but they can *bully*. It's your husband, your dear Horace, and a million other dear Horaces who are going to do the bullying and frightening this time. The women are going to stay quiet, at home. By tomorrow, perhaps before, Horace will be marching to Westminster shouting out 'Votes for Women!'

ETHEL: Winnie, how absurd you are! (You know how often you've tried to convert Horace and failed.) Is it likely that he will become a Suffragette just because–

WINIFRED: Just because–? Go on, Ethel.

ETHEL: Well, you know – all this you've been telling me about his relations coming here and asking him to support them. Of course, I don't believe it. Agatha, for instance, would never dream of giving up her situation. But if they did come Horace would just tell them he *couldn't* keep them. How could he on £4 a week?

WINIFRED: How could he? That's the point! He couldn't, of course. That's why he'll want to get rid of them at any cost – even the cost of letting women have the vote. That's why he and the majority of men in this country shouldn't for years have kept alive the foolish superstition that all women are supported by men. For years we have told them it was a delusion, but they could not take our arguments seriously. Their method of answering us was exactly that of the little boy in the street who cries 'Yah – Suffragette!' or 'Where's your "'ammer"?' when he sees my badge.

ETHEL: I always wish you wouldn't wear it when you come here . . . Horace does so dislike it. He thinks it unwomanly.

WINIFRED: Oh! does he? Tomorrow he may want to borrow it – when he and the others have had their object-lesson. They wouldn't listen to argument . . . so we had to expose their pious fraud about woman's place in the world in a very practical and sensible way. At this very minute working women of every grade in every part of England are ceasing work, and going to demand support and the necessities of life from their nearest male relatives, however distant the nearest relative may be. I hope, for your sake, Ethel, that Horace's relatives aren't an exacting lot!

ETHEL: There wasn't a word about it in the *Daily Mail* this morning.

WINIFRED: Never mind. The evening papers will make up for that.

ETHEL: What male relative are you going to, Winnie? Uncle Joseph?

WINIFRED: Oh, I'm in the fighting line, as usual, so our dear uncle will be spared. My work is with the great army of women who have no male belongings of any kind! I shall be busy till midnight marshalling them to the workhouse . . .

This is perhaps the most important part of the strike. By this we shall hit men as ratepayers even when they have escaped us as relatives! Every man, either in a public capacity or a private one, will find himself face to face with the appalling problem of maintaining millions of women in idleness. Do you think the men will take up the burden? Not they!(*Looks at her watch.*) Good heavens! The strike began ages ago. I must be off. I've wasted too much time here already.

ETHEL (*looking at the clock*): I had no idea it was so late. I must see about Horace's tea. He may be home any minute. (*Rings the bell, left.*)

WINIFRED: Poor Horace!

ETHEL (*annoyed*): Why 'poor Horace'? I don't think he has anything to complain of. (*Rings again.*)

WINIFRED: At this minute I feel some pity for all men.

ETHEL: What can have happened to Martha?

WINIFRED: She's gone, my dear, that's all.

ETHEL: Gone! Nonsense. She's been with me ever since I was married, and I pay her very good wages.

Enter LILY, a shabby little maid-of-all-work, dressed for walking, the chief effort of the toilette being a very cheap and very smart hat.

ETHEL: Where's Martha, Lily?

LILY: She's left, m'm.

ETHEL: Left! She never gave me notice.

LILY: No, m'm, we wasn't to give no notice, but at three o'clock we was to quit.

ETHEL: But why? Don't be a silly little girl. And you mustn't come in here in your hat.

LILY: I was just goin' when you rang. That's what I've got me 'at on for.

ETHEL: Going! Where? It's not your afternoon out.

LILY: I'm goin' back to the Union. There's dozens of others goin' with me.

ETHEL: But why –?

LILY: Miss Christabel – she told us. She says to us: 'Now look 'ere, all of yer – you who've got no men to go to on Thursday – yer've got to go to the Union, she says: 'and the one who 'angs back' – and she looked at me she did – 'may be the person 'oo the 'ole strain of the movement is restin' on, the traitor 'oo's sailin' under the 'ostile flag,' she says: and I says, 'That won't be me – not much!')

During this speech WINIFRED *puts on a sandwich board which bears the inscription: 'This way to the Workhouse.'*

WINIFRED: Well, Ethel, are you beginning to believe?

ETHEL: Oh, I think it's very unkind – very wicked. How am I to get Horace anything to eat with no servants?

WINIFRED: Cheer up, my dear. Horace and the others can end the strike when they choose. But they're going to have a jolly bad time first. Goodbye. (*Exit* WINNIE, *singing the 'Marseillaise.'*)

LILY: Wait a bit, Miss. I'm comin' with yer. (*Sings the 'Marseillaise' too.*)

ETHEL: No, no. Oh, Lily, please don't go, or at any rate bring up the kettle first, and the chops, and the frying pan. Please! Then I think I can manage.

LILY (*coming back into the room and speaking impressively*): There's no ill-feeling. It's an objick-lesson – that's all.

Exit LILY. ETHEL *begins to cry weakly; then lays the table; gets bread, cruet, tea, cups, etc. from the cupboard, right.* LILY *re-enters with a frying pan, a kettle, and two raw chops.*

LILY: 'Ere you are – it's the best I can do. You see, mum, I've got to be recognised by the State. I don't think I'm a criminal nor a lunatic, and I oughtn't to be treated as sich.

ETHEL: You poor little simpleton. Do you suppose that, even if this absurd plan succeeds, *you* will get a vote?

LILY: I may – you never know your luck; but that's not why I'm giving it up work. It's so as I shan't stop them as ought to 'ave it. The 'ole strain's on me, and I'm goin' to the Union – so goodbye, mum. (*Exit* LILY.)

ETHEL: And I've always been so kind to you! Oh, you little brute! What *will* Horace say? (*Looking out of the window.*) It can't be true. Everything looks the same as usual. (HORACE'S *voice outside*))

HORACE: We must have at least sixteen more Dreadnoughts this year. (WILLIAMS' *voice outside*)

WILLIAMS: You can't get 'em, old chap, unless you expect the blooming colonies to pay for 'em.

ETHEL: Ah, here is Horace, and Gerald Williams with him. Oh, I hope Horace hasn't asked him to tea! (*She powders her nose at the glass, then pretends to be busy with the kettle.*)

Enter HORACE COLE – *an English master in his own house – and* GERALD WILLIAMS, *a smug young man stiff with self-consciousness.*

ETHEL: You're back early, aren't you, Horry? How do you do, Mr Williams?

GERALD WILLIAMS: How do you do, Mrs Cole. I've just dropped in to fetch a book your husband's promised to lend me.

HORACE *rummages in book-shelves.*

ETHEL: Had a good day, Horry?

HORACE: Oh, much as usual. (Ah, here it is (*Reading out the title:*) 'Where's the Wash-tub now?' with a preface by Lord Curzon of Kedleston, published by the Men's League for Opposing Women's Suffrage. If that doesn't settle your missus, nothing will.)

ETHEL: Is Mrs Williams a Suffragette?

GERALD: Rather, and whenever I say anything, all she can answer is, 'You know nothing about it.' I call that illogical. Thank you, old man. I'll read it to her after tea. So long. Goodbye, Mrs Cole.

ETHEL: Did Mrs Williams tell you anything this morning . . . before you went to the City?

GERALD: About Votes for Women, do you mean? Oh, no. Not allowed at breakfast. In fact, not allowed at all. I tried to stop her going to these meetings where they fill the women's heads with all sorts of rubbish, and she said she'd give 'em up if I'd give up footer matches on Saturday afternoons; so we agreed to disagree. See you tomorrow, old chap. Goodbye, Mrs Cole.

Exit GERALD WILLIAMS.

(HORACE: You might have asked him to stop to tea. You made him very welcome – I don't think.

ETHEL: I'm sorry; but I don't think he would have stayed if I *had* asked him.

HORACE: Very likely not, but you should always be hospitable. Tea ready?)

ETHEL: Not quite, dear. It will be in a minute.

HORACE: What on earth is all this!

ETHEL: Oh, nothing. I thought I would cook your chop for you up here today – just for fun.

HORACE: I really think, Ethel, that as long as we can afford a servant, it's rather unnecessary.

ETHEL: You know you're always complaining of Martha's cooking. I thought you would like me to try.

(HORACE: My dear child! It's very nice of you. But why not cook in the kitchen? Raw meat in the drawing room! Do you want to turn me into a poor miserable vegetarian?)

ETHEL: Oh, Horry, don't!

She puts her arms round his neck and sobs. The chop at the end of the toasting fork in her hand dangles in his face.

HORACE: What on earth's the matter? Ethel, dear, don't be hysterical. If you knew what it was to come home fagged to death and be worried like this . . . I'll ring for Martha and tell her to take away those beastly chops. They're getting on my nerves.

ETHEL: Martha's gone.

HORACE: When? Why? Did you have a row? I suppose you had to give her a month's wages. I can't afford that sort of thing, you know.

ETHEL (*soothing*): It's not you who afford it, anyhow. Don't I pay Martha out of my own money?

HORACE: Do you call it ladylike to throw that in my face . . .

ETHEL (*incoherently*): I'm not throwing it in your face . . . but as it happens I didn't pay her anything. She went off without a word . . . and Lily's gone, too. (*She puts her head down on the table and cries.*)

HORACE: Well, that's a good riddance. I'm sick of her dirty face and slovenly ways. If she ever does clean my boots, she makes them look worse than when I took them off. We must get a char-woman.

ETHEL: We shan't be able to. Isn't it in the papers?

HORACE: What *are* you talking about?

ETHEL: Winifred said it would be in the evening papers.

HORACE: Winifred! She's been here, has she? That accounts for everything. How that woman comes to be your sister I can't imagine. Of course, she's mixed up with this wild-cat scheme.

ETHEL: Then you know about it!

(HORACE: Oh. I saw something about 'Suffragettes on Strike' on the posters on my way home. Who cares if they do strike? They're no use to anyone. Look at Winifred. What does she ever do except go round making speeches, and kicking up a row outside the House of Commons until she forces the police to arrest her. Then she goes to prison and poses as a martyr. Martyr! We all know she could go home at once if she would promise the magistrate to behave herself. What they ought to do is to try all these hysterical women privately and sentence them to be ducked – privately. Then they'd soon give up advertising themselves.)

ETHEL: Winnie has a splendid answer to that, but I forget what it is. Oh, Horry, was there anything on the posters about the nearest male relative?

HORACE: Ethel, my dear, you haven't gone dotty, have you? When you have quite done with my chair, I – (*He helps her out of the chair and sits down.*) Thank you.

ETHEL: Winnie said that not only are all the working women going to strike, but they are going to make their nearest male relatives support them.

HORACE: Rot!

ETHEL: I thought how dreadful it would be if Agatha came, or that cousin of yours on the stage whom you won't let me know, or your Aunt Lizzie! Martha and Lily have gone to *their* male relatives at least, Lily's gone to the workhouse – it's all the same thing. Why shouldn't it be true? Oh, look, Horace, there's a cab – with luggage. Oh, what shall we do?

HORACE: Don't fuss! It's stopping next door, not here at all.

ETHEL: No, no; it's here. (*She rushes out.*)

HORACE (*calling after her*): Come back! You can't open the door yourself. It will look as if we didn't keep a servant.

Re-enter ETHEL followed after a few seconds by AGATHA. AGATHA is a weary-looking woman of about thirty-five. She wears the National Union colours, and is dowdily dressed.

ETHEL: It *is* Agatha – and such a big box. Where *can* we put it?

AGATHA (*mildly*): How do you do, Horace. (*Kisses him.*) Dear Ethel! (*Kisses her.*) You're not looking so well as usual. Would you mind paying the cabman two shillings, Horace, and helping him with my box? It's rather heavy, but then it contains all my wordly belongings.

HORACE: Agatha – you haven't lost your situation! You haven't left the Lewises?

AGATHA: Yes, Horace; I left at three o'clock.

HORACE: My dear Agatha – I'm extremely sorry – but we can't put you up here.

AGATHA: Hadn't you better pay the cab? Two shillings so soon becomes two-and-six. (*Exit HORACE.*) I am afraid my brother doesn't realise that I have some claim on him.

ETHEL: We thought you were so happy with the Lewises.

AGATHA: So were the slaves in America when they had kind masters. They didn't want to be free.

ETHEL: Horace said you always had late dinner with them when they had no company.

AGATHA: Oh, I have no complaint against my late employers. In fact, I was sorry to inconvenience them by leaving so suddenly. But I had a higher duty to perform than my duty to them.

ETHEL: I don't know what to do. It will worry Horace dreadfully.

Re-enter HORACE.

HORACE: The cab *was* two-and-six, and I had to give a man twopence to help me in with that Noah's ark. Now, Agatha, what does this mean? Surely in your position it was very unwise to leave the Lewises. You can't stay here. We must make some arrangement.

AGATHA: Any arrangement you like, dear, provided you support me.

HORACE: I support you!

AGATHA: As my nearest male relative, I think you are obliged to do so. If you refuse, I must go to the workhouse.

HORACE: But why can't you support yourself? You've done it for years.

AGATHA: Yes – ever since I was eighteen. Now I am going to give up work, until my work is recognised. Either my proper place is the home –the home provided for me by some dear father, brother, husband, cousin, or uncle – or I am a self-supporting member of the State, who ought not to be shut out from the rights of citizenship.

HORACE: All this sounds as if you had become a Suffragette! Oh, Agatha, I always thought you were a lady.

AGATHA: Yes, I *was* a lady – such a lady that at eighteen I was thrown upon the world, penniless, with no training whatever which fitted me to earn my own living. When women become citizens I believe that daughters will be given the same chance as sons, and such a life as mine will be impossible.

HORACE: Women are so illogical. What on earth has all this to do with your planting yourself on me in this inconsiderate way? You put me in a most unpleasant position. You must see, Agatha, that I haven't the means to support a sister as well as a wife. Couldn't you go to some friends until you find another situation?

AGATHA: No, Horace. I'm going to stay with you.

HORACE (*changing his tone, and turning nasty*): Oh, indeed! And for how long – if I may ask?

AGATHA: Until a Bill for the removal of the sex disability is passed.

HORACE (*impotently angry*): Nonsense. I can't keep you, and I won't. I have always tried to do my duty by you. I think hardly a week passes that I don't write to you. But now that you have deliberately thrown up an excellent situation as a governess, and come here and threatened me – yes, threatened me – I think it's time to say that, sister or no sister, I intend to be master in my own house!

Enter MOLLY, *a good-looking young girl of about twenty. She is dressed in well-cut, tailor-made clothes, wears a neat little hat, and carries some golf-clubs and a few books.*

MOLLY: How are you, Uncle Horace? Is that Aunt Aggie? How d'ye do? I haven't seen you since I was a kid.

HORACE: Well, what have you come for?

MOLLY: There's a charming welcome to give your only neice!

HORACE: You know perfectly well, Molly, that I disapprove of you in every way. I hear – I have never read it, of course – but I hear that you have written a most scandalous book. You live in lodgings by yourself, when if you chose you could afford some really nice and refined boarding-house. You have most undesirable acquaintances, and altogether –

MOLLY: Cheer up, Uncle. Now's your chance of reforming me. I've come to live with you. You can support me and improve me at the same time.

HORACE: I never heard such impertinence. I have always understood from you that you earn more than I do.

MOLLY: Ah, yes; but you never *liked* my writing for money, did you? You called me 'sexless' once because I said that as long as I could support myself I didn't feel an irresistible temptation to marry

that awful little bounder Weekes.

ETHEL: Reginald Weekes! How can you call him a bounder! He was at Oxford.

MOLLY: Hullo, Auntie Ethel! I didn't notice you. You'll be glad to hear I haven't brought much luggage – only a night-gown and some golf clubs.

HORACE: I suppose this is a joke!

(MOLLY: Well, of course, that's one way of looking at it. I'm not going to support myself any longer. I'm going to be a perfect lady, and depend on my Uncle Horace – my nearest male relative – for the necessities of life. (*A motor horn is heard outside.*) Aren't you glad that I am not going to write another scandalous book, or live in lodgings by myself?)

ETHEL (*at the window*): Horace! Horace! There's someone getting out of a motor – a grand motor. Who can it be? And there's no one to answer the door.

MOLLY: That doesn't matter. I found it open, and left it open to save trouble.

ETHEL: She's got luggage, too! The chauffeur is bringing in a dressing-case.

HORACE: I'll turn her into the street – and the dressing-case, too.

He goes fussily to the door, and meets MADAME CHRISTINE *on the threshold. The lady is dressed smartly and tastefully. Age about forty, manners elegant, smile charming, speech resolute. She carries a jewel-case, and consults a legal document during her first remarks.*

MADAME CHRISTINE: You are Mr Cole?

HORACE: No! Certainly not! (*Wavering.*) At least, I was this morning, but –

MADAME CHRISTINE: Horace Cole, son of John Hay Cole, formerly of Streatham, where he carried on the business of a –

A motor horn sounds outside.

HORACE: I beg your pardon, but my late father's business has really nothing to do with this matter, and to a professional man it's rather trying to have these things raked up against him. Excuse me, but do you want your motor to go?

MADAME CHRISTINE: It's not my motor any longer; and – yes, I do want it to go, for I may be staying here some time. I think you had one sister, Agatha, and one brother, Samuel, now dead. Samuel was much older than you –

AGATHA: Why don't you answer, Horace? Yes, that's perfectly correct. I am Agatha.

MADAME CHRISTINE: Oh, are you? How d'ye do?

MOLLY: And Samuel Cole was my father.

MADAME CHRISTINE: I'm very glad to meet you. I didn't know I had such charming relations. Well, Mr Cole, my father was John Hay Cole's first cousin; so you, I think, are my second cousin, and my nearest male relative.

HORACE (*distractedly*): If anyone calls me that again I shall go mad.

MADAME CHRISTINE: I am afraid you aren't quite pleased with the relationship!

HORACE: You must excuse me – but I don't consider a second cousin a relation. A second cousin is a – well –

MADAME CHRISTINE: Oh, it answers the purpose. I suddenly find myself destitute, and I want you to support me. I am sure you would not like a Cole to go the workhouse.

HORACE: I don't care a damn where any of you go.

ETHEL (*shocked*): Horry! How can you!

MADAME CHRISTINE: That's frank, at any rate; but I am sure, Cousin Horace, that in spite of your manners, your heart's in the right place. You won't refuse me board and lodging, until Parliament makes it possible for me to resume my work?

HORACE: My dear madam, do you realise that my salary is £3.10s. a week – and that my house will hardly hold your luggage, much less you?

MADAME CHRISTINE: Then you must agitate. Your female relatives have supported themselves up till now, and asked nothing from you. I myself, dear cousin, was, until this morning, running a profitable dressmaking business in Hanover Square. In my public capacity I am Madame Christine.

MOLLY: I know! You make sweet gowns, but I've never been able to afford you.

HORACE: And do you think, Madame Christine –

MADAME CHRISTINE: Cousin Susan, please.

HORACE: Do you think that you are justified in coming to a poor clerk, and asking him to support you – you, who could probably turn over my yearly income in a single week! Didn't you come here in your own motor?

MADAME CHRISTINE: At three o'clock that motor became the property of the Women's Social and Political Union. All the rest of my property and all available cash have been divided equally between the National Union and the Women's Freedom League. Money is the sinews of war, you know.

HORACE: Do you mean to tell me that you've given all your money to the Suffragettes! It's a pity you haven't a husband. He'd very soon put an end to such folly.

MADAME CHRISTINE: I had a husband once. He liked me to do foolish things – for instance, to support him. After that unfortunate experience, Cousin Horace, you may imagine how glad I am to find a man who really is a man, and will support me instead. By the way, I should *so* much like some tea. Is the kettle boiling?

ETHEL (*feebly*): There aren't enough cups! Oh, what *shall* I do?

HORACE: Never mind, Ethel; I shan't want any. I am goind to dine in town, and go to the theatre. I shall hope to find you all gone when I come back. If not, I shall send for the police.

Enter MAUDIE SPARK, *a young woman with an aggressively cheerful manner, a voice raucous from much bellowing of music-hall songs, a hat of huge size, and a heart of gold.*

MAUDIE: 'Ullo! 'Ullo! Who's talking about the police? Not my dear cousin Horry?

HORACE: How dare you come here?

MAUDIE: Necessity, old dear. If I could have found a livelier male relative, you may bet I'd have gone to him! But you, Horace, are the only first cousin of this poor orphan. What are you in such a hurry for?

HORACE: Let me pass! I'm going to the theatre.

(MAUDIE: Silly jay! the theatres are all closed – and the halls, too. The actresses have gone on strike – resting indefinitely. I've done my little bit towards that. They won't get any more work out of Maudie Spark, Queen of Comédiennes, until the women have got the vote. Ladies and fellow-relatives, you'll be pleased to hear the strike's going fine. The big drapers can't open tomorrow. One man can't fill the place of fifteen young ladies at once, you see. The duchesses are out in the streets begging people to come in and wash their kids. The City men are trying to get taxi men in to do their typewriting. Every man, like Horry here, has his house full of females. Most of 'em thought, like Horry, that they'd go to the theatre to escape. But there's not a blessed theatre to go to! Oh, what a song it'll make. 'A woman's place is the home – I don't think, I don't think, I don't think.')

HORACE: Even if this is not a plot against me personally, even if there are other women in London at this minute disgracing their sex –

MAUDIE: Here, stop it – come off it! If it comes to that, what are *you* doing – threatening your womankind with the police and the workhouse.

HORACE: I was not addressing myself to you.

AGATHA: Why not, Horace? She's your cousin. She needs your protection just as much as we do.

HORACE: I regard that woman as the skeleton in the cupboard of a respectable family; but that's neither here nor there. I address myself to the more ladylike portion of this gathering, and I say that whatever is going on the men will know what to do, and will do it with dignity and firmness. (*The impressiveness of this statement is marred by the fact that* HORACE'S

hand, in emphasising it, comes down heavily on the loaf of bread on the table.*) A few exhibitions of this kind won't frighten them.

(MAUDIE: Oh, won't it! I like that! They're being so firm and so dignified that they's running down to the House of Commons like lunatics, and blackguarding the Government for not having given us the vote before! (*Shouts outside of newsboys in the distance.*))

MOLLY: Splendid! Have they begun already?

MADAME CHRISTINE: Get a paper, Cousin Horace. I know some men will never believe anything till they see it in the paper.

ETHEL: The boys are shouting out something now. Listen.

(*Shouts outside: 'Extry special. Great strike of women. Women's strike. Theatres closed. Extry special edition. "Star!" "News!" 6.30 edition'.*

MOLLY: You see. Since this morning Suffragettes have become women!)

ETHEL (*at window*): Here, boy, paper! *Cries go on: 'Extra special "Star". Men petition the Government. Votes for Women. Extry special.'* Oh, heavens, here's Aunt Lizzie!

As ETHEL *pronounces the name* HORACE *dives under the table. Enter* AUNT LIZZIE *leading a fat spaniel and carrying a bird cage with a parrot in it.* MISS ELIZABETH WILKINS *is a comfortable, middle-aged body of a type well known to those who live in the less fashionable quarter of Bloomsbury. She looks as if she kept lodgers, and her looks do not belie her. She is not very well educated, but has a good deal of native intelligence. Her features are homely, and her clothes about thirty years behind the times.*

AUNT LIZZIE: Well, dears, all here? That's right. Where's Horace? Out? Just as well; we can talk more freely. I'm sorry I'm late, but animals do so hate a move. It took a long time to make them understand the strike. But I think they will be very comfortable here. You love dogs, don't you, Ethel?

ETHEL: Not Ponto. He always growls at me.

AUNT LIZZIE: Clever dog! he knows you don't sympathise with the cause.

ETHEL: But I do, Aunt; only I have always said that as I was happily married I thought it had very little to do with me.

AUNT LIZZIE: You've changed your mind about that today, I should think! What a day it's been! We never expected everything would go so smoothly. They say the Bill's to be rushed through at once. No more deceitful promises, no more dishonest 'facilities'; deeds, not words, at last! Seen the papers? The Press are not boycotting us today, my dears.
(MADAME CHRISTINE, MOLLY, and MAUDIE *each take a paper.*) The boy who sold them to me put the money back into Ponto's collecting box. That dog must have made five pounds for the cause since this morning.

HORACE (*puts his head out*): 'Liar!'

MOLLY: Oh, do listen to this. It's too splendid! (*Reading from the paper.*) 'Women's Strike. – Latest: Messrs Lyons and Co. announce that by special arrangement with the War Office the places of their defaulting waitresses will be filled by the non-commissioned officers and men of the 2nd Battalion Coldstream Guards. Business will therefore be carried on as usual.'

MADAME CHRISTINE: What do you think of this? (*Reading:*) 'Latest Intelligence. – It is understood that the Naval Volunteers have been approached by the authorities with the object of inducing them to act as charwomen to the House of Commons.'

AUNT LIZZIE (*to* ETHEL): Well, my dear! What have you got there? Read what the *Star* says.

ETHEL (*tremulously reading*): 'The queue of women waiting for admission to Westminster Workhouse is already a mile and a half in length. As the entire police force are occupied in dealing with the men's processions, Lord Haldane has been approached with a view to ascertaining if the Territorials can be sworn in as special constables.'

MAUDIE (*laughing*): This is a little bit of all right. (*Reading*) 'Our special

representative, on calling upon the Prime Minister with the object of ascertaining his views on the situation, was informed that the Right Honourable gentleman was unable to receive him, as with the assistance of the boot-boy and a Foreign Office messenger, he was actively engaged in making his bed.'

AUNT LIZZIE: Always unwilling to receive people, you see! Well, he must be feeling sorry now that he never received us. Everyone's putting the blame on him. It's extraordinary how many men – and newspapers, too – have suddenly found out that they have always been in favour of woman's suffrage! That's the sensible attitude, of course. It would be humiliating for them to confess that it was not until we held a pistol to their heads that they changed their minds. Well, at this minute I would rather be the man who has been our ally all along than the one who has been our enemy. It's not the popular thing to be an 'anti' any more. Any man who tries to oppose us today is likely to be slung up to the nearest lamp post.

ETHEL (*rushing wildly to the table*): Oh, Horry! My Horry!

HORACE *comes out from under the table.*

AUNT LIZZIE: Why, bless the boy, what are you doing there?

HORACE: Oh, nothing. I merely thought I might be less in the way here, that's all.

AUNT LIZZIE: You didn't hide when I came in, by any chance!

HORACE: I hide from you! Aren't you always welcome in this house?

AUNT LIZZIE: Well, I haven't noticed it particularly; and I'm not calling today, you understand, I've come to stay.

HORACE, *dashed and beaten, begins to walk up and down the room, and consults* ETHEL.

Well, well! I won't deny it was a wrench to leave 118a, Upper Montagu Place, where I've done my best for boarders, old and young, gents and ladies, for twenty-five years – and no complaints! A home from home, they always call it. All my ladies had left before I started out, on the same business as ourselves –

but what those poor boys will do for their dinner tonight I don't know. They're a helpless lot! Well, it's all over; I've given up my boarding-house, and I depend on you, Horace, to keep me until I am admitted to citizenship. It may take a long time.

(HORACE: It must *not* take a long time! I shan't allow it. It shall be done at once. Well, you needn't all look so surprised. I know I've been against it, but I didn't realise things. I thought only a few hooligan window-smashers wanted the vote; but when I find that *you* – Aunt Fancy a woman of your firmness of character, one who has always been so careful with her money, being declared incapable of voting! The thing is absurd.

MAUDIE: Bravo! Our Horry's waking up.

HORACE (*looking at her scornfully*): If there are a few women here and there who *are* incapable – I mention no names, mind – it doesn't affect the position. What's going to be done? Who's going to do it? If this rotten Government think we're going to maintain millions of women in idleness just because they don't like the idea of my Aunt Lizzie making a scratch on a bit of paper and shoving it into a ballot-box once every five years, this Government have reckoned without the men – (*General cheering.*) I'll show 'em what I've got a vote for! What do they expect? You can't all marry. There aren't enough men to go round, and if you're earning your own living and paying taxes you ought to have a say; it's only fair. (*General cheering and a specially emphatic* 'Hear, hear' *from* MADAME CHRISTINE.) The Government are narrow-minded idiots!)

MADAME CHRISTINE: Hear, hear!

HORACE: They talk as if all the women ought to stay at home washing and ironing. Well, before a woman has a wash-tub, she must have a home to put it in, mustn't she? And who's going to give it her? I'd like them to tell me that. Do they expect *me* to do it?

AGATHA: Yes, dear.

HORACE: I say if she can do it herself and keep herself, so much the better for everyone. Anyhow, who are the Government? They're only representing *me*, and being paid thousands a year by *me* for carrying out *my* wishes.

MOLLY: Oh, er – what ho!

HORACE (*turns on her angrily*): I like a woman to be a woman – that's the way I was brought up; but if she insists on having a vote – and apparently she does.

ALL: She does! she does!

HORACE: – I don't see why she shouldn't have it. Many a woman came in here at the last election and tried to wheedle me into voting for her particular candidate. If she has time to do that – and I never heard the member say then that she ought to be at home washing and ironing the baby – I don't see why she hasn't time to vote. It's never taken up much of *my* time, or interfered with *my* work. I've only voted once in my life – but that's neither here nor there. I know what the vote does for me. It gives me a status; that's what you women want – a status.)

ALL: Yes, yes, a status.

HORACE: I might even call it a *locus standi*. If I go now and tell these rotten Cabinet Ministers what I think of them, it's my *locus standi*–

MAUDIE: That's a good word.

HORACE: – that will force them to listen to me. Oh, I know. And, by gum! I'll give them a bit of my mind. They shall hear a few home truths for once. 'Gentlemen,' I shall say – well, that won't be true of all of them to start with, but one must give 'em the benefit of the doubt – 'gentlemen, the men of England are sick and tired of your policy. Who's driven the women of England into this? *You* – (*he turns round on* ETHEL, *who jumps violently.*) – because you were too stupid to know that they meant business – because you couldn't read the writing on the wall.' (*Hear, hear.*) It may be nothing to you, gentlemen, that every industry in this country is paralysed and every Englishman's home turned into a howling wilderness –

MOLLY: Draw it mild, Uncle.

HORACE: A howling wilderness, I repeat – by your refusal to see what's as plain as the nose on your face; but I would have you know, gentlemen, that it *is* something to us. We aren't slaves. We never will be slaves –

AGATHA: Never, never!

HORACE: And we insist on reform. Gentlemen, conditions have changed, and women have to work. Don't men encourage them to work, *invite* them to work?

AGATHA: *Make* them work.

HORACE: And women are placed in the battle of life on the same terms as we are, short of one thing, the *locus standi* of a vote.

MAUDIE: Good old *locus standi!*

HORACE: If you aren't going to give it them, gentlemen, and if they won't go back to their occupations without it, we ask you how they're going to live? Who's going to support them? Perhaps you're thinking of giving them all old age pensions and asking the country to pay the piper! The country will see you damned first, if, gentlemen, you'll pardon the expression. It's dawning upon us all that the women would never have taken such a step as this if they hadn't been the victims of a gross injustice.

ALL: Never.

HORACE: Why shouldn't they have a voice in the laws which regulate the price of food and clothes? Don't they pay for their food and clothes?

MAUDIE: Paid for mine since the age of six.

HORACE: Why shouldn't they have a voice in the rate of wages and the hours of labour in certain industries? Aren't they working at those industries? If you had a particle of common sense or decent feeling, gentlemen –'

Enter GERALD WILLIAMS *like a souvenir of Mafeking night. He shouts incoherently and in a hoarse voice. He is utterly transformed from the meek, smug being of an hour before. He is wearing several ribbons and badges and carries a banner bearing this inscription: 'The men of Brixton demand votes for women this evening.'*

WILLIAMS: Cole, Cole! Come on! Come on! You'll be late. The procession's forming up at the town hall. There's no time to lose. What are you slacking here for? Perhaps this isn't good enough for you. I've got twelve of them in my drawing-room. We shall be late for the procession if we don't start at once. Hurry up! Come on! Votes for Women! Where's your banner? Where's your badge? Down with the Government! Rule Britannia! Votes for Women! D'you want to support a dozen women for the rest of your life, or don't you? ... Every man in Brixton is going to Westminster. Borrow a ribbon and come along. Hurry up, now! Hooray! (*Rushes madly out crying* 'Votes for Women! Rule Britannia; Women never, never shall be slaves! Votes for Women!)

All the women who are wearing ribbons decorate HORACE.

ETHEL: My hero! (*She throws her arms round him.*)

HORACE: You may depend on me – all of you – to see justice done. When you want a thing done, get a man to do it! Votes for Women!

AGATHA *gives him a flag which he waves triumphantly.*

Curtain tableau: HORACE *marching majestically out of the door, with the women cheering him enthusiastically.*

VOTES FOR WOMEN

VOTES FOR WOMEN
Elizabeth Robins
(First performed at the Court Theatre, London, in 1907)

Elizabeth Robins was born in the United States, given a good education, and sent to Vassar College in the 1870s to study medicine. She ran away to go on the stage and arrived in London in the late 1880s. In England she not only became one of the leading actresses, she also became one of the most prominent literary figures and she was – in the words of Jane Marcus – 'a propagandist of genius'.

Angered by the exclusion of women from anything other than severely constrained, stereotyped and supportive parts in the theatre, Elizabeth Robins recognised that the only way to escape the tyranny of the actor-manager was to have actress-managers, and she proceeded to bring this about with some of the other leading actresses of the day. Elizabeth Robins championed Ibsen (who at least wrote parts that actresses could identify with and find challenging) and her first venture as a manager – with Marion Lee – was in 1892 at the Vaudeville Theatre where they put on a production of *Karin*, a play written by a Norwegian woman, Alfhild Agrell. One result of this pioneering effort was that by '1912 there were four actresses running London theatres, and more importantly, at the Victoria Music Hall in Waterloo Road, the young manager Lilian Bayliss, had secured a theatre licence from the Lord Chamberlain's office' (Julie Holledge, p. 42).

Elizabeth Robins' first play was written in collaboration with Lady Bell and was entitled *Alan's Wife*. It caused an uproar when it was performed in 1893 because the main character, Jean Creyke, departed so far from the Victorian ideal of womanhood. Like so many other women writers however, Elizabeth Robins did not acknowledge her authorship because she was aware that the admission that the playwright was a woman was sufficient to damn any play.

In 1907 Elizabeth Robins published *The Convert*, a novel designed to publicise the suffragette movement. It was based on her own verbatim reports of speeches made by the suffragettes (particularly Christabel Pankhurst), and on the heckling they aroused. Not only was the novel a best-seller (it was republished in 1980 by the Women's Press), but Elizabeth Robins' experience of these huge public meetings is reflected in her dramatic skill in the construction of the Trafalgar Square scenes of *Votes for Women*. Even the critics granted that this was a significant achievement. *Votes for Women* makes many serious points, and not just about the vote. One of the fundamental issues raised is that of the double sexual standard which condemns a woman who has an affair outside marriage, while 'allowances are made' for the man. Homeless women, the poverty of women, the hardship of women's lives, are all the substance of this propaganda play which never loses its dramatic tension and which was extremely well received by its West End audiences.

A fervent worker for women's rights, and for women to be able to control their own work place, Elizabeth Robins was among the first to see the potential of the popular theatre as a platform for women's suffrage. *Votes for Women* was written with this express purpose and was first staged at the Court Theatre in 1907. It was this play 'which heralded the beginning of a suffrage theatre' wrote Julie Holledge; Elizabeth Robins helped to change the theatre and to organise actresses, and with 'their involvement with the women's rights movement and their dissatisfaction with a male dominated theatre, these women had begun to develop a drama that could express the reality of women's lives ... With the emergence of the mass suffrage movement in the Edwardian era, over a thousand actresses were thrust into the fight for votes for women. Out of their struggle the first women's theatre movement of the twentieth century was born' (p. 46).

Dale Spender

Characters

LORD JOHN WYNNSTAY
LADY JOHN WYNNSTAY, *his wife*
MRS HERIOT, *sister of Lady John*
MISS JEAN DUNBARTON, *niece to Lady John and Mrs Heriot*
THE HON. GEOFFREY STONOR, *Unionist M.P. affianced to Jean Dunbarton*
MR ST JOHN GREATOREX, *Liberal M.P.*
THE HON. RICHARD FARNBOROUGH
MR FREDDY TUNBRIDGE
MRS FREDDY TUNBRIDGE
MR ALLEN TRENT
MISS ERNESTINE BLUNT, *a Suffragette*
MR PILCHER, *a working man*
A WORKING WOMAN
MISS VIDA LEVERING
PERSONS IN THE CROWD; SERVANTS IN THE TWO HOUSES

Votes for Women was first performed at the Court Theatre, London, in 1907, with the following cast:

LORD JOHN WYNNSTAY	Mr Athol Forde
THE HON. GEOFFREY STONOR	Mr Aubrey Smith
MR ST JOHN GREATOREX	Mr E. Holman Clark
MR RICHARD FARNBOROUGH	Mr. P. Clayton Greene
MR FREDDY TUNBRIDGE	Mr Percy Marmont
MR ALLEN TRENT	Mr Lewis Casson
MR WALKER*	Mr Edmund Gwenn
LADY JOHN WYNNSTAY	Miss Maud Milton
MRS HERIOT	Miss Frances Ivor
MISS VIDA LEVERING	Miss Wynne-Matthison
MISS BEATRICE DUNBARTON*	Miss Jean MacKinlay
MRS FREDDY TUNBRIDGE	Miss Gertrude Burnett
MISS ERNESTINE BLUNT	Miss Dorothy Minto
A WORKING WOMAN	Miss Agnes Thomas

* In the text these characters have been altered to MR PILCHER and MISS JEAN DUNBARTON

ACT I	Wynnstay House in Hertfordshire
ACT II	Trafalgar Square, London
ACT III	Eaton Square, London

The Entire Action of the Play takes place between Sunday noon and six o'clock in the evening of the same day.

Note on Performance

Votes for Women is not a comedy though it has, in the first act particularly, some very witty dialogue. It is a drama with a strong and angry moral centre. Vida Levering is a woman of great integrity and dignity, she is also clever, witty and very attractive. She is a person of moral stature, a stature wrested from the blows she has been dealt by life and by men, in particular by one man, Geoffrey Stonor. Though heroic, she is also human and shows at the end of the play that she can be magnanimous in victory. Though men have demonstrated irrefutably that they are unable, in power, to create a decent world, she will give them another chance. She is ready to work side by side with men to right the wrongs she sees. The play also argues strongly that what happens to one woman happens to *all* women. It's not just individual bad luck but part of a universal bad deal.

Again it could be staged with a minimum of set and props. The first act furniture can be rearranged for the third act to create a different space and the second act could be done with either a bare stage or an arrangement of rostra or boxes to create the platform. There are some excellent characters and the first act is full of lively drawing-room behaviour. The character descriptions are very useful. Who does not know the man with John Greatorex's hair? The women are completely in charge of this act. They support and indulge the men whilst actually, invisibly, creating the social warp and weft of their life. The womens' most significant relationships however are with each other; as Lady John says to Lord Freddy, 'My dear boy, you know as little of what's in a woman's line as most men.' Some of the women are 'right wing'. They think prostitutes 'like' the life they lead and that the Suffragettes are degraded people who probably eat babies. Their comments are similar to those I have heard women express on the dwellers at Greenham Common. They should be played straight. Any caricature of these attitudes lets the audience off the hook. They bear out a serious problem, as Lady John says . . . 'You can never get men to realise . . . you can't always get women'. As for John Greatorex's damning of feminists as old, ugly, and frigid . . . it could have come out of any of today's newspapers.

Act Two presents some problems, unless the cast is enormous. I suggest the cast of Act One double as Newspaper Vendor, Poetic Young Man etc, or that all the crowd speakers are kept offstage and shout their lines from the wings. This will create a feeling of size and space much better than a handful of actors trying to look like a crush of hundreds (Of course if you are determined, see Michael Green *The Art of Coarse Acting* and get a lot of hats) I would put the rostra centre stage facing the real audience and have Stonor's party enter downstage to watch, they will then be close to the audience and therefore audible over the public speaking. This act contains many arguments of the suffrage movement now central to the womens' movement, and also gives some idea of the sort of invective used then (and now) against it.

Act Three is the emotional climax of the play and needs committed playing. The story of Vida and Geoffrey might seem melodramatic today, but the double standard of judging male and female behaviour survives all attempts to balance rights.

Carole Hayman

ACT ONE

Hall of Wynnstay House.

Twelve o'clock, Sunday morning, end of June. With the rising of the curtain, enter the BUTLER. *As he is going, with majestic port, to answer the door, enter briskly from the garden, by the lower French window,* LADY JOHN WYNNSTAY, *flushed, and flapping a garden hat to fan herself. She is a pink-cheeked woman of fifty-four, who has plainly been a beauty, keeps her complexion, but is 'gone to fat.'*

LADY JOHN: Has Miss Levering come down yet?

BUTLER (*pausing*): I haven't seen her, m'lady.

LADY JOHN (*almost sharply as* BUTLER *turns*): I won't have her disturbed if she's resting. (*To herself as she goes to the writing table.*) She certainly needs it.

BUTLER: Yes, m'lady.

LADY JOHN (*sitting at the writing table, her back to the front door*): But I want her to know the moment she comes down that the new plans arrived by the morning post.

BUTLER (*pausing nearly at the door*): Plans, m'la–

LADY JOHN: She'll understand. There they are. (*Glancing at the clock.*) It's very important she should have them in time to look over before she goes –

BUTLER *opens the door.*

(*Over her shoulder.*) Is that Miss Levering?

BUTLER: No, m'lady. Mr Farnborough.

Exit BUTLER.
Enter the HON. R. FARNBOROUGH.
He is twenty-six; reddish hair, high-coloured, sanguine, self-important.

FARNBOROUGH: I'm afraid I'm scandalously early. It didn't take me nearly as long to motor over as Lord John said.

LADY JOHN (*shaking hands*): I'm afraid my husband is no authority on motoring – and he's not home yet from church.

FARNBOROUGH: It's the greatest luck finding *you*. I thought Miss Levering was the only person under this roof who was ever allowed to observe Sunday as a real Day of Rest.

LADY JOHN: If you've come to see Miss Levering –

FARNBOROUGH: Is she here? I give you my word I didn't know it.

LADY JOHN (*unconvinced*): Oh?

FARNBOROUGH: Does she come every weekend?

LADY JOHN: Whenever we can get her to. But we've only known her a couple of months.

FARNBOROUGH: And I have only known her three weeks! Lady John, I've come to ask you to help me.

LADY JOHN (*quickly*): With Miss Levering? I can't do it!

FARNBOROUGH: No, no – all that's no good. She only laughs.

LADY JOHN (*relieved*): Ah! – she looks upon you as a boy.

FARNBOROUGH (*firing up*): Such rot! What do you think she said to me in London the other day?

LADY JOHN: That she was four years older than you?

FARNBOROUGH: Oh, I knew that. No. She said she knew she was all the charming things I'd been saying, but there was only one way to prove it – and that was to marry some one young enough to be her son. She'd noticed that was what the *most* attractive women did – and she named names.

LADY JOHN (*laughing*): *You* were too old!

FARNBOROUGH (*nods*): Her future husband, she said, was probably just entering Eton.

LADY JOHN: Just like her!

FARNBOROUGH (*waving the subject away*): No. I wanted to see you about the Secretaryship.

LADY JOHN: You didn't get it, then?

FARNBOROUGH: No. It's the grief of my life.

LADY JOHN: Oh, if you don't get one you'll get another.

FARNBOROUGH: But there *is* only one.

LADY JOHN: Only one vacancy?

FARNBOROUGH: Only one man I'd give my ears to work for.

LADY JOHN (*smiling*): I remember.

FARNBOROUGH (*quickly*): Do I always talk about Stonor? Well, it's a habit people have got into.

LADY JOHN: I forget, do you know Mr Stonor personally, or (*smiling*) are you just dazzled from afar?

FARNBOROUGH: Oh, I know him. The trouble is he doesn't know me. If he did he'd realise he can't be sure of winning his election without my valuable services.

LADY JOHN: Geoffrey Stonor's re-election is always a foregone conclusion.

FARNBOROUGH: That the great man shares that opinion is precisely his weak point. (*Smiling.*) His only one.

LADY JOHN: You think because the Liberals swept the country the last time –

FARNBOROUGH: How can we be sure any Conservative seat is safe after – (*As* LADY JOHN *smiles and turns to her papers:*) Forgive me, I know you're not interested in politics *qua* politics. But this concerns Geoffrey Stonor.

LADY JOHN: And you count on my being interested in him like all the rest of my sex.

FARNBOROUGH (*leans forward*): Lady John, I've heard the news.

LADY JOHN: What news?

FARNBOROUGH: That your little niece – the Scotch heiress – is going to become Mrs Geoffrey Stonor.

LADY JOHN: Who told you that?

FARNBOROUGH: Please don't mind my knowing.

LADY JOHN (*visibly perturbed*): She had set her heart upon having a few days with just her family in the secret, before the flood of congratulations breaks loose.

FARNBOROUGH: Oh, that's all right. I always hear things before other people.

LADY JOHN: Well, I must ask you to be good enough to be very circumspect. I wouldn't have my niece think that I –

FARNBOROUGH: Oh, of course not.

LADY JOHN: She will be here in a hour.

FARNBOROUGH (*jumping up delighted*): What? Today? The future Mrs Stonor!

LADY JOHN (*harassed*): Yes. Unfortunately we had one or two people already asked for the weekend –

FARNBOROUGH: And I go and invite myself to luncheon! Lady John, you can buy me off. I'll promise to remove myself in five minutes if you'll –

LADY JOHN: No, the penalty is you shall stay and keep the others amused between church and luncheon, and so leave me free. (*Takes up the plan.*) Only *remember* –

FARNBOROUGH: Wild horses won't get a hint out of me! I only mentioned it to you because – since we've come back to live in this part of the world you've been so awfully kind – I thought, I hoped maybe you – you'd put in a word for me.

LADY JOHN: With – ?

FARNBOROUGH: With your nephew that is to be. Though I'm *not* the slavish satellite people make out, you can't doubt –

LADY JOHN: Oh, I don't doubt. But you know Mr Stonor inspires a similar enthusiasm in a good many young –

FARNBOROUGH: They haven't studied the situation as I have. They don't know what's at stake. They don't go to that hole Dutfield as I did just to hear his Friday speech.

LADY JOHN: Ah! But you were rewarded. Jean – my niece – wrote me it was 'glorious.'

FARNBOROUGH (*judicially*): Well, you know, *I* was disappointed. He's too content just to criticise, just to make his delicate pungent fun of the men who are grappling – very inadequately, of course – still *grappling* with the big questions. There's a carrying power (*gets up and faces an imaginary audience*) – some of Stonor's friends ought to point it out – there's a driving power in the poorest constructive policy that makes the most brilliant criticism look barren.

LADY JOHN (*with good-humoured malice*): Who told you that?

FARNBOROUGH: You think there's nothing in it because *I* say it. But now that he's coming into the family, Lord John or somebody really ought to point out – Stonor's overdoing his rôle of magnificent security.

LADY JOHN: I don't see even Lord John offering to instruct Mr Stonor.

FARNBOROUGH: Believe me, that's just Stonor's danger! Nobody saying a word, everybody hoping he's on the point of adopting some definite line, something strong and original that's going to fire the public imagination and bring the Tories back into power.

LADY JOHN: So he will.

FARNBOROUGH (*hotly*): Not if he disappoints meetings – goes calmly up to town – and leaves the field to the Liberals.

LADY JOHN: When did he do anything like that?

FARNBOROUGH: Yesterday! (*With a harassed air.*) And now that he's got this other preoccupation –

LADY JOHN: You mean –

FARNBOROUGH: Yes, your niece – that spoilt child of Fortune. Of course! (*Stopping suddenly.*) She kept him from the meeting last night. Well! (*Sits down.*) If that's the effect she's going to have it's pretty serious!

LADY JOHN (*smiling*): You are!

FARNBOROUGH: I can assure you the election agent's more so. He's simply tearing his hair.

LADY JOHN (*more gravely and coming nearer*): How do you know?

FARNBOROUGH: He told me so himself – yesterday. I scraped acquaintance with the agent just to see if – if –

LADY JOHN: It's not only here that you manœuvre for that Secretaryship!

FARNBOROUGH (*confidentially*): You can never tell when your chance might come! That election chap's promised to keep me posted.

The door flies open and JEAN DUNBARTON *rushes in.*

JEAN: Aunt Ellen – here I –

LADY JOHN (*astonished*): My dear child!

They embrace. Enter LORD JOHN *from the garden – a benevolent, silver-haired despot of sixty-two.*

LORD JOHN: I thought that was you running up the avenue.

JEAN *greets her uncle warmly, but all the time she and her aunt talk together. 'How did you get here so early?' 'I knew you'd be surprised – wasn't it clever of me to manage it? I don't deserve all the credit.' 'But there isn't any train between –' 'Yes, wait till I tell you.' 'You walked in the broiling sun –' 'No, no.' 'You must be dead. Why didn't you telegraph? I ordered the carriage to meet the 1.10. Didn't you say the 1.10? Yes, I'm sure you did – here's your letter.'*

LORD JOHN (*has shaken hands with* FARNBOROUGH *and speaks through the torrent*): Now they'll tell each other for ten minutes that she's an hour earlier than we expected.

LORD JOHN *leads* FARNBOROUGH *towards the garden.*

FARNBOROUGH: The Freddy Tunbridges said *they* were coming to you this week.

LORD JOHN: Yes, they're dawdling through the park with the Church Brigade.

FARNBOROUGH: Oh! (*With a glance back at* JEAN.) I'll go and meet them.

Exit FARNBOROUGH.

LORD JOHN (*as he turns back*): That discreet young man will get on.

LADY JOHN (*to* JEAN): But *how* did you get here?

JEAN (*breathless*): 'He' motored me down.

LADY JOHN: Geoffrey Stonor? (JEAN *nods.*) Why, where is he, then?

JEAN: He dropped me at the end of the avenue and went on to see a supporter about something.

LORD JOHN: You let him go off like that without –

LADY JOHN (*taking JEAN'S two hands*): Just tell me, my child, is it all right?

JEAN: My engagement? (*Radiantly.*) Yes, absolutely.

LADY JOHN: Geoffrey Stonor isn't going to be – a little too old for you?

JEAN (*laughing*): Bless me, am I such a chicken?

LADY JOHN: Twenty-four used not to be so young – but it's become so.

JEAN: Yes, we don't grow up so quick. (*Gaily.*) But on the other hand we *stay* up longer.

LORD JOHN: You've got what's vulgarly called 'looks,' my dear, and that will help to *keep* you up!

JEAN (*smiling*): I know what Uncle John's thinking. But I'm not the only girl who's been left 'what's vulgarly called' money.

LORD JOHN: You're the only one of our immediate circle who's been left so beautifully much.

JEAN: Ah, but remember Geoffrey could – everybody *knows* he could have married any one in England.

LADY JOHN (*faintly ironic*): I'm afraid everybody does know it – not excepting Mr Stonor.

LORD JOHN: Well, how spoilt is the great man?

JEAN: Not the least little bit in the world. You'll see! He so wants to know my best-loved relations better. (*Another embrace.*) An orphan has so few belongings, she has to make the most of them.

LORD JOHN (*smiling*): Let us hope he'll approve of us on more intimate acquaintance.

JEAN (*firmly*): He will. He's an angel. Why, he gets on with my grandfather!

LADY JOHN: *Does* he? (*Teasing.*) You mean to say Mr Geoffrey Stonor isn't

just a tiny bit – 'superior' about Dissenters.

JEAN (*stoutly*): Not half as much as Uncle John and all the rest of you! My grandfather's been ill again, you know, and rather difficult – bless him! (*Radiantly.*) But Geoffrey – (*Clasps her hands.*)

LADY JOHN: He must have powers of persuasion! – to get that old Covenanter to let you come in an abhorred motor car – on Sunday, too!

JEAN (*half whispering*): Grandfather didn't know!

LADY JOHN: Didn't know?

JEAN: I honestly meant to come by train. Geoffrey met me on my way to the station. We had the most glorious run. Oh, Aunt Ellen, we're so happy! (*Embracing her.*) I've so looked forward to having you to myself the whole day just to talk to you about –

LORD JOHN (*turning away with affected displeasure*): Oh, very well –

JEAN (*catches him affectionately by the arm*): You'd find it dreffly dull to hear me talk about Geoffrey the whole blessed day!

LADY JOHN: Well, till luncheon, my dear, you mustn't mind if I – (*To LORD JOHN, as she goes to the writing table.*) Miss Levering wasn't only tired last night, she was ill.

LORD JOHN: I thought she looked very white.

JEAN: Who is Miss – You don't mean to say there are other people?

LADY JOHN: One or two. Your uncle's responsible for asking that old cynic, St. John Greatorex, and I –

JEAN (*gravely*): Mr. Greatorex – he's a Radical, isn't he?

LORD JOHN (*laughing*): Jean! Beginning to 'think in parties'!

LADY JOHN: It's very natural now that she should –

JEAN: I only meant it was odd he should be here. Naturally at my grandfather's –

LORD JOHN: It's all right, my child. Of course we expect now that you'll begin to think like Geoffrey Stonor, and to feel like Geoffrey Stonor, and to talk like Geoffrey Stonor. And quite proper too.

JEAN (*smiling*): Well, if I do think with my husband and feel with him – as, of course, I shall – it will surprise me if I ever find myself talking a tenth as well – (*Following her uncle to the French window.*) You should have heard him at Dutfield – (*Stopping short, delighted.*) Oh! The Freddy Tunbridges. What? Not Aunt Lydia! Oh-h! (*Looking back reproachfully at* LADY JOHN, *who makes a discreet motion 'I couldn't help it.'*)

Enter the TUNBRIDGES. MR FREDDY, *of no profession and of independent means. Well-groomed, pleasant-looking; of few words. A 'nice man' who likes 'nice women', and has married one of them.* MRS FREDDY *is thirty. An attractive figure, delicate face, intelligent grey eyes, over-sensitive mouth, and naturally curling dust-coloured hair.*

MRS FREDDY: What a delightful surprise!

JEAN (*shaking hands warmly*): I'm so glad. How d'ye do, Mr Freddy?

Enter LADY JOHN'S *sister,* MRS HERIOT – *smart, pompous, fifty – followed by* FARNBOROUGH.

MRS HERIOT: My dear Jean! My darling child!

JEAN: How do you do, aunt?

MRS HERIOT (*sotto voce*): *I* wasn't surprised. I always prophesied –

JEAN: Sh! *Please!*

FARNBOROUGH: We haven't met since you were in short skirts. I'm Dick Farnborough.

JEAN: Oh, I remember.

They shake hands.

MRS FREDDY (*looking round*): Not down yet – the Elusive One?

JEAN: Who is the Elusive One?

MRS FREDDY: Lady John's new friend.

LORD JOHN (*to* JEAN): Oh, I forgot you hadn't seen Miss Levering; such a nice creature! (*To* MRS FREDDY.) – don't you think?

MRS FREDDY: Of course I do. You're lucky to get her to come so often. She won't go to other people.

LADY JOHN: She knows she can rest here.

FREDDY (*who has joined* LADY JOHN *near the writing table*): What does she do to tire her?

LADY JOHN: She's been helping my sister and me with a scheme of ours.

MRS HERIOT: She certainly knows how to inveigle money out of the men.

LADY JOHN: It would sound less equivocal, Lydia, if you added that the money is to build baths in our Shelter for Homeless Women.

MRS FREDDY: Homeless women?

LADY JOHN: Yes, in the most insanitary part of Soho.

FREDDY: Oh – a – really.

FARNBOROUGH: It doesn't sound quite in Miss Levering's line!

LADY JOHN: My dear boy, you know as little about what's in a woman's line as most men.

FREDDY (*laughing*): Oh, I say!

LORD JOHN (*indulgently to* MR FREDDY *and* FARNBOROUGH): Philanthropy in a woman like Miss Levering is a form of restlessness. But she's a *nice* creature; all she needs is to get some 'nice' fella to marry her.

MRS FREDDY (*laughing as she hangs on her husband's arm*): Yes, a woman needs a balance wheel – if only to keep her from flying back to town on a hot day like this.

LORD JOHN: Who's proposing anything so –

MRS FREDDY: The Elusive One.

LORD JOHN: Not Miss –

MRS FREDDY: Yes, before luncheon!

Exit FARNBOROUGH *to the garden.*

LADY JOHN: She must be in London by this afternoon, she says.

LORD JOHN: What for in the name of –

LADY JOHN: Well, *that* I didn't ask her. But (*consults her watch*) I think I'll just go up and see if she's changed her plans.

Exit LADY JOHN.

LORD JOHN: Oh, she must be *made* to. Such a nice creature! All she needs –

Voices outside. Enter fussily, talking and gesticulating, ST JOHN GREATOREX, *followed by* MISS LEVERING *and* FARNBOROUGH. GREATOREX *is sixty, wealthy, a county magnate, and Liberal MP. He is square, thick-set, square-bearded. His shining bald pate has two strands of coal-black hair trained across his crown from left ear to right and securely pasted there. He has small, twinkling eyes and a reputation for telling good stories after dinner when ladies have left the room. He is carrying a little book for* MISS LEVERING. *She (parasol over shoulder), an attractive, essentially feminine, and rather 'smart' woman of thirty-two, with a somewhat foreign grace; the kind of whom men and women alike say, 'What's her story? Why doesn't she marry?'*

GREATOREX: I protest! Good Lord! what are the women of this country coming to? I *protest* against Miss Levering being carried off to discuss anything so revolting. Bless my soul! what can a woman like you *know* about it?

MISS LEVERING (*smiling*): Little enough. Good morning.

GREATOREX (*relieved*): I should think so indeed!

LORD JOHN (*aside*): You aren't serious about going –

GREATOREX (*waggishly breaking in*): We were so happy out there in the summer-house, weren't we?

MISS LEVERING: Ideally.

GREATOREX: And to be haled out to talk about Public *Sanitation* forsooth! (*Hurries after* MISS LEVERING *as she advances to speak to the* FREDDYS & co.) Why, God bless my soul, do you realise that's *drains*?

MISS LEVERING: I'm dreadfully afraid it is! (*Holds out her hand for the small book* GREATOREX *is carrying.*)

GREATOREX *returns* MISS LEVERING'S *book open; he has been keeping the place with his finger. She opens it and shuts her handkerchief in.*

GREATOREX: And we in the act of discussing Italian literature! Perhaps you'll tell me that isn't a more savoury topic for a lady.

MISS LEVERING: But for the tramp population less conducive to savouriness, don't you think, than – baths?

GREATOREX: No, I can't understand this morbid interest in vagrants. *You're* much too – leave it to the others.

JEAN: What others?

GREATOREX (*with smiling impertinence*): Oh, the sort of woman who smells of indiarubber. The typical English spinster. (*To* MISS LEVERING.) *You* know –Italy's full of her. She never goes anywhere without a mackintosh and a collapsible bath – rubber. When you look at her, it's borne in upon you that she doesn't only smell of rubber. *She's* rubber too.

LORD JOHN (*laughing*): This is my neice, Miss Jean Dunbarton, Miss Levering.

JEAN: How do you do? (*They shake hands.*)

GREATOREX (*to* JEAN): I'm sure *you* agree with me.

JEAN: About Miss Levering being too –

GREATOREX: For that sort of thing – *much* too –

MISS LEVERING: What a pity you've exhausted the more eloquent adjectives.

GREATOREX: But I haven't!

MISS LEVERING: Well, you can't say to me as you did to Mrs Freddy: 'You're too young and too happily married – and too – (*Glances round smiling at* MRS FREDDY, *who, oblivious, is laughing and talking to her husband and* MRS HERIOT.)

JEAN: For what was Mrs Freddy too happily married and all the rest?

MISS LEVERING (*lightly*): Mr Greatorex was repudiating the horrid rumour that Mrs Freddy had been speaking in public; about Women's

Trade Unions – wasn't that what you said, Mrs Heriot?

LORD JOHN (*chuckling*): Yes, it isn't made up as carefully as your aunt's parties usually are. Here we've got Greatorex (*takes his arm*) who hates political women, and we've got in that mild and inoffensive looking little lady – (*Motion over his shoulder towards* MRS FREDDY.)

GREATOREX (*shrinking down stage in comic terror*): You don't mean she's *really* –

JEAN (*simultaneously and gaily rising*): Oh, and you've got me!

LORD JOHN (*with genial affection*): My dear child, he doesn't hate the charming wives and sweethearts who help to win seats.

JEAN *makes her uncle a discreet little signal of warning.*

MISS LEVERING: Mr Greatorex objects only to the unsexed creatures who – a –

LORD JOHN (*hastily to cover up his slip*): Yes, yes, who want to act independently of men.

MISS LEVERING: Vote, and do silly things of that sort.

LORD JOHN (*with enthusiasm*): Exactly.

MRS HERIOT: It will be a long time before we hear any more of *that* nonsense.

JEAN: You mean that rowdy scene in the House of Commons?

MRS HERIOT: Yes. No decent woman will be able to say 'Suffrage' without blushing for another generation, thank Heaven!

MISS LEVERING (*smiling*): Oh? I understood that so little I almost imagined people were more stirred up about it than they'd ever been before.

GREATOREX (*with a quizzical affectation of gallantry*): Not people like you.

MISS LEVERING (*teasingly*): How do you know?

GREATOREX (*with a start*): God bless my soul!

LORD JOHN: She's saying that only to get a rise out of you.

GREATOREX: Ah, yes, your frocks aren't serious enough.

MISS LEVERING: I'm told it's an exploded notion that the Suffrage women are all dowdy and dull.

GREATOREX: Don't you believe it!

MISS LEVERING: Well, of course we know you've been an authority on the subject for – let's see, how many years is it you've kept the House in roars whenever Woman's Rights are mentioned?

GREATOREX (*flattered but not entirely comfortable*): Oh, as long as I've known anything about politics there have been a few discontented old maids and hungry widows –

MISS LEVERING: 'A few!' That's really rather forbearing of you, Mr Greatorex. I'm afraid the number of the discontented and the hungry was 96,000 – among the mill operatives alone. (*Hastily.*) At least the papers said so, didn't they?

GREATOREX: Oh, don't ask me; that kind of woman doesn't interest me, I'm afraid. Only I am able to point out to the people who lose their heads and seem inclined to treat the phenomenon seriously that there's absolutely nothing new in it. There have been women for the last forty years who haven't had anything more pressing to do than petition Parliament.

MISS LEVERING (*reflectively*): And that's as far as they've got.

LORD JOHN (*turning on his heel*): It's as far as they'll ever get.

Meets the group coming down.

MISS LEVERING (*chaffing* GREATOREX): Let me see, wasn't a deputation sent to you not long ago? (*Sits*)

GREATOREX: H'm! (*Irritably.*) Yes, yes.

MISS LEVERING (*as though she has just recalled the circumstances*): Oh, yes, I remember. I thought at the time, in my modest way, it was nothing short of heroic of them to go asking audience of their arch opponent.

GREATOREX (*stoutly*): It didn't come off.

MISS LEVERING (*innocently*): Oh! I thought they insisted on bearding the lion in his den.

GREATOREX: Of course I wasn't going to be bothered with a lot of –

MISS LEVERING: You don't mean you refused to go out and face them!

GREATOREX (*with a comic look of terror*): I wouldn't have done it for worlds. But a friend of mine went and had a look at 'em.

MISS LEVERING (*smiling*): Well, did he get back alive?

GREATOREX: Yes, but he advised me not to go. 'You're quite right,' he said. 'Don't you think of bothering,' he said. 'I've looked over the lot,' he said, 'and there isn't a weekender among 'em.'

JEAN (*gaily precipitates herself into the conversation*): You remember Mrs Freddy's friend who came to tea here in the winter? (*To* GREATOREX.) He was a member of Parliament too – quite a little young one – he said women would never be respected till they had the vote!

GREATOREX *snorts, the other men smile and all the women except* MRS HERIOT.

MRS HERIOT (*sniffing*): I remember telling him that he was too young to know what he was talking about.

LORD JOHN: Yes, I'm afraid you all sat on the poor gentleman.

LADY JOHN (*entering*): Oh, *there* you are! (*Greets* MISS LEVERING.)

JEAN: It was such fun. He was flat as a pancake when we'd done with him. Aunt Ellen told him with her most distinguished air she didn't want to be 'respected.'

MRS FREDDY (*with a laugh of remonstrance*): My *dear* Lady John!

FARNBOROUGH: Quite right! Awful idea to think you're *respected*!

MISS LEVERING (*smiling*): Simply revolting.

LADY JOHN (*at writing-table*): Now, you frivolous people, go away. We've only got a few minutes to talk over the terms of the late Mr Soper's

munificence before the carriage comes for Miss Levering –

MRS FREDDY (*to* FARNBOROUGH): Did you know she'd got that old horror to give Lady John £8,000 for her charity before he died?

MRS FREDDY: Who got him to?

LADY JOHN: Miss Levering. He wouldn't do it for me, but she brought him round.

FREDDY: Yes. Bah-ee Jove! I expect so.

MRS FREDDY (*turning enthusiastically to her husband*): Isn't she wonderful?

LORD JOHN (*aside*): Nice creature. All she needs is –

MR *and* MRS FREDDY *and* FARNBOROUGH *stroll off to the garden.* LADY JOHN *is on the far side of the writing-table.* MRS HERIOT *is at the top.* JEAN *and* LORD JOHN *on the left.*

GREATOREX (*on divan centre, aside to* MISS LEVERING): Too 'wonderful' to waste your time on the wrong people.

MISS LEVERING: I shall waste less of my time after this.

GREATOREX: I'm relieved to hear it. I can't see you wheedling money for shelters and rot of that sort out of retired grocers.

MISS LEVERING: You see, you call it rot. We couldn't have got £8,000 out of *you*.

GREATOREX (*very low*): I'm not sure.

MISS LEVERING *looks at him.*

GREATOREX: If I gave you that much – for your little projects – what would you give me?

MISS LEVERING (*speaking quietly*): Soper didn't ask that.

GREATOREX (*horrified*): Soper! I should think not!

LORD JOHN (*turning to* MISS LEVERING): Soper? You two still talking Soper? How flattered the old beggar'd be!

LORD JOHN (*lower*): Did you hear what Mrs Heriot said about him? 'So kind; so munificent – so *vulgar*, poor soul, we couldn't know him in London – *but we shall meet him in heaven.'*

GREATOREX *and* LORD JOHN *go off laughing.*

LADY JOHN (*to* MISS LEVERING): Sit over there, my dear. (*Indicating chair in front of the writing table.*) You needn't stay, Jean. This won't interest you.

MISS LEVERING (*in the tone of one agreeing*): It's only an effort to meet the greatest evil in the world?

JEAN (*pausing as she's following the others*): What do you call the greatest evil in the world?

Looks pass between MRS HERIOT *and* LADY JOHN.

MISS LEVERING (*without emphasis*): The helplessness of women.

JEAN *stands still.*

LADY JOHN (*rising and putting her arm about the girl's shoulder*): Jean, darling, I know you can think of nothing but (*aside*) him – so just go and –

JEAN (*brightly*): Indeed, indeed, I can think of everything better than I ever did before. He has lit up everything for me – made everything vivider, more – more significant.

MISS LEVERING (*turning round*): Who has?

JEAN: Oh, yes, I don't care about other things less but a thousand times more.

LADY JOHN: You *are* in love.

MISS LEVERING: Oh, that's it! (*Smiling at* JEAN.) I congratulate you.

LADY JOHN (*returning to the outspread plan*): Well – *this*, you see, obviates the difficulty you raised.

MISS LEVERING: Yes, quite.

MRS HERIOT: But it's going to cost a great deal more.

MISS LEVERING: It's worth it.

MRS HERIOT: We'll have nothing left for the organ at St Pilgrim's.

LADY JOHN: My dear Lydia, we're putting the organ aside.

MRS HERIOT (*with asperity*): We can't afford to 'put aside' the elevating effect of music.

LADY JOHN: What we must make for, first, is the cheap and humanely conducted lodging-house.

MRS HERIOT: There are several of those already, but poor St Pilgrim's –

MISS LEVERING: There are none for the poorest women.

LADY JOHN: No, even the excellent Soper was for multiplying Rowton Houses. You can never get men to realise – you can't always get women –

MISS LEVERING: It's the work least able to wait.

MRS HERIOT: I don't agree with you, and I happen to have spent a great deal of my life in works of charity.

MISS LEVERING: Ah, then you'll be interested in the girl I saw dying in a Tramp Ward a little while ago. *Glad* her cough was worse – only she mustn't die before her father. Two reasons. Nobody but her to keep the old man out of the workhouse – and 'father is so proud.' If she died first, he would starve; worst of all he might hear what had happened up in London to his girl.

MRS HERIOT: She didn't say, I suppose, how she happened to fall so low.

MISS LEVERING: Yes, she had been in service. She lost the train back one Sunday night and was too terrified of her employer to dare ring him up after hours. The wrong person found her crying on the platform.

MRS HERIOT: She should have gone to one of the Friendly Societies.

MISS LEVERING: At eleven at night?

MRS HERIOT: And there are the Rescue Leagues. I myself have been connected with one for twenty years –

MISS LEVERING (*reflectively*): 'Twenty years!' Always arriving 'after the train's gone' – after the girl and the Wrong Person have got to the journey's end.

MRS HERIOT'S *eyes flash.*

JEAN: Where is she now?

LADY JOHN: Never mind.

MISS LEVERING: Two nights ago she was waiting at a street corner in the rain.

MRS HERIOT: Near a public-house, I suppose.

MISS LEVERING: Yes, a sort of 'public-house.' She was plainly dying – she was told she shouldn't be out in the rain. 'I mustn't go in yet,' she said. '*This* is what he gave me,' and she began to cry. In her hand were two pennies silvered over to look like half-crowns.

MRS HERIOT: I don't believe that story. It's just the sort of thing some sensation-monger trumps up – now, who tells you such –

MISS LEVERING: Several credible people. I didn't believe them till –

JEAN: Till –?

MISS LEVERING: Till last week I saw for myself.

LADY JOHN: *Saw*? Where?

MISS LEVERING: In a low lodging-house not a hundred yards from the church you want a new organ for.

MRS HERIOT: How did *you* happen to be there?

MISS LEVERING: I was on a pilgrimage.

JEAN: A pilgrimage?

MISS LEVERING: Into the Underworld.

LADY JOHN: *You* went?

JEAN: How *could* you?

MISS LEVERING: I put on an old gown and a tawdry hat – (*Turns to* LADY JOHN.) You'll never know how many things are hidden from a woman in good clothes. The bold, free look of a man at a woman he believes to be destitute – you must *feel* that look on you before you can understand – a good half of history.

MRS HERIOT (*rises*): Jean! –

JEAN: But where did you go – dressed like that?

MISS LEVERING: Down among the homeless women – on a wet night looking for shelter.

LADY JOHN (*hastily*): No wonder you've been ill.

JEAN (*under her breath*): And it's like that?

MISS LEVERING: No.

JEAN: No?

MISS LEVERING: It's so much worse I dare not tell about it – even if you weren't here I couldn't.

MRS HERIOT (*to* JEAN): You needn't suppose, darling, that those wretched creatures feel it as we would.

MISS LEVERING: The girls who need shelter and work aren't all serving-maids.

MRS HERIOT (*with an involuntary flash*): We know that all the women who – *make mistakes* aren't.

MISS LEVERING (*steadily*): That is why *every* woman ought to take an interest in this – every girl too.

JEAN   Yes – oh, yes!
LADY (*simultaneously*): No. This is a
JOHN   matter for us
                        older –

MRS HERIOT (*with an air of sly challenge*): Or for a person who has some special knowledge. (*Significantly.*) *We* can't pretend to have access to such sources of information as Miss Levering.

MISS LEVERING (*meeting* MRS HERIOT'S *eye steadily*): Yes, for I can give you access. As you seem to think, I have some first-hand knowledge about homeless girls.

LADY JOHN (*cheerfully turning it aside*): Well, my dear, it will all come in convenient. (*Tapping the plan.*)

MISS LEVERING: It once happened to me to take offence at an ugly thing that was going on under my father's roof. Oh, *years* ago! I was an impulsive girl. I turned my back on my father's house –

LADY JOHN (*for* JEAN'S *benefit*): That was ill-advised.

MRS HERIOT: Of course, if a girl does *that* –

MISS LEVERING: That was what all my relations said (*with a glance at* JEAN), and I couldn't explain.

JEAN: Not to your mother?

MISS LEVERING: She was dead. I went to London to a small hotel and tried to find employment. I wandered about all day and every day from agency to agency. I was supposed to be educated.

I'd been brought up partly in Paris; I could play several instruments, and sing little songs in four different tongues. (*Slight pause.*)

JEAN: Did nobody want you to teach French or sing the little songs?

MISS LEVERING: The heads of schools thought me too young. There were people ready to listen to my singing, but the terms – they were too hard. Soon my money was gone. I began to pawn my trinkets. *They* went.

JEAN: And still no work?

MISS LEVERING: No; but by that time I had some real education – an unpaid hotel bill, and not a shilling in the world. (*Slight pause.*) Some girls think it hardship to have to earn their living. The horror is not to be allowed to –

JEAN (*bending forward*): What happened?

LADY JOHN (*rises*): My dear (*to* MISS LEVERING:) have your things been sent down? Are you quite ready?

MISS LEVERING: Yes, all but my hat.

JEAN: Well?

MISS LEVERING: Well, by chance I met a friend of my family.

JEAN: That was lucky.

MISS LEVERING: I thought so. He was nearly ten years older than I. He said he wanted to help me. (*Pause.*)

JEAN: And didn't he?

LADY JOHN *lays her hand on* MISS LEVERING'S *shoulder.*

MISS LEVERING: Perhaps after all he did. (*With sudden change of tone.*) Why do I waste time over myself? I belonged to the little class of armed women. My body wasn't born weak, and my spirit wasn't broken by the *habit* of slavery. But, as Mrs Heriot was kind enough to hint, I do know something about the possible fate of homeless girls. I found there were pleasant parks, museums, free libraries in our great rich London – and not one single place where destitute women can be sure of work that isn't killing or food that isn't worse than prison fare. That's why women ought not to sleep o' nights till this Shelter stands spreading out wide arms.

JEAN: No, no –

MRS HERIOT (*gathering up her gloves, fan, prayer-book, etc.*): Even when it's built – you'll see! Many of those creatures will prefer the life they lead. They *like* it.

MISS LEVERING: A woman told me – one of the sort that knows – told me many of them 'like it' so much that they are indifferent to the risk of being sent to prison. '*It gives them a rest*,' she said.

LADY JOHN: A rest!

MISS LEVERING *glances at the clock as she rises to go upstairs.*

LADY JOHN *and* MRS HERIOT *bend their heads over the plan, covertly talking.*

JEAN (*intercepting* MISS LEVERING): I want to begin to understand something of – I'm horribly ignorant.

MISS LEVERING (*Looks at her searchingly*): I'm a rather busy person –

JEAN (*interrupting*): I have quite a special reason for wanting *not* to be ignorant. (*Impulsively.*) I'll go to town tomorrow, if you'll come and lunch with me.

MISS LEVERING: Thank you – I (*catches* MRS HERIOT's *eye*) – I must go and put my hat on.

Exit upstairs.

MRS HERIOT (*aside*): How little she minds all these horrors!

LADY JOHN: They turn me cold. Ugh! (*Rising, harassed.*) I wonder if she's signed the visitors' book!

MRS HERIOT: For all her Shelter schemes, she's a hard woman.

JEAN: Miss Levering is?

MRS HERIOT: Oh, of course *you* won't think so. She has angled very adroitly for your sympathy.

JEAN: She doesn't look hard.

LADY JOHN (*glancing at* JEAN *and taking alarm*): I'm not sure but what she does. Her mouth – always like this ... as if she were holding back something by main force!

MRS HERIOT (*half under her breath*): Well, so she is.

Exit LADY JOHN *into the lobby to look at the visitors' book.*

JEAN: Why haven't I seen her before?

MRS HERIOT: Oh, she's lived abroad. (*Debating with herself.*) You don't know about her, I suppose?

JEAN: I don't know how Aunt Ellen came to know her.

MRS HERIOT: That was my doing. But I didn't bargain for her being introduced to you.

JEAN: She seems to go everywhere. And why shouldn't she?

MRS HERIOT (*quickly*): You mustn't ask her to Eaton Square.

JEAN: I have.

MRS HERIOT: Then you'll have to get out of it.

JEAN (*with a stubborn look*): I must have a reason. And a very good reason.

MRS HERIOT: Well, it's not a thing I should have preferred to tell you, but I know how difficult you are to guide . . . so I suppose you'll have to know. (*Lowering her voice.*) It was ten or twelve years ago. I found her horribly ill in a lonely Welsh farmhouse. We had taken the Manor for that August. The farmer's wife was frightened, and begged me to go and see what I thought. I soon saw how it was – I thought she was dying.

JEAN: *Dying!* What was the –

MRS HERIOT: I got no more out of her than the farmer's wife did. She had had no letters. There had been no one to see her except a man down from London, a shady-looking doctor – nameless, of course. And then this result. The farmer and his wife, highly respectable people, were incensed. They were for turning the girl out.

JEAN: *Oh!* but –

MRS HERIOT: Yes. Pitiless some of these people are! I insisted they should treat the girl humanely, and we became friends . . . that is, 'sort of'. In spite of all I did for her –

JEAN: What did you do?

MRS HERIOT: I–I've told you, and I lent her money. No small sum either.

JEAN: Has she never paid it back?

MRS HERIOT: Oh, yes, after a time. But I *always* kept her secret – as much as I knew of it.

JEAN: But you've been telling me!

MRS HERIOT: That was my duty – and I *never* had her full confidence.

JEAN: Wasn't it natural she –

MRS HERIOT: Well, all things considered, she might have wanted to tell me who was responsible.

JEAN: Oh! Aunt Lydia!

MRS HERIOT: All she ever said was that she was ashamed – (*losing her temper and her fine feeling for the innocence of her auditor*) – ashamed that she 'hadn't had the courage to resist' – not the original temptation but the pressure brought to bear on her 'not to go through with it,' as she said.

JEAN (*wrinkling her brows*): You are being so delicate – I'm not sure I understand.

MRS HERIOT (*irritably*): The only thing you need understand is that she's not a desirable companion for a young girl.

Pause.

JEAN: When did you see her after – after –

MRS HERIOT (*with a slight grimace*): I met her last winter at the Bishop's. (*Hurriedly.*) She's a connection of his wife's. They'd got her to help with some of their work. Then she took hold of ours. Your aunt and uncle are quite foolish about her, and I'm debarred from taking any steps, at least till the Shelter is out of hand.

JEAN: I do rather wonder she can bring herself to talk about – the unfortunate women of the world.

MRS HERIOT: The effrontery of it!

JEAN: Or . . . the courage! (*Puts her hand up to her throat as if the sentence had caught there.*)

MRS HERIOT: Even presumes to set *me* right! Of course I don't *mind* in the least, poor soul . . . but I feel I owe it to your dead mother to tell you about her, especially as you're old enough now to know something about life –

JEAN (*slowly*): – and since a girl needn't be very old to suffer for her ignorance. (*Moves a little away.*) I *felt* she was rather wonderful.

MRS HERIOT: *Wonderful!*

JEAN (*pausing*): ... To have lived through *that* when she was ... how old?

MRS HERIOT (*rising*): Oh, nineteen or thereabouts.

JEAN: Five years younger than I. To be abandoned and to come out of it like this!

MRS HERIOT (*laying her hand on the girl's shoulder*): It was too bad to have to tell you such a sordid story today of all days.

JEAN: It is a very terrible story, but this wasn't a bad time. I feel very sorry today for women who aren't happy.

Motor horn heard faintly.

(*Jumping up.*) That's Geoffrey!

MRS HERIOT: Mr Stonor! What makes you think ...?

JEAN: Yes, yes. I'm sure, I'm sure –

Checks herself as she is flying off. Turns and sees LORD JOHN *entering from the garden.*

Motor horn louder.

LORD JOHN: Who do you think is motoring up the drive?

JEAN (*catching hold of him*): Oh, dear! How am I ever going to be able to behave like a girl who isn't engaged to the only man in the world worth marrying?

MRS HERIOT: You were expecting Mr Stonor all the time!

JEAN: He promised he'd come to luncheon if it was humanly possible; but I was afraid to tell you for fear he'd be prevented.

LORD JOHN (*laughing as he crosses to the lobby*): You felt we couldn't have borne the disappointment.

JEAN: I felt I couldn't.

The lobby door opens. LADY JOHN *appears radiant, followed by a tall*

figure in a dustcoat, etc., no goggles. He has straight, firm features, a little blunt; fair skin, high coloured; fine, straight hair, very fair; grey eyes, set somewhat prominently and heavy when not interested; lips full, but firmly moulded. GEOFFREY STONOR *is heavier than a man of forty should be, but otherwise in the pink of physical condition. The* FOOTMAN *stands waiting to help him off with his motor coat.*

LADY JOHN: Here's an agreeable surprise!

JEAN *has gone forward only a step, and stands smiling at the approaching figure.*

LORD JOHN: How do you do? (*As he comes between them and briskly shakes hands with* STONOR.)

FANBOROUGH *appears at the French window.*

FARNBOROUGH: Yes, by Jove! (*Turning to the others clustered round the window.*) What gigantic luck!

Those outside crane and glance, and then elaborately turn their backs and pretend to be talking among themselves, but betray as far as manners permit the enormous sensation the arrival has created.

STONOR: How do you do?

Shakes hands with MRS HERIOT, *who has rushed up to him with both hers outstretched. He crosses to* JEAN, *who meets him half way; they shake hands, smiling into each other's eyes.*

JEAN: Such a long time since we met!

LORD JOHN (*to* STONOR): You're growing very enterprising. I could hardly believe my ears when I heard you'd motored all the way from town to see a supporter on Sunday.

STONOR: I don't know how we covered the ground in the old days. (*To* LADY JOHN.) It's no use to stand for your borough any more. The American, you know, he 'runs' for Congress. By and by we shall all be flying after the thing we want. (*Smiles at* JEAN.)

JEAN: Sh! (*Smiles and then glances over her shoulder and speaks low.*) All sorts of irrelevant people here.

FARNBOROUGH (*unable to resist the temptation, comes forward*): How do you do, Mr Stonor?

STONOR: Oh – how d'you do.

FARNBOROUGH: Some of them were arguing in the smoking-room last night whether it didn't hurt a man's chances going about in a motor.

LORD JOHN: Yes, we've been hearing a lot of stories about the unpopularity of motor cars – among the class that hasn't got 'em, of course. What do you say?

LADY JOHN: I'm sure you gain more votes by being able to reach so many more of your constituency than we used –

STONOR: Well, I don't know – I've sometimes wondered whether the charm of our presence wasn't counterbalanced by the way we tear about smothering our fellow-beings in dust and running down their pigs and chickens, not to speak of their children.

LORD JOHN (*anxiously*): What on the whole are the prospects?

FARNBOROUGH *cranes forward.*

STONOR (*gravely*): We shall have to work harder than we realised.

FARNBOROUGH: Ah! (*Retires towards group.*)

JEAN (*in a half-aside as she slips her arm in her uncle's and smiles at GEOFFREY*): He says he believes I'll be able to make a real difference to his chances. Isn't it angelic of him?

STONOR (*in a jocular tone*): Angelic? Macchiavelian. I pin all my hopes on your being able to counteract the pernicious influence of my opponent's glib wife.

JEAN: You want me to have a *real* share in it all, don't you, Geoffrey?

STONOR (*smiling into her eyes*): Of course I do.

FARNBOROUGH *drops down again on pretence of talking to MRS HERIOT.*

LORD JOHN: I don't gather you're altogether sanguine. Any complication?

JEAN *and* LADY JOHN *stand close together, the girl radiant, following STONOR with her eyes and whispering to the sympathetic elder woman.*

STONOR: Well, (*taking Sunday paper out of pocket*) there's this agitation about the Woman Question. Oddly enough, it seems likely to affect the issue.

LORD JOHN: Why should it? Can't you do what the other four hundred have done?

STONOR (*laughs*): Easily. But, you see, the mere fact that four hundred and twenty members have been worried into promising support – and then once in the House have let the matter severely alone –

LORD JOHN (*to* STONOR): Let it alone! Bless my soul, I should think so indeed.

STONOR: Of course. Only it's a device that's somewhat worn.

Enter MISS LEVERING, *with hat on; gloves and veil in her hand.*

LORD JOHN: Still if they think they're getting a future Cabinet Minister on their side –

STONOR: . . .it will be sufficiently embarassing for the Cabinet Minister.

STONOR *turns to speak to* JEAN. *He stops dead seeing* MISS LEVERING.

JEAN (*smiling*): You know one another?

MISS LEVERING (*looking at* STONOR *with intentness but quite calmly*): Everybody in this part of the world knows Mr Stonor, but he doesn't know me.

LORD JOHN: Miss Levering.

They bow.

Enter GREATOREX, *sidling in with an air of giving* MRS FREDDY *a wide berth.*

JEAN (*to* MISS LEVERING *with artless enthusiasm*): Oh, have you been hearing him speak?

MISS LEVERING: Yes, I was visiting some relations near Dutfield. They took me to hear you.

STONOR: Oh – the night the Suffragettes made their customary row.

MISS LEVERING: The night they asked you –

STONOR (*flying at the first chance of distraction, shakes hands with* MRS FREDDY): Well, Mrs Freddy, what do you think of your friends now?

MRS FREDDY: My friends?

STONOR (*offering her the Sunday paper*): Yes, the disorderly women.

MRS FREDDY (*with dignity*): They are not my friends, but I don't think you must call them –

STONOR: Why not? (*Laughs.*) I can forgive them for worrying the late Government. But they *are* disorderly.

MISS LEVERING (*quietly*): Isn't the phrase consecrated to a different class?

GREATOREX (*who has got hold of the Sunday paper*): He's perfectly right. How do you do? Disorderly women! That's what they are!

FARNBOROUGH (*reading over his shoulder*): Ought to be locked up! Every one of 'em.

GREATOREX (*assenting angrily*): Public nuisances! Going about with dog whips and spitting in policemen's faces.

FREDDY (*with a harassed air*): I wonder if they did spit?

GREATOREX (*exulting*): Of *course* they did.

MRS FREDDY (*turns on him*): You're no authority on what they do. *You* run away.

GREATOREX (*trying to turn the laugh*): Run away? Yes. (*Backing a few paces.*) And if ever I muster up courage to come back, it will be to vote for better manners in public life, not worse than we have already.

MRS FREDDY (*meekly*): So should I. Don't think that *I* defend the Suffragette methods.

JEAN (*with cheerful curiosity*): Still, you *are* an advocate of the Suffrage, aren't you?

MRS FREDDY: Here? (*Shrugs.*) I don't beat the air.

GREATOREX (*mocking*): Only policemen.

MRS FREDDY (*plaintively*): If you cared to know the attitude of the real workers in the reform, you might have noticed in any paper last week we lost no time in dissociating ourselves from the little group of hysterical – (*Catches her husband's eye, and instantly checks her flow of words.*)

MRS HERIOT: They have lowered the whole sex in the eyes of the entire world.

JEAN (*joining* GEOFFREY STONOR): I can't quite see what they want – those Suffragettes.

GREATOREX: Notoriety.

FARNBOROUGH: What they want? A good thrashin' – that's what I'd give 'em.

MRS HERIOT (*murmurs*): Spirited fellow!

LORD JOHN: Well, there's one sure thing – they've dished their goose. (GREATOREX *chuckles, still reading the account.*) I believe these silly scenes are a pure joy to you.

GREATOREX: Final death-blow to the whole silly business!

JEAN (*mystified, looking from one to the other*): The Suffragettes don't seem to *know* they're dead.

GREATOREX: They still keep up a sort of death-rattle. But they've done for themselves.

JEAN (*clasping her hands with fervour*): Oh, I hope they'll last till the election's over.

FARNBOROUGH (*stares*): Why?

JEAN: Oh, we want them to get the working man to – (*stumbling and a little confused*) – to vote for . . . the Conservative candidate. Isn't that so?

Looking round for help. General laughter.

LORD JOHN: Fancy, Jean –!

GREATOREX: The working man's a good deal of an ass, but even he won't listen to –

JEAN (*again appealing to the silent*

STONOR): But he *does* listen like anything! I asked why there were so few at the Long Mitcham meeting, and I was told, 'Oh, they've all gone to hear Miss –'

STONOR: Just for a lark, that was.

LORD JOHN: It has no real effect on the vote.

GREATOREX: Not the smallest.

JEAN (*wide-eyed to* STONOR): Why, I thought you said –

STONOR (*hastily, rubbing his hand over the lower part of his face and speaking quickly*): I've a notion a little soap and water wouldn't do me any harm.

LORD JOHN: I'll take you up. You know Freddy Tunbridge.

STONOR *pauses to shake hands. Exeunt all three.*

JEAN (*perplexed, as* STONOR *turns away, says to* GREATOREX): Well, if women are of no importance in politics, it isn't for the reason you gave. There is now and then a weekender among them.

GREATOREX (*shuffles about uneasily*): Hm – Hm. (*Finds himself near* MRS FREDDY.) Lord! The perils that beset the feet of man! (*With an air of comic caution, moves away, left.*)

JEAN (*to* FARNBOROUGH, *aside, laughing*): Why does he behave like that?

FARNBOROUGH: His moral sense is shocked.

JEAN: Why, I saw him and Mrs Freddy together at the French Play the other night – as thick as thieves.

MISS LEVERING: Ah, that was before he knew her revolting views.

JEAN: What revolting views?

GREATOREX: Sh! Sunday.

As GREATOREX *sidles cautiously further away.*

JEAN (*laughing in spite of herself*): I can't believe women are so helpless when I see men so afraid of them.

GREATOREX: The great mistake was in teaching them to read and write.

JEAN (*over* MISS LEVERING'S *shoulder, whispers*): Say something.

MISS LEVERING (*to* GREATOREX, *smiling*): Oh no, that wasn't the worst mistake.

GREATOREX: Yes, it was.

MISS LEVERING: No. Believe me. The mistake was in letting women learn to talk.

GREATOREX: Ah! (*Wheels about with sudden rapture.*) I see now what's to be the next great reform.

MISS LEVERING (*holding up the little volume*): When women are all dumb, no more discussions of the 'Paradiso.'

GREATOREX (*with a gesture of mock rapture*): The thing itself! (*Aside.*) That's a great deal better than talking about it, as I'm sure *you* know.

MISS LEVERING: Why do you think I know?

GREATOREX: Only the plain women are in any doubt.

JEAN *joins* MISS LEVERING.

GREATOREX: Wait for me, Farnborough. I cannot go about unprotected.

Exeunt FARNBOROUGH *and* GREATOREX.

MRS FREDDY: It's true what that old cynic says. The scene in the House has put back the reform a generation.

JEAN: I wish I'd been there.

MRS FREDDY: I *was.*

JEAN: Oh, was it like the papers said?

MRS FREDDY: Worse. I've never been so moved in public. No tragedy, no great opera ever gripped an audience as the situation in the House did that night. There we all sat breathless – with everything more favourable to us than it had been within the memory of women. Another five minutes and the Resolution would have passed. Then . . . all in a moment –

LORD JOHN (*to* MRS HERIOT): Listen – they're talking about the female hooligans.

MRS HERIOT: No, thank you! (*Sits apart with the 'Church Times.'*)

MRS FREDDY (*excitedly*): All in a moment a horrible dingy little flag was poked through the grille of the Woman's Gallery – cries – insults – scuffling – the police – the ignominious turning out of the women – *us* as well as the – Oh, I can't *think* of it without – (*Jumps up and walks to and fro. Pauses.*) Then the next morning! The people gloating. Our friends antagonised – people who were wavering – nearly won over – all thrown back – heart breaking! Even my husband! Freddy's been an angel about letting me take my share when I felt I must – but of course I've always known he doesn't really like it. It makes him shy. I'm sure it gives him a horrid twist inside when he sees my name among the speakers on the placards. But he's always been an angel about it before this. After the disgraceful scene he said, 'It just shows how unfit women are for any sort of coherent thinking or concerted action.'

JEAN: To think that it should be women who've given the Cause the worst blow it ever had!

MRS FREDDY: The work of forty years destroyed in five minutes!

JEAN: They must have felt pretty sick when they woke up the next morning – the Suffragettes.

MRS FREDDY: I don't waste any sympathy on *them*. I'm thinking of the penalty *all* women have to pay because a handful of hysterical –

JEAN: Still I think I'm sorry for them. It must be dreadful to find you've done such a lot of harm to the thing you care most about in the world.

MISS LEVERING: Do you picture the Suffragettes sitting in sackcloth?

MRS FREDDY: Well, they can't help realising *now* what they've done.

MISS LEVERING (*quietly*): Isn't it just possible they realise they've waked up interest in the Woman Question so that it's advertised in every paper and discussed in every house from Land's End to John O'Groats? Don't you think *they* know there's been more said and written about it in these ten days since the scene, than in the ten years before it?

MRS FREDDY: You aren't saying you think it was a good way to get what they wanted?

MISS LEVERING (*shrugs*): I'm only pointing out that it seems not such a bad way to get it known they *do* want something – and (*smiling*) 'want it bad'.

JEAN (*getting up*): Didn't Mr Greatorex say women had been politely petitioning Parliament for forty years?

MISS LEVERING: And men have only laughed.

JEAN: But they'd come round. (*She looks from one to the other.*) Mrs Tunbridge says, before that horrid scene, everything was favourable at last.

MISS LEVERING: At last? Hadn't it been just as 'favourable' before?

MRS FREDDY: No. We'd never had so many members pledged to our side.

MISS LEVERING: I thought I'd heard somebody say the Bill had got as far as that, time and time again.

JEAN: Oh no. Surely not –

MRS FREDDY (*reluctantly*): Y-yes. This was only a Resolution. The Bill passed a second reading thirty-seven years ago.

JEAN (*with wide eyes*): And what difference did it make?

MISS LEVERING: The men laughed rather louder.

MRS FREDDY: Oh, it's got as far as a second reading several times – but we never had so many friends in the House before –

MISS LEVERING (*with a faint smile*): 'Friends!'

JEAN: Why do you say it like that?

MISS LEVERING: Perhaps because I was thinking of a funny story – he said it was funny – a Liberal Whip told me the other day. A Radical Member went out of the House after his speech in favour of the Woman's Bill, and as he came back half an hour later, he heard some Members talking in the Lobby about the astonishing number who were going to vote for the measure. And the Friend of Woman dropped his jaw and clutched the man next to him: 'My God!'

he said, 'you don't mean to say they're going to give it to them!'

JEAN: Oh!

MRS FREDDY: You don't think all men in Parliament are like that!

MISS LEVERING: I don't think all men are burglars, but I lock my doors.

JEAN (*below her breath*): You think that night of the scene – you think the men didn't *mean* to play fair?

MISS LEVERING (*her coolness in contrast to the excitement of the others*): Didn't the women sit quiet till ten minutes to closing time?

JEAN: Ten minutes to settle a question like that!

MISS LEVERING (*quietly to* MRS FREDDY): Couldn't you see the men were at their old game?

LADY JOHN (*coming forward*): You think they were just putting off the issue till it was too late?

MISS LEVERING (*in a detached tone*): *I* wasn't there, but I haven't heard anybody deny that the women waited till ten minutes to eleven. Then they discovered the policeman who'd been sent up at the psychological moment to the back of the gallery. Then, I'm told, when the women saw they were betrayed once more, they utilised the few minutes left, to impress on the country at large the fact of their demands – did it in the only way left them. (*Sits leaning forward reflectively smiling, chin in hand.*) It does rather look to the outsider as if the well-behaved women had worked for forty years and made less impression on the world then those fiery young women made in five minutes.

MRS FREDDY: Oh, come, be fair!

MISS LEVERING: Well, you must admit that, next day, every newspaper reader in Europe and America knew there were women in England in such dead earnest about the Suffrage that the men had stopped laughing at last, and turned them out of the House. Men even advertised how little they appreciated the fun by sending the women to gaol in pretty sober earnest. And all the world was talking about it.

MRS HERIOT *lays down the 'Church Times' and joins the others.*

LADY JOHN: I have noticed, whenever the men aren't there, the women sit and discuss that scene.

JEAN (*cheerfully*): *I* shan't have to wait till the men are gone. (*Leans over* LADY JOHN'S *shoulder and says half aside*) He's in sympathy.

LADY JOHN: How do you know?

JEAN: He told the interrupting women so.

MRS FREDDY *looks mystified. The others smile.*

LADY JOHN: Oh!

MR FREDDY *and* LORD JOHN *appear by the door they went out of. They stop to talk.*

MRS FREDDY: Here's Freddy! (*Lower, hastily to* MISS LEVERING): You're judging from the outside. Those of us who have been working for years – we all realise it was a perfectly lunatic proceeding. Why, *think*! The only chance of our getting what we want is by *winning over* the men. (*Her watchful eye, leaving her husband for a moment, catches* MISS LEVERING'S *little involuntary gesture.*) What's the matter?

MISS LEVERING: 'Winning over the men' has been the woman's way for centuries. Do you think the result should make us proud of our policy? Yes? Then go and walk in Piccadilly at midnight. (*The older women glance at* JEAN.) No, I forgot –

MRS HERIOT (*with majesty*): Yes, it's not the first time you've forgotten.

MISS LEVERING: I forgot the magistrate's ruling. He said no decent woman had any business to be in London's main thoroughfare at night unless she has *a man with her*. I heard that in Nine Elms, too. 'You're obliged to take up with a chap!' was what the woman said.

MRS HERIOT (*rising*): JEAN! Come!

She takes JEAN *by her arm and draws her to the window, where she signals* GREATOREX *and* FARNBOROUGH. MRS FREDDY *joins her husband and* LORD JOHN.

LADY JOHN (*kindly, aside to* MISS LEVERING): My dear, I think Lydia Heriot's right. We oughtn't to do anything or *say* anything to encourage this ferment of feminism, and I'll tell you why: it's likely to bring a very terrible thing in its train.

MISS LEVERING: What terrible thing?

LADY JOHN: Sex antagonism.

MISS LEVERING (*rising*): It's here.

LADY JOHN (*very gravely*): Don't say that.

JEAN *has quietly disengaged herself from* MRS HERIOT, *and the group at the window returns and stands behind* LADY JOHN, *looking up into* MISS LEVERING'S *face.*

MISS LEVERING (*to* LADY JOHN): You're so conscious it's here, you're afraid to have it mentioned.

LADY JOHN (*turning and seeing* JEAN. *Rising hastily*): If it's here, it is the fault of those women agitators.

MISS LEVERING (*gently*): No woman *begins* that way. (*Leans forward with clasped hands looking into vacancy.*) Every woman's in a state of natural subjection (*smiles at* JEAN) – no, I'd rather say allegiance to her idea of romance and her hope of motherhood. They're embodied for her in man. They're the strongest things in life – till man kills them. (*Rousing herself and looking into* LADY JOHN'S *face.*) Let's be fair. Each woman knows why that allegiance died.

LADY JOHN *turns hastily, sees* LORD JOHN *coming down with* MR FREDDY *and meets them at the foot of the stairs.* MISS LEVERING *has turned to the table looking for her gloves, etc., among the papers; unconsciously drops the handkerchief she had in her little book.*

JEAN (*in a low voice to* MISS LEVERING): All this talk against the wicked Suffragettes – it makes me want to go and hear what they've got to say for themselves.

MISS LEVERING (*smiling with a non-committal air as she finds the veil she's been searching for*): Well, they're

holding a meeting in Trafalgar Square at three o'clock.

JEAN: This afternoon? But that's no use to people out of town – Unless I could invent some excuse . . .

LORD JOHN (*benevolently*): Still talking over the Shelter plans?

MISS LEVERING: No. We left the Shelter some time ago.

LORD JOHN (*to* JEAN): Then what's all the chatterment about?

JEAN, *a little confused, looks at* MISS LEVERING.

MISS LEVERING: The latest thing in veils. (*Ties hers round her hat.*)

GREATOREX: The invincible frivolity of woman!

LORD JOHN (*genially*): Don't scold them. It's a very proper tonic.

MISS LEVERING (*whimsically*): Oh, I was afraid you'd despise us for it.

BOTH MEN (*with condescension*): Not at all – not at all.

JEAN (*to* MISS LEVERING *as* FOOTMAN *appears*): Oh, they're coming for you. Don't forget your book. (FOOTMAN *holds out a salver with a telegram on it for* JEAN.) Why, it's for me!

MISS LEVERING: But it's time I was –

She crosses to the table.

JEAN (*opening the telegram*): May I? (*Reads, and glances over the paper at* MISS LEVERING.) I've got your book. (*Crosses to* MISS LEVERING, *and, looking at the back of the volume*) Dante! Whereabouts are you? (*Opening at the marker.*) Oh, the 'Inferno.'

MISS LEVERING: No; I'm in a worse place.

JEAN: I didn't know there was a worse.

MISS LEVERING: Yes; it's worse with the Vigliacchi.

JEAN: I forget. Were they Guelf or Ghibelline?

MISS LEVERING (*smiling*): They weren't either, and that was why Dante couldn't stand them. (*More gravely.*) He said there was not place in Heaven nor in Purgatory – not even a corner in Hell

– for the souls who had stood aloof from strife. (*Looking steadily into the girl's eyes.*) He called them 'wretches who never lived,' Dante did, because they'd never felt the pangs of partizanship. And so they wander homeless on the skirts of limbo among the abortions and off-scourings of Creation.

JEAN (*a long breath after a long look. When* MISS LEVERING *has turned away to make her leisurely adieux* JEAN'S *eyes fall on the open telegram*): Aunt Ellen, I've got to go to London.

STONOR, *re-entering, hears this, but pretends to talk to* MR FREDDY, *etc.*

LADY JOHN: My dear child!

MRS HERIOT: Nonsense! Is your grandfather worse?

JEAN (*folding the telegram*): No-o. I don't think so. But it's necessary I should go, all the same.

MRS HERIOT: Go away when Mr Stonor –

JEAN: He said he'd have to leave directly after luncheon.

LADY JOHN: I'll just see Miss Levering off, and then I'll come back and talk about it.

LORD JOHN (*to* MISS LEVERING): Why are you saying goodbye as if you were never coming back?

MISS LEVERING (*smiling*): One never knows. Maybe I shan't come back. (*To* STONOR.) Goodbye.

STONOR *bows ceremoniously. The others go up laughing.* STONOR *comes down.*

JEAN (*impulsively*): There mayn't be another train! Miss Levering –

STONOR (*standing in front of her*): What if there isn't? I'll take you back in the motor.

JEAN (*rapturously*): Will you? (*Inadvertently drops the telegram.*) I must be there by three!

STONOR (*picks up the telegram and a handkerchief lying near, glances at the message*): Why, it's only an invitation to dine – Wednesday!

JEAN: Sh! (*Takes the telegram and puts it in her pocket.*)

STONOR: Oh, I see! (*Lower, smiling.*) It's rather dear of you to arrange our going off like that. You *are* a clever little girl!

JEAN: It's not that I was arranging. I want to hear those women in Trafalgar Square – the Suffragettes.

STONOR (*incredulous, but smiling*): How perfectly absurd! (*Looking after* LADY JOHN.) Besides, I expect she wouldn't like my carrying you off like that.

JEAN: Then she'll have to make an excuse and come too.

STONOR: Ah, it wouldn't be quite the same –

JEAN (*rapidly thinking it out*): We could get back here in time for dinner.

GEOFFREY STONOR *glances down at the handkerchief still in his hand, and turns it half mechanically from corner to corner.*

JEAN (*absent-mindedly*): Mine?

STONOR (*hastily, without reflection*): No. (*He hands it to* MISS LEVERING *as she passes*): Yours.

MISS LEVERING, *on her way to the lobby with* LORD JOHN *seems not to notice.*

JEAN (*takes the handkerchief to give it to her, glancing down at the embroidered corner; stops*): But that's not an L! It's Vi –!

GEOFFREY STONOR *suddenly turns his back and takes up the newspaper.*

LADY JOHN (*from the lobby*): Come, Vida, since you will go.

MISS LEVERING: Yes; I'm coming.

Exit MISS LEVERING.

JEAN: *I* didn't know her name was Vida; how did you?

STONOR *stares silently over the top of his paper.*

ACT TWO

Scene: the north side of the Nelson Column in Trafalgar Square. The Curtain rises on an uproar. The crowd, which momentarily increases, is composed chiefly of weedy youths and wastrel old men. There are a few decent artisans; three of four 'beery' out-o'-works; three or four young women of the domestic servant or Strand restaurant cashier class; one aged woman in rusty black peering with faded, wondering eyes, consulting the faces of men and laughing nervously and apologetically from time to time; one or two quiet-looking, business-like women, thirty to forty; two middle-class men, who stare and whisper and smile. A quiet old man with a lot of unsold Sunday papers under one arm stands in an attitude of rapt attention, with the free hand round his deaf ear. A brisk-looking woman of forty-five or so, wearing pince-nez, goes round with a pile of propagandist literature on her arm. Many of the men smoking cigarettes – the old ones pipes. On the outskirts of this crowd, of several hundred, a couple of smart men in tall shining hats hover a few moments, single eyeglass up, and then saunter off. Against the middle of the Column, where it rises above the stone platform, is a great red banner, one supporting pole upheld by a grimy sandwichman, the other by a small, dirty boy of eight. If practicable only the lower portion of the banner need be seen, bearing the final words of the legend –
'VOTES FOR WOMEN!' *in immense white letters. It will be well to get, to the full, the effect of the height above the crowd of the straggling group of speakers on the pedestal platform. These are, as the Curtain rises, a working-class woman who is waving her arms and talking very earnestly, her voice for the moment blurred in the uproar. She is dressed in brown serge and looks pinched and sallow. At her side is the* CHAIRMAN *urging that she be given a fair hearing.* ALLEN TRENT *is a tall, slim, brown-haired man of twenty-eight, with a slight stoop, an agreeable aspect, well-bred voice, and the gleaming brown eye of the visionary. Behind these two, looking on or talking among themselves, are several other carelessly dressed women; one,*

better turned out than the rest, is quite young, very slight and gracefully built, with round, very pink cheeks, full, scarlet lips, naturally waving brown hair, and an air of childish gravity. She looks at the unruly mob with imperturbable calm. The CHAIRMAN'S *voice is drowned.*

WORKING WOMAN (*with lean, brown finger out and voice raised shriller now above the tumult*): I've got boys o' me own and we laugh at all sorts o' things, but I should be ashymed and so would they if ever they was to be'yve as you're doin' to-d'y.

In laughter the noise dies.

People 'ave been sayin' this is a middle-class woman's movement. It's a libel. I'm a workin' woman myself, the wife of a working man. (*Voice:* 'Pore devil!') I'm a Poor Law Guardian and a –

NOISY YOUNG MAN: Think of that, now – gracious me!

Laughter and interruption.

OLD NEWSVENDOR (*to the noisy young man near him*): Oh, shut up, cawn't yer?

NOISY YOUNG MAN: Not fur *you!*

VOICE: Go 'ome and darn yer old man's stockens!

VOICE: Just clean yer *own* doorstep!

WORKING WOMAN: It's a pore sort of 'ousekeeper that leaves 'er doorstep till Sunday afternoon. Maybe that's when you would do *your* doorstep. I do mine in the mornin' before you men are awake.

OLD NEWSVENDOR: It's true, wot she says! – every word.

WORKING WOMAN: You say we women 'ave got no business servin' on boards and thinkin' about politics. Wot's *politics?*

A derisive roar.

It's just 'ousekeepin' on a big scyle. 'Oo among you working' men 'as the most comfortable 'omes? Those of you that gives yer wives yer wyges.

Loud laughter and jeers.

VOICES: { That's it!
{ Wantin' our money.
{ Lord 'Igh 'Ousekeeper of England.

WORKING WOMAN: If it wus only to use fur *our* comfort, d'ye think many o' you workin' men would be found turnin' over their wyges to their wives? No! Wot's the reason thousands do – and the best and the soberest? Because the workin' man knows that wot's a pound to *'im* is twenty shillin's to 'is wife. And she'll myke every penny in every one o' them shillin's *tell*. She gets more fur *'im* out of 'is wyges than wot 'e can! Some o' you know wot the 'omes is like where the men don't let the women manage. Well, the Poor Laws and the 'ole Government is just in the same muddle because the men 'ave tried to do the national 'ousekeepin' without the women.

Roars.

But, like I told you before, it's a libel to say it's only the well-off women wot's wantin' the vote. Wot about the 96,000 textile workers? Wot about the Yorkshire tailoresses? I can tell you wot plenty o' the poor women think about it. I'm one of them, and I can tell you we see there's reforms needed. *We ought to 'ave the vote (jeers)*, and we know 'ow to appreciate the other women 'oo go to prison fur tryin' to get it fur us!

With a little final bob of emphasis and a glance over shoulder at the old woman and the young one behind her, she seems about to retire, but pauses as the murmur in the crowd grows into distinct phrases. 'They get their 'air cut free..' 'Naow they don't, that's only us!' 'Silly Suffragettes!' 'Stop at 'ome!' ''Inderin' policemen – mykin' rows in the streets!'

VOICE (*louder than the others*): They sees yer ain't fit t'ave –

OTHER VOICES: 'Ha, ha!' 'Shut up!' 'Keep quiet, cawn't yer?' (*General uproar.*)

CHAIRMAN: You evidently don't know what had to be done by *men* before the extension of the Suffrage in '67. If it hadn't been for demonstrations of violence. (*His voice is drowned.*)

WORKING WOMAN (*coming forward again, her shrill note rising clear*): You s'y woman's plyce is 'ome! Don't you know there's a third of the women o' this country can't afford the luxury of stayin' in their 'omes? They *got* to go out and 'elp make money to p'y the rent and keep the 'ome from bein' sold up. Then there's all the women that 'aven't got even miseerable 'omes. They 'aven't got any 'omes *at all*.

NOISY YOUNG MAN: You said *you* got one. W'y don't you stop in it?

WORKING WOMAN: Yes, that's like a man. If one o' you is all right, he thinks the rest don't matter. We women –

NOISY YOUNG MAN: The lydies! God bless 'em!

Voices drown her and the CHAIRMAN.

OLD NEWSVENDOR (*to* NOISY YOUNG MAN): Oh, take that extra 'alf pint 'ome and *sleep it off!*

WORKING WOMAN: P'r'aps *your* 'omes are all right. P'r'aps you aren't livin', old and young, married and single, in one room. I come from a plyce where many fam'lies 'ave to live like that if they're to go on livin' *at all*. If you don't believe me, come and let me show you! (*She spreads out her lean arms.*) Come with me to Canning Town! – come with me to Bromley – come to Poplar and to Bow! No. You won't even *think* about the overworked women and the underfed children and the 'ovels they live in. And you want that we shouldn't think neither –

A VAGRANT: We'll do the thinkin'. You go 'ome and nuss the byby.

WORKING WOMAN: I do nurse my byby! I've nursed seven. What 'ave you done for yours? P'r'aps your children never goes 'ungry, and maybe you're satisfied – though I must say I wouldn't a' thought it from the *look* o' you.

VOICE: Oh, I s'y!

WORKING WOMAN: But we women are not satisfied. We don't only want better things for our own children. We want better things for all. *Every* child is our child. We know in our 'earts we oughtn't to rest till we've mothered 'em every one.

VOICE: 'Women' – 'children' – wot about the *men*? Are *they* all 'appy?

Derisive laughter and 'No! no!' 'Not precisely.' ''Appy? Lord!'

WORKING WOMAN: No, there's lots o' you men I'm sorry for (*Shrill Voice: 'Thanks awfully!'*), an' we'll 'elp you if you let us.

VOICE: 'Elp us? You tyke the bread out of our mouths. You women are black-leggin' the men!

WORKING WOMAN: *W'y* does any woman tyke less wyges than a man for the same work? Only because we can't get anything better. That's part the reason w'y we're yere to-d'y. Do you reely think we tyke them there low wyges because we got a *lykin'* for low wyges? No. We're just like you. We want as much as ever we can get. (*'Ear! 'Ear!' and laughter.*) We got a gryte deal to do with our wyges, we women has. We got the children to think about. And w'en we got our rights, a woman's flesh and blood won't be so much cheaper than a man's that employers can get rich on keepin' you out o' work, and sweatin' us. If you men only could see it, we got the *syme* cause, and if you 'elped us you'd be 'elpin yerselves.

VOICES: 'Rot!' 'Drivel.'

OLD NEWSVENDOR: True as gospel!

She retires against the banner with the others. There is some applause.

A MAN (*patronisingly*): Well, now, that wusn't so bad – fur a woman.

ANOTHER: Nnaw. *Not fur a woman.*

CHAIRMAN (*speaking through this last* Miss Ernestine Blunt will now address you.

Applause, chiefly ironic, laughter, a general moving closer and knitting up of attention. ERNESTINE BLUNT *is about twenty-four, but looks younger. She is very downright, not to say pugnacious – the something amusing and attractive about her is there, as it were, against her will, and the more fetching for that. She has no conventional gestures, and none of any sort at first. As she warms to her work she uses her slim hands to enforce her emphasis, but as though unconsciously. Her manner of speech is less monotonous than that of the average woman-speaker, but she, too, has a fashion of leaning all her weight on the end of the sentence. She brings out the*

final word or two with an effort of underscoring, and makes a forward motion of the slim body as if the better to drive the last nail in. She evidently means to be immensely practical – the kind who is pleased to think she hasn't a grain of sentimentality in her composition, and whose feeling, when it does all but master her, communicates itself magnetically to others.

MISS ERNESTINE BLUNT: Perhaps I'd better begin by explaining a little about our 'tactics'.

Cries of 'Tactics! We know!' 'Mykin' trouble!' 'Public scandal!'

To make you understand what we've done, I must remind you of what others have done. Perhaps you don't know that women first petitioned Parliament for the Franchise as long ago as 1866.

VOICE: How do *you* know?

She pauses a moment, taken off her guard by the suddenness of the attack.

VOICE: You wasn't there!

VOICE: That was the trouble. Haw! haw!

MISS ERNESTINE BLUNT: And the petition was presented –

VOICE: Give 'er a 'earin' now she 'as got out of 'er crydle.

MISS ERNESTINE BLUNT: – presented to the House of Commons by that great Liberal, John Stuart Mill. (*Voice:* 'Mill? Who is he when he's at home?') Bills or Resolutions have been before the House on and off for the last thirty-six years. That, roughly, is our history. We found ourselves, towards the close of the year 1905, with no assurance that if we went on in the same way any girl born into the world in this generation would live to exercise the rights of citizenship, though she lived to be a hundred. So we said all this has been in vain. We must try some other way. How did the working man get the Suffrage, we asked ourselves? Well, we turned up the records, and we *saw* –

VOICES: 'Not by scratching people's faces!' ... 'Disraeli give it 'em!' 'Dizzy? Get out!' 'Cahnty Cahncil scholarships!' 'Oh, Lord, this education!' 'Chartists riots, she's thinkin' of!' (*Noise in the crowd.*)

MISS ERNESTINE BLUNT: But we don't *want* to follow such a violent example. We would much rather *not* – but if that's the only way we can make the country see we're in earnest, we are prepared to show them.

VOICE: An' they'll show you! – Give you another month 'ard.

MISS ERNESTINE BLUNT: Don't think that going to prison has any fears for us. We'd go *for life* if by doing that we could get freedom for the rest of the women.

VOICES: 'Hear, hear!' 'Rot!' 'W'ye don't the men 'elp ye to get your rights?'

MISS ERNESTINE BLUNT: Here's some one asking why the men don't help. It's partly they don't understand yet – they *will* before we've done! (*Laughter.*) Partly they don't understand yet what's at stake–

RESPECTABLE OLD MAN (*chuckling*): Lord, they're a 'educatin' of us!

VOICE: Wot next?

MISS ERNESTINE BLUNT: – and partly that the bravest man is afraid of ridicule. Oh, yes; we've heard a great deal all our lives about the timidity and the sensitiveness of women. And it's true. We *are* sensitive. But I tell you, ridicule crumples a man up. It steels a woman. We've come to know the value of ridicule. We've educated ourselves so that we welcome ridicule. We owe our sincerest thanks to the comic writers. The cartoonist is our unconscious friend. Who cartoons people who are of no importance? What advertisement is so sure of being remembered?

POETIC YOUNG MAN: I admit that.

MISS ERNESTINE BLUNT: If we didn't know it by any other sign, the comic papers would tell us *we've arrived*! But our greatest debt of gratitude we owe, to the man who called us female hooligans.

The crowd bursts into laughter.

We aren't hooligans, but we hope the fact will be overlooked. If everybody said we were nice, well-behaved women, who'd come to hear us? *Not the men.*

Roars.

Men tell us it isn't womanly for us to care about politics. How do they know what's womanly? It's for women to decide that. Let the men attend to being manly. It will take them all their time.

VOICE: Are we down-'earted? Oh no!

MISS ERNESTINE BLUNT: And they say it would be dreadful if we got the vote, because then we'd be pitted against men in the economic struggle. But that's come about already. Do you know that out of every hundred women in this country eighty-two are wage-earning women? It used to be thought unfeminine for women to be students and to aspire to the arts – that bring fame and fortune. But nobody has ever said it was unfeminine for women to do the heavy drudgery that's badly paid. That kind of work had to be done by *some*body – and the men didn't hanker after it. Oh, no.

Laughter and interruption.

A MAN ON THE OUTER FRINGE: She can talk – the little one can.

ANOTHER: Oh, they can all 'talk'.

A BEERY, DIRTY FELLOW OF FIFTY: I wouldn't like to be 'er 'usban'. Think o' comin' 'ome to *that*!

HIS PAL: I'd soon learn 'er!

MISS ERNESTINE BLUNT (*speaking through the noise*): Oh, no! *Let* the women scrub and cook and wash. That's all right! But if they want to try their hand at the better paid work of the liberal professions – oh, very unfeminine indeed! Then there's another thing. Now I want you to listen to this, because it's *very* important. Men say if we persist in competing with them for the bigger prizes, they're dreadfully afraid we'd lose the beautiful protecting chivalry that – Yes, I don't wonder you laugh. *We* laugh. (*Bending forward with lit eyes.*) But the women I found at the Ferry Tin Works working for five shillings a week – I didn't see them laughing. The beautiful chivalry of the employers of women doesn't prevent them from paying women tenpence a day for sorting coal and loading and unloading carts – doesn't prevent them from forcing women to earn bread in ways worse still. So we won't talk about chivalry. It's being over-sarcastic. We'll just let this poor ghost of chivalry go – in exchange for a little plain justice.

VOICE: If the House of Commons won't give you justice, why don't you go to the House of Lords?

MISS ERNESTINE BLUNT: What?

VOICE: Better 'urry up. Case of early closin'.

Laughter. A man at the back asks the speaker something.

MISS ERNESTINE BLUNT (*unable to hear*): You'll be allowed to ask any question you like at the end of the meeting.

NEWCOMER (*boy of eighteen*): Oh, is it question time? I s'y, Miss, 'oo killed cock robin?

She is about to resume, but above the general noise the voice of a man at the back reaches her indistinct but insistent. She leans forward trying to catch what he says. While the indistinguishable murmur has been going on GEOFFREY STONOR has appeared on the edge of the crowd, followed by JEAN and LADY JOHN in motor veils.

JEAN (*pressing forward eagerly and raising her veil*): Is she one of them? That little thing!

STONOR (*doubtfully*): I–I suppose so.

JEAN: Oh, ask some one, Geoffrey. I'm so disappointed. I did so hope we'd hear one of the – the worst.

MISS ERNESTINE BLUNT (*to the interrupter – on the other side*): What? What do you say? (*She screws up her eyes with the effort to hear, and puts a hand up to her ear. A few indistinguishable words between her and the man.*)

LADY JOHN (*who has been studying the figures on the platform through her lorgnon, turns to a working man beside her*): Can you tell me, my man, which are the ones that – a – that make the disturbances?

WORKING MAN: Don't you be took in, Miss.

MISS ERNESTINE BLUNT: Oh, yes – I see. There's a man over here asking –

A YOUNG MAN: *I've* got a question, too. Are – you – married?

ANOTHER (*sniggering*): Quick! There's yer chawnce. 'E's a bachelor.

Laughter.

MISS ERNESTINE BLUNT (*goes straight on as if she had not heard*): – man asking: if the women get full citizenship, and a war is declared, will the women fight?

POETIC YOUNG MAN: No, really – no, really, now!

The Crowd: 'Haw! Haw!' 'Yes!' 'Yes, how about that?'

MISS ERNESTINE BLUNT (*smiling*): Well, you know, some people say the whole trouble about us is that we *do* fight. But it is only hard necessity makes us do that. We don't *want* to fight – as men seem to – just for fighting's sake. Women are for peace.

VOICE: Hear, hear.

MISS ERNESTINE BLUNT: And when we have a share in public affairs there'll be less likelihood of war. But that's not to say women can't fight. The Boer women did. The Russian women face conflicts worse than any battlefield can show. (*Her voice shakes a little, and the eyes fill, but she controls her emotion gallantly, and dashes on.*) But we women know all that is evil, and we're for peace. Our part – we're proud to remember it – our part has been to go about after you men in war time, and – *pick up the pieces*!

A great shout.

Yes – seems funny, doesn't it? You men blow them to bits, and then we come along and put them together again. If you know anything about military nursing, you know a good deal of our work has been done in the face of danger – *but it's always been done.*

OLD NEWSVENDOR: That's so. That's so.

MISS ERNESTINE BLUNT: You complain that more and more we're taking away from you men the work that's always been yours. You can't any longer keep women out of the industries. The only question is upon what terms shall she continue to be in? As long as she's in on bad terms, she's not only hurting herself – she's hurting you. But if you're feeling discouraged about our competing with you, we're willing to leave you your trade in war. *Let* the men take life! We *give* life! (*Her voice is once more moved and proud.*) No one will pretend ours isn't one of the dangerous trades either. I won't say any more to you now, because we've got others to speak to you, and a new woman helper that I want you to hear.

She retires to the sound of clapping. There's a hurried consultation between her and the CHAIRMAN. *Voices in the Crowd:* 'The little 'un's all right' 'Ernestine's a corker,' *etc.*

JEAN (*looking at* STONOR *to see how he's taken it*): Well?

STONOR (*smiling down at her*): Well –

JEAN: Nothing reprehensible in what *she* said, was there?

STONOR (*shrugs*): Oh, reprehensible!

JEAN: It makes me rather miserable all the same.

STONOR (*draws her hand protectingly through his arm*): You mustn't take it as much to heart as all that.

JEAN: I can't help it – I can't indeed, Geoffrey. I shall *never* be able to make a speech like that!

STONOR (*taken aback*): I hope not, indeed.

JEAN: Why, I thought you said you wanted me –?

STONOR (*smiling*): To make nice little speeches with composure – so I did! So I – (*Seems to lose his thread as he looks at her.*)

JEAN (*with a little frown*): You *said* –

STONOR: That you have very pink cheeks? Well, I stick to that.

JEAN (*smiling*): Sh! Don't tell everybody.

STONOR: And you're the only female creature I ever saw who didn't look a fright in motor things.

JEAN (*melted and smiling*): I'm glad you don't think me a fright.

CHAIRMAN: I will now ask (*name indistinguishable*) to address the meeting.

JEAN (*as she sees* LADY JOHN *moving to one side*): Oh, don't go yet, Aunt Ellen!

LADY JOHN: Go? Certainly not. I want to hear another. (*Craning her neck.*) I can't believe, you know, she was really one of the worst.

A big, sallow Cockney has come forward. His scanty hair grows in wisps on a great bony skull.

VOICE: That's Pilcher.

ANOTHER: 'Oo's Pilcher?

ANOTHER: If you can't afford a bottle of Tatcho, w'y don't you get yer 'air cut.

MR PILCHER (*not in the least discomposed*): I've been addressin' a big meetin' at 'Ammersmith this morning, and w'en I told 'em I was comin' 'ere this awfternoon to speak fur the women – well – then the usual thing began!

An appreciative roar from the crowd.

In these times if you want peace and quiet at a public meetin' –

The crowd fills' in the hiatus with laughter.

There was a man at 'Ammersmith, too, talkin' about women's sphere bein' 'ome. 'Ome do you call it? You've got a kennel w'ere you can munch your tommy. You've got a corner w'ere you can curl up fur a few hours till you go out to work again. No, my man, there's too many of you ain't able to *give* the women 'omes – fit to live in, too many of you in that fix fur you to go on jawin' at those o' the women 'oo want to myke the 'omes a little decenter.

VOICE: If the vote ain't done us any good, 'ow'll it do the women any good?

MR PILCHER: Looke 'ere! Any men here belongin' to the Labour Party?

Shouts and applause.

Well, I don't need to tell these men the vote 'as done us *some* good. They know it. And it'll do us a lot more good w'en you know 'ow to use the power you got in your 'and.

VOICE: Power! It's those fellers at the bottom o' the street that's got the power.

MR PILCHER: It's you, and men like you, that gave it to 'em. You carried the

Liberals into Parliament Street on your own shoulders.

Complacent applause.

You believed all their fine words. You never asked yourselves, 'Wot's a Liberal, anyw'y?'

A VOICE: He's a jolly good fellow.

Cheers and booing.

MR PILCHER: No, 'e ain't, or if 'e is jolly, it's only because 'e thinks you're such silly codfish you'll go swellin' his majority again. (*Laughter, in which* STONOR *joins.*) It's enough to make any Liberal jolly to see sheep like you lookin' on, proud and 'appy, while you see Liberal leaders desertin' Liberal principles.

Voices in agreement and protest.

You show me a Liberal, and I'll show you a Mr Fycing-both-W'ys. Yuss.

STONOR *moves closer with an amused look.*

'E sheds the light of 'is warm and 'andsome smile on the working man, and round on the other side 'e's tippin' a wink to the great landowners. That's to let 'em know 'e's standin' between them and the Socialists. Huh! Socialists. Yuss, *Socialists!*

General laughter, in which STONOR *joins.*

The Liberal, e's the judicial sort o'chap that sits in the middle –

VOICE: On the fence!

MR PILCHER: Tories one side – Socialists the other. Well it ain't always so comfortable in the middle. You're like to get squeezed. Now, I s'y to the women, the Conservatives don't promise you much but what they promise they *do!*

STONOR (*to* JEAN): This fellow isn't half bad.

MR PILCHER: The Liberals – they'll promise you the earth, and give yer . . . the whole o' nothing.

Roars of approval.

JEAN: *Isn't* it fun? Now, aren't you glad I brought you?

STONOR (*laughing*): This chap's rather amusing!

MR PILCHER: We men 'ave seen it 'appen over and over. But the women can tyke a 'int quicker 'n what we can. They won't stand the nonsense men do. Only they 'aven't got a fair chawnce even to agitate fur their rights. As I wus comin' up 'ere I 'eard a man sayin', 'Look at this big crowd. W'y, we're all *men!* If the women want the vote w'y ain't they 'ere to s'y so? Well, I'll tell you w'y. It's because they've 'ad to get the dinner fur you and me, and now they're washin' up the dishes.

A VOICE: D'you think *we* ought to st'y 'ome and wash the dishes?

MR PILCHER (*laughs good-naturedly*): If they'd leave it to us once or twice per'aps we'd understand a little more about the Woman Question. I know w'y *my* wife isn't here. It's because she *knows* I ain't much use round the 'ouse, and she's 'opin' I can talk to some purpose. Maybe she's mistaken. Any'ow, here I am to vote for her and all the other women.

VOICES: 'Hear! hear!', 'Oh-h!'

MR PILCHER: And to tell you men what improvements you can expect to see when women 'as the share in public affairs they *ought* to 'ave!

VOICE: What do you know about it? You can't even talk grammar.

MR PILCHER (*is dashed a fraction of a moment, for the first and only time*): I'm not 'ere to talk grammar but to talk Reform. I ain't defendin' my grammar – but I'll say in pawssing that if my mother 'ad 'ad 'er rights, maybe my grammar would have been better.

STONOR *and* JEAN *exchange smiles. He takes her arm again and bends his head to whisper something in her ear. She listens with lowered eyes and happy face. The discreet love-making goes on during the next few sentences. Interruption. One voice insistent but not clear. The speaker waits only a second and then resumes. 'Yes, if the women,' but he cannot instantly makes himself heard. The boyish* CHAIRMAN *looks harassed and anxious.* MISS ERNESTINE BLUNT *alert, watchful.*

MR PILCHER: Wait a bit – 'arf a minute, my man!

VOICE: 'Oo yer talkin' to? I ain't your man.

MR PILCHER: Lucky for me! There seems to be a *gentleman* 'ere who doesn't think women ought to 'ave the vote.

VOICE: *One?* Oh-h!

Laughter.

MR PILCHER: Per'aps 'e doesn't know much about women?

Indistinguishable repartee.

Oh, the gentleman says 'e's married. Well, then, fur the syke of 'is wife we mustn't be too sorry 'e's 'ere. No doubt she's s'ying: "Eaven by prysed those women are mykin' a Demonstrytion in Trafalgar Square, and I'll 'ave a little peace and quiet at 'ome for one Sunday in my life.'

The crowd laughs and there are jeers for the interruptor – and at the speaker.

(*Pointing.*) Why, *you're* like the man at 'Ammersmith this morning. 'E was awskin' me: 'Ow would you like men to st'y at 'ome and do the family washin'?'

Laughter.

I told 'im I wouldn't advise it. I 'ave too much respect fur – me clo'es.

VAGRANT: It's their place – the women ought to do the washin'.

MR PILCHER: I'm not sure you ain't right. For a good many o' you fellas, from the look o' you – you cawn't even wash yerselves.

Laughter.

VOICE (*threatening*): 'Oo are you talkin' to?

CHAIRMAN *more anxious than before – movement in the crowd.*

THREATENING VOICE: Which of us d'you mean?

MR PILCHER (*coolly looking down*): Well, it takes about ten of your sort to myke a man, so you may take it I mean the lot of you.

Angry indistinguishable retorts and the crowd sways. MISS ERNESTINE BLUNT, *who has been watching the fray with serious face, turns suddenly, catching sight of someone just arrived at the end of the platform.* MISS BLUNT *goes right with alacrity, saying audibly to* PILCHER *as she passes, 'Here she is,' and proceeds to offer her hand helping some one to get up the improvised steps. Laughter and interruption in the crowd.*

LADY JOHN: Now, there's another woman going to speak.

JEAN: Oh, is she? Who? Which? I do hope she'll be one of the wild ones.

MR PILCHER (*speaking through this last. Glancing at the new arrival whose hat appears above the platform.*): That's all right, then. (*Turns to the left.*) When I've attended to this microbe that's vitiating the air on my right –

Laughter and interruptions from the crowd.

STONOR *stares, one dazed instant, at the face of the new arrival; his own changes.*

JEAN *withdraws her arm from his and quite suddenly presses a shade nearer the platform.* STONOR *moves forward and takes her by the arm.*

STONOR: We're going now.

JEAN: Not yet – oh, please not yet. (*Breathless, looking back.*): Why I – I do believe –

STONOR (*to* LADY JOHN, *with decision*): I'm going to take Jean out of this mob. Will you come?

LADY JOHN: What? Oh yes, if you think – (*Another look through her glasses.*) But isn't that – *surely* it's – !!!

VIDA LEVERING *comes forward. She wears a long, plain, dark green dustcloak. Stands talking to* ERNESTINE BLUNT *and glancing a little apprehensively at the crowd.*

JEAN: Geoffrey!

STONOR (*trying to draw* JEAN *away*): Lady John's tired –

JEAN: But you don't see who it is, Geoffrey –! (*Looks into his face, and is arrested by the look she finds there.*)

LADY JOHN *has pushed in front of them amazed, transfixed, with glass up.*

GEOFFREY STONOR *restrains a gesture of annoyance, and withdraws behind two big policemen.* JEAN *from time to time turns to look at him with a face of perplexity.*

MR PILCHER (*resuming through a fire of indistinct interruption*): I'll come down and attend to that microbe while a lady will say a few words to you (*raises his voice*) – if she can myke 'erself 'eard.

PILCHER *retires in the midst of booing and cheers.*

CHAIRMAN (*harassed and trying to creat a diversion*): Some one suggests – and it's such a good idea I'd like you to listen to it –

Noise dies down.

that a clause shall be inserted in the next Suffrage Bill that shall expressly reserve to each Cabinet Minister, and to any respectable man, the power to prevent the Franchise being given to the female members of his family on his public declaration of their lack of sufficient intelligence to entitle them to vote.

VOICES: Oh! oh.

CHAIRMAN: Now, I ask you to listen, as quietly as you can, to a lady who is not accustomed to speaking – a – in Traflagar Square – or a ... as a matter of fact, at all.

VOICES: 'A dumb lady.' 'Hooray!' 'Three cheers for the dumb lady!'

CHAIRMAN: A lady who, as I've said, will tell you, if you'll behave yourselves, her impressions of the administration of police court justice in this country.

JEAN *looks wondering at* STONOR'S *sphinx-like face as* VIDA LEVERING *comes to the edge of the platform.*

MISS LEVERING: Mr Chairman, men and women –

VOICES (*off*): Speak up.

MISS LEVERING *flushes, comes quite to the edge of the platform and raises her voice a little.*

MISS LEVERING: I just wanted to tell you that I was – I was – present in the police court when the women were charged for creating a disturbance.

VOICE: Y' oughtn't t' get mixed up in wot didn't concern you.

MISS LEVERING: I – I – (*Stumbles and stops.*)

Talking and laughing increases. 'Wot's 'er name?' 'Mrs or Miss?' 'Ain't seen this one before.'

CHAIRMAN (*anxiously*): Now, see here, men; don't interrupt –

A GIRL (*shrilly*): I don't like this one's 'at. Ye can see she ain't one of 'em.

MISS LEVERING (*trying to recommence*): I –

VOICE: They're a disgrace – them women be'ind yer.

A MAN WITH A FATHERLY AIR: It's the w'y they goes on as mykes the Government keep ye from gettin' yer rights.

CHAIRMAN (*losing his temper*): It's the way *you* go on that –

Noise increases. CHAIRMAN *drowned, waves his arms and moves his lips.* MISS LEVERING *discouraged, turns and looks at* ERNESTINE BLUNT and pantomimes 'It's no good. I can't go on.' ERNESTINE BLUNT *comes forward, says a word to the* CHAIRMAN, *who ceases gyrating, and nods.*

MISS ERNESTINE BLUNT (*facing the crowd*): Look here. If the Government withhold the vote because they don't like the way some of us ask for it – *let them give it to the Quiet Ones.* Does the Government want to punish *all* women because they don't like the manners of a handful? Perhaps that's you men's notion of justice. It isn't women's.

VOICES: Haw! haw!

MISS LEVERING: Yes. Thi-this is the first time I've ever 'gone on,' as you call it, but they never gave me a vote.

MISS ERNESTINE BLUNT (*with energy*): No! And there are one – two – three – four women on this platform. Now, we all want the vote, as you know. Well, we'd agree to be disfranchised all our lives, if they'd give the vote to all the other women.

VOICE: Look here, you made one speech, give the lady a chawnce.

MISS ERNESTINE BLUNT (*retires smiling*): That's *just* what I wanted *you* to do!

MISS LEVERING: Perhaps you – you don't know – you don't know –

VOICE (*sarcastic*): 'Ow 're we goin' to know if you can't tell us?

MISS LEVERING (*flushing and smiling*): Thank you for that. We couldn't have a better motto. How *are* you to know if we can't somehow manage to tell you? (*With a visible effort she goes on.*) Well, I certainly didn't know before that the sergeants and policemen are instructed to deceive the people as to the time such cases are heard. You ask, and you're sent to Marlborough Police Court instead of to Marylebone.

VOICE: They ought ter sent yer to 'Olloway – do y' good.

OLD NEWSVENDOR: You go on, Miss, don't mind 'im.

VOICE: Wot d'you expect from a pig but a grunt?

MISS LEVERING: You're told the case will be at two o'clock, and it's really called for eleven. Well, I took a great deal of trouble, and I didn't believe what I was told –

Warming a little to her task.

Yes, that's almost the first thing we have to learn – to get over our touching faith that, because a man tells us something, it's true. I got to the right court, and I was so anxious not to be late, I was too early. The case before the women's was just coming on. I heard a noise. At the door I saw the helmets of two policemen, and I said to myself: 'What sort of crime shall I have to sit and hear about? Is this a burglar coming along between the two big policemen, or will it be a murderer? What sort of felon is to stand in the dock before the women whose crime is they ask for the vote?' But, try as I would, I couldn't see the prisoner. My heart misgave me. Is it a woman, I wondered? Then the policemen got nearer, and I saw – (*she waits an instant*) – a little, thin, half-starved boy. What do you think he was

charged with? Stealing. What had he been stealing – that small criminal? *Milk.* It seemed to me as I sat there looking on, that the men who had the affairs of the world in their hands from the beginning, and who've made so poor a business of it –

VOICES: Oh! oh! Pore benighted man! Are we down-'earted? *Oh*, no!

MISS LEVERING: – so poor a business of it as to have the poor and the unemployed in the condition they're in today – when your only remedy for a starving child is to hale him off to the police court – because he had managed to get a little milk – well, I *did* wonder that the men refuse to be helped with a problem they've so notoriously failed at. I began to say to myself: 'Isn't it time the women lent a hand?'

A VOICE: Would you have women magistrates?

She is stumped by the suddenness of the demand.

VOICES: Haw! Haw! Magistrates!

ANOTHER: Women! Let 'em prove first they deserve –

A SHABBY ART STUDENT: (*his hair longish, soft hat, and flowing tie*): They study music by thousands; where's their Beethoven? Where's their Plato? Where's the woman Shakespeare?

ANOTHER: Yes – what 'a' they ever done?

The speaker clenches her hands, and is recovering her presence of mind, so that by the time the CHAIRMAN *can makes himself heard with, 'Now men, give this lady a fair hearing – don't interrupt' – she, with the slightest of gestures, waves him aside with a low 'It's all right.'*

MISS LEVERING (*steadying and raising her voice*): These questions are quite proper! They are often asked elsewhere; and I would like to ask in return: Since when was human society held to exist for its handful of geniuses? How many Platos are there here in this crowd?

A VOICE (*very loud and shrill*): Divil a wan!

Laughter.

MISS LEVERING: Not one. Yet that doesn't keep you men off the register. How many Shakespeares are there in all England today? Not one. Yet the State doesn't tumble to pieces. Railroads and ships are built – homes are kept going, and babies are born. The world goes on! (*Bending over the crowd.*) It goes on *by virtue of its common people.*

VOICES (*subdued*): Hear! hear!

MISS LEVERING: I am not concerned that you should think we women can paint great pictures, or compose immortal music, or write good books. I am content that we should be classed with the common people – who keep the world going. But (*Straightening up and taking a fresh start.*) I'd like the world to go a great deal better. We were talking about justice. I have been inquiring into the kind of lodging the poorest class of homeless women can get in this town of London. I find that only the men of that class are provided for. Some measure to establish Rowton Houses for women has been before the London County Council. They looked into the question 'very carefully,' so their apologists say. And what did they decide? They decided that *they could do nothing.*

LADY JOHN (*having forced her way to* STONOR'S *side*): Is that true?

STONOR (*speaking through* MISS LEVERING'S *next words*): I don't know.

MISS LEVERING: Why could that great, all-powerful body do nothing? Because, if these cheap and decent houses were opened, they said, the homeless women in the streets would make use of them! You'll think I'm not in earnest. But that was actually the decision and the reason given for it. Women that the bitter struggle for existence has forced into a life of horror –

STONOR (*sternly to* LADY JOHN): You think this is the kind of thing – (*A motion of the head towards* JEAN.)

MISS LEVERING: – the outcast women might take advantage of the shelter these decent, cheap places offered. But the *men,* I said! Are all who avail themselves of Lord Rowton's hostels, are *they* all angels? Or does wrong-doing in a man not matter? Yet women are recommended to depend on the chivalry of men.

The two policemen, who at first had been strolling about, have stood during this scene in front of GEOFFREY STONOR. *They turn now and walk away, leaving* STONOR *exposed. He, embarrassed, moves uneasily, and* VIDA LEVERING'S *eye falls upon his big figure. He still has the collar of his motor coat turned up to his ears. A change passes over her face, and her nerve fails her an instant.*

MISS LEVERING: Justice and chivalry!! (*She steadies her voice and hurries on.*) – they both remind me of what those of you who read the police court news – (I have begun only lately to do that) – but you've seen the accounts of the girl who's been tried in Manchester lately for the murder of her child. Not pleasant reading. Even if we'd noticed it, we wouldn't speak of it in my world. A few months ago I should have turned away my eyes and forgotten even the headline as quickly as I could. But since that morning in the police court, I read these things. This, as you'll remember, was about a little working girl – an orphan of eighteen – who crawled with the dead body of her new born child to her master's back door, and left the baby there. She dragged herself a little way off and fainted. A few days later she found herself in court, being tried for the murder of her child. Her master – a married man – had of course reported the 'find' at his back door to the police, and he had been summoned to give evidence. The girl cried out to him in the open court, 'You are the father!' He couldn't deny it. The Coroner at the jury's request censured the man, and regretted that the law didn't make him responsible. But he went scot-free. And that girl is now serving her sentence in Strangeways Gaol.

Murmuring and scraps of indistinguishable comment in the crowd, through which only JEAN'S *voice is clear.*

JEAN (*who has wormed her way to* STONOR'S *side*): Why do you dislike her so?

STONOR: I? Why should you think –

JEAN (*with a vaguely frightened air*): I never saw you look as you did – as you do.

CHAIRMAN: Order, please – give the lady a fair –

MISS LEVERING (*signing to him 'It's all right'*): Men make boast that an English citizen is tried by his peers. What woman is tried by hers?

A sombre passion strengthens her voice and hurries her on.

A woman is arrested by a man, brought before a man judge, tried by a jury of men, condemned by men, taken to prison by a man, and by a man she's hanged! Where in all this were *her* 'peers'? Why did men so long ago insist on trial by 'a jury of their peers'? So that justice shouldn't miscarry – wasn't it? A man's peers would best understand his circumstances, his temptation, the degree of his guilt. Yet there's no such unlikeness between different classes of men as exists between man and woman. What man has the knowledge that makes him a fit judge of woman's deeds at that time of anguish – that hour – (*lowers her voice and bends over the crowd*) – that hour that some woman struggled through to put each man here into the world. I noticed when a previous speaker quoted the Labour Party you applauded. Some of you here – I gather – call yourselves Labour men. Every woman who has borne a child is a Labour woman. No man among you can judge what she goes through in her hour of darkness –

JEAN (*with frightened eyes on her lover's set, white face, whispers*): Geoffrey –

MISS LEVERING (*catching her fluttering breath, goes on very low*) – in that great agony when, even under the best conditions that money and devotion can buy, many a woman falls into temporary mania, and not a few go down to death. In the case of this poor little abandoned working girl, what man can be the fit judge of her deeds in that awful moment of half-crazed temptation? Women know of these things as those know burning who have walked through fire.

STONOR *makes a motion towards* JEAN *and she turns away fronting the audience. Her hands go up to her throat as though she suffered a choking sensation. It is in her face that she 'knows'.* MISS LEVERING *leans over the platform and speaks with a low and thrilling earnestness.*

I would say in conclusion to the women here, it's not enough to be sorry for these unfortunate sisters. We must get the conditions of life made fairer. We women must organise. We must learn to work together. We have all (rich and poor, happy and unhappy) worked so long and so exclusively for *men*, we hardly know how to work for one another. But we must learn. Those who can, may give money –

VOICES (*grumbling*): Oh, yes – Money! Money!

MISS LEVERING: Those who haven't pennies to give – even those people aren't so poor they can't give some part of their labour – some share of their sympathy and support. (*Turns to hear something the* CHAIRMAN *is whispering to her.*)

JEAN (*low to* LADY JOHN): Oh, I'm glad I've got power!

LADY JOHN (*bewildered*): Power! – you?

JEAN: Yes, all that money –

LADY JOHN *tries to make her way to* STONOR.

MISS LEVERING (*suddenly turning from the* CHAIRMAN *to the crowd*): Oh, yes, I hope you'll all join the Union. Come up after the meeting and give your names.

LOUD VOICE: You won't get many men.

MISS LEVERING (*with fire*): Then it's to the women I appeal!

She is about to retire when, with a sudden gleam in her lit eyes, she turns for the last time to the crowd, silencing the general murmur and holding the people by the sudden concentration of passion in her face.

I don't mean to say it wouldn't be better if men and women did this work together – shoulder to shoulder. But the mass of men won't have it so. I only hope they'll realise in time the good they've renounced and the spirit they've aroused. For I know as well as any man could tell me, it would be a bad day for England if all women felt about all men as I do.

She retires in a tumult. The others on the platform close about her. The CHAIRMAN tries in vain to get a hearing from the excited crowd.

JEAN tries to make her way through the knot of people surging round her.

STONOR (*calls*): Here – Follow me!

JEAN: No – no – I –

STONOR: You're going the wrong way.

JEAN: *This* is the way I must go.

STONOR: You can get out quicker on this side.

JEAN: I don't *want* to get out.

STONOR: What! Where are you going?

JEAN: To ask that woman to let me have the honour of working with her.

She disappears in the crowd.

Curtain.

ACT THREE

Scene: The drawing room at old MR DUNBARTON'S *house in Eaton Square. Six o'clock the same evening. As the Curtain rises the door opens and* JEAN *appears on the threshold. She looks back into her own sitting room, then crosses the drawing room, treading softly on the parquet spaces between the rugs. She goes to the window and is in the act of parting the lace curtains when the folding doors are opened by the* BUTLER.

JEAN (*to the Servant*): Sh!

She goes softly back to the door she has left open and closes it carefully. When she turns, the BUTLER *has stepped aside to admit* GEOFFREY STONOR, *and departed, shutting the folding doors.* STONOR *comes rapidly forward.*

(*Before he gets a word out.*) Speak low, please.

STONOR (*angrily*): I waited about a whole hour for you to come back.

JEAN turns away as though vaguely looking for the nearest chair.

If you don't mind leaving *me* like that you might have considered Lady John.

JEAN (*pausing*): Is she here with you?

STONOR: No. My place was nearer than this, and she was very tired. I left her to get some tea. We couldn't tell whether you'd be here, or *what* had become of you.

JEAN: Mr Trent got us a hansom.

STONOR: Trent?

JEAN: The Chairman of the meeting.

STONOR: 'Got us –'?

JEAN: Miss Levering and me.

STONOR (*incensed*): MISS L –

BUTLER (*opens the door and announces*): Mr Farnborough.

Enter MR RICHARD FARNBOROUGH – *more flurried than ever.*

FARNBOROUGH (*seeing* STONOR): At last! You'll forgive this incursion, Miss Dunbarton, when you hear –

(*Turns abruptly back to* STONOR.)
They've been telegraphing you all over
London. In despair they set me on your
track.

STONOR: Who did? What's up.

FARNBOROUGH (*lays down his hat
and fumbles agitatedly in his breast
pocket*): There was the devil to pay at
Dutfield last night. The Liberal chap
tore down from London and took over
your meeting!

STONOR: Oh? – Nothing about it in the
Sunday paper *I* saw.

FARNBOROUGH: Wait till you see the
Press tomorrow morning! There was a
great rally and the beggar made a
rousing speech.

STONOR: What about?

FARNBOROUGH: Abolition of the
Upper House –

STONOR: They were at that when I was
at Eton!

FARNBOROUGH: Yes. But this new
man has got a way of putting things! –
the people went mad. (*Pompously.*) The
Liberal platform as defined at Dutfield
is going to make a big difference.

STONOR (*drily*): You think so.

FARNBOROUGH: Well, your agent says
as much. (*Opens telegram.*)

STONOR: My – (*Taking telegram.*) 'Try
find Stonor' – Hm! Hm!

FARNBOROUGH (*pointing*): –
'tremendous effect of last night's Liberal
manifesto ought to be counteracted in
tomorrow's papers.' (*Very earnestly.*)
You see, Mr Stonor, it's a battle cry we
want.

STONOR (*turns on his heel*): Claptrap!

FARNBOROUGH (*a little dashed*):
Well, they've been saying we have
nothing to offer but personal popularity.
No practical reform. No –

STONOR: No truckling to the masses, I
suppose. (*Walks impatiently away.*)

FARNBOROUGH (*snubbed*): Well, in
these democratic days – (*Turns to
JEAN for countenance.*) I hope you'll
forgive my bursting in like this. (*Struck
by her face.*) But I can see you realise
the gravity – (*Lowering his voice with

an air of speaking for her ear alone.*) It
isn't as if he were going to be a mere
private member. Everybody knows he'll
be in the Cabinet.

STONOR (*drily*): It may be a Liberal
Cabinet.

FARNBOROUGH: Nobody thought so
up to last night. Why, even your brother
– but I am afraid I'm seeming officious.
(*Takes up his hat.*)

STONOR (*coldly*): What about my
brother?

FARNBOROUGH: I met Lord
Windlesham as I rushed out of the
Carlton.

STONOR: Did he say anything?

FARNBOROUGH: I told him the
Dutfield news.

STONOR (*impatiently*): Well?

FARNBOROUGH: He said it only
confirmed his fears.

STONOR (*half under his breath*): Said
that, did he?

FARNBOROUGH: Yes. Defeat is
inevitable, he thinks, unless – (*Pause.*)

GEOFFREY STONOR *who has been
pacing the floor, stops but doesn't raise
his eyes.*

unless you can 'manufacture some
political dynamite within the next few
hours.' Those were his words.

STONOR (*resumes his walking to and
fro, raises his head and catches sight of
JEAN'S white, drawn face. Stops
short*): You are very tired.

JEAN: No. No.

STONOR (*to FARNBOROUGH*): I'm
obliged to you for taking so much
trouble. (*Shakes hands by way of
dismissing FARNBOROUGH.*) I'll see
what can be done.

FARNBOROUGH (*offering the reply-
paid form*): If you'd like to wire I'll take
it.

STONOR (*faintly amused*): You don't
understand, my young friend. Moves of
this kind are not rushed at by
responsible politicians. I must have time
for consideration.

FARNBOROUGH (*disappointed*): Oh,

well, I only hope someone else won't jump into the breach before you – (*Watch in hand.*) I tell you. (*To* JEAN.) I'll find out what time the newspapers go to press on Sunday. Goodbye (*To* STONOR.) I'll be at the Club just *in case* I can be of any use.

STONOR (*firmly*): No, don't do that. If I should have anything new to say –

FARNBOROUGH (*feverishly*): B-b-but with our party, as your brother said – 'heading straight for a vast electoral disaster –'

STONOR: If I decide on a counterblast I shall simply telegraph to headquarters. Goodbye.

FARNBOROUGH: Oh – a – g-goodbye. (*A gesture of 'The country's going to the dogs.'*)

JEAN *rings the bell. Exit* FARNBOROUGH.

STONOR (*studying the carpet*): 'Political dynamite,' eh? (*Pause.*) After all . . . women are much more conservative than men – aren't they?

JEAN *looks straight in front of her, making no attempt to reply.*

Especially the women the property qualification would bring in. (*He glances at* JEAN *as though for the first time conscious of her silence.*) You see now (*He throws himself into the chair by the table.*) one reason why I've encouraged you to take an interest in public affairs. Because people like us don't go screaming about it, is no sign we don't (some of us) see what's on the way. However little they want to, women of our class will have to come into line. All the best things in the world – everything that civilisation has won will be in danger if – when this change comes – the only women who have practical political training are the women of the lower classes. Women of the lower classes, and (*His brows knit heavily.*) – women inoculated by the Socialist virus.

JEAN: Geoffrey.

STONOR (*draws the telegraph form towards him*): Let us see, how we shall put it – when the time comes – shall we? (*He detaches a pencil from his watch chain and bends over the paper, writing.*)

JEAN *opens her lips to speak, moves a shade nearer the table and then falls back upon her silent, half-incredulous misery.*

STONOR (*holds the paper off, smiling*): Enough dynamite in that! Rather too much, isn't there, little girl?

JEAN: Geoffrey, I know her story.

STONOR: Whose story?

JEAN: Miss Levering's

STONOR: *Whose?*

JEAN: Vida Levering's

STONOR *stares speechless. Slight pause.*

(*The words escaping from her in a miserable cry.*) Why did you desert her?

STONOR (*staggered*): I! *I?*

JEAN: Oh, why did you do it?

STONOR (*bewildered*): What in the name of – What has she been saying to you?

JEAN: Someone else told me part. Then the way you looked when you saw her at Aunt Ellen's – Miss Levering's saying you didn't know her – then your letting out that you knew even the curious name on the handkerchief – Oh, I pieced it together –

STONOR (*with recovered self-possession*): Your ingenuity is undeniable!

JEAN: – and then, when she said that at the meeting about 'the dark hour' and I looked at your face – it flashed over me – Oh, *why* did you desert her?

STONOR: I *didn't* desert her.

JEAN: Ah-h! (*Puts her hands before her eyes.*)

STONOR *makes a passionate motion towards her, is checked by her muffled voice saying.*

I'm glad – I'm glad!

He stares bewildered. JEAN *drops her hands in her lap and steadies her voice.*

She went away from you, then?

STONOR: You don't expect me to enter into –

JEAN: She went away from you?

STONOR (*with a look of almost uncontrollable anger*): Yes!

JEAN: Was that because you wouldn't marry her?

STONOR: I couldn't marry her – and she knew it.

JEAN: Did you want to?

STONOR (*an instant's angry scrutiny and then turning away his eyes*): I thought I did – *then*. It's a long time ago.

JEAN: And why 'couldn't' you?

STONOR (*a movement of strong irritation cut short*): Why are you catechising me? It's a matter that concerns another woman.

JEAN: If you're saying that it doesn't concern me, you're saying – (*her lip trembles*) – that *you* don't concern me.

STONOR (*commanding his temper with difficulty*): In those days I – I was absolutely dependent on my father.

JEAN: Why, you must have been thirty, Geoffrey.

STONOR (*slight pause*): What? Oh – thereabouts.

JEAN: And everybody says you're so clever.

STONOR: Well, everybody's mistaken.

JEAN (*drawing nearer*): It must have been terribly hard –

STONOR *turns towards her.*

for you both –

He arrests his movement and stands stonily.

that a man like you shouldn't have had the freedom that even the lowest seem to have.

STONOR: Freedom?

JEAN: To marry the woman they choose.

STONOR: She didn't break off our relations because I couldn't marry her.

JEAN: Why was it, then?

STONOR: You're too young to discuss such a story. (*Half turns away.*)

JEAN: I'm not so young as she was when –

STONOR (*wheeling upon her*): Very well, then, if you will have it! The truth is, it didn't seem to weigh upon her, as it

seems to on you, that I wasn't able to marry her.

JEAN: Why are you so sure of that?

STONOR: Because she didn't so much as hint such a thing when she wrote that she meant to break off the – the –

JEAN: What made her write like that?

STONOR (*with suppressed rage*): Why *will* you go on talking of what's so long over and ended?

JEAN: What reason did she give?

STONOR: If your curiosity has so got the upper hand – *ask her.*

JEAN (*her eyes upon him*): You're afraid to tell me.

STONOR (*putting pressure on himself to answer quietly*): I still hoped – at *that* time – to win my father over. She blamed me because (*goes to the window and looks blindly out and speaks in a low tone.*) if the child had lived it wouldn't have been possible to get my father to – to overlook it.

JEAN (*faintly*): You wanted it *overlooked*? I don't underst–

STONOR (*turning passionately back to her*): Of course you don't. (*He seizes her hand and tries to draw her to him.*) If you did, you wouldn't be the beautiful, tender, innocent child you are –

JEAN (*has withdrawn her hand and shrunk from him with an impulse – slight as is its expression – so tragically eloquent, that fear for the first time catches hold of him*): I am glad you didn't mean to desert her, Geoffrey. It wasn't your fault after all – only some misunderstanding that can be cleared up.

STONOR: *Cleared up?*

JEAN: Yes. Cleared up.

STONOR (*aghast*): You aren't thinking that this miserable old affair I'd as good as forgotten –

JEAN (*in a horror struck whisper, with a glance at the door which he doesn't see*): Forgotten!

STONOR: No, no. I don't mean exactly forgotten. But you're torturing me so I don't know what I'm saying. (*He goes closer.*) You aren't – Jean! you – you aren't going to let it come between you and me!

JEAN (*presses her handkerchief to her lips, and then, taking it away, answers steadily*): I can't make or unmake what's past. But I'm glad, at least, that you didn't *mean* to desert her in her trouble. You'll remind her of that first of all, won't you? (*Moves to the door.*)

STONOR: Where are you going? (*Raising his voice.*) Why should I remind anybody of what I want only to forget?

JEAN (*finger on lip*): Sh!

STONOR (*with eyes on the door*): You don't mean that *she's* –

JEAN: Yes. I left her to get a little rest.

He recoils in an access of uncontrollable rage. She follows him. Speechless, he goes to get his hat.

Geoffrey, don't go before you hear me. I don't know if what I think matters to you now – but I hope it does. (*With tears.*) You can still make me think of you without shrinking – if you will.

STONOR (*fixes her a moment with his eyes. Then sternly*): What is it you are asking of me?

JEAN: To make amends, Geoffrey.

STONOR (*with an outburst*): You poor little innocent!

JEAN: I'm poor enough. But (*locking her hands together.*) I'm not so innocent but what I know you must right that old wrong now, if you're ever to right it.

STONOR: You aren't insane enough to think I would turn round in these few hours and go back to something that ten years ago was ended for ever! Why, it's stark, staring madness!

JEAN: No. (*Catching on his arm*): What you did ten years ago – *that* was mad. This is paying a debt.

STONOR: Look here, Jean, you're dreadfully wrought up and excited – tired too –

JEAN: No, not tired – though I've travelled so far today. I know you smile at sudden conversions. You think they're hysterical – worse – vulgar. But people must get their revelation how they can. And, Geoffrey, if I can't make you see

this one of mine – I shall know your love could never mean strength to me. Only weakness. And I shall be afraid. So afraid I'll never dare to give you the *chance* of making me loathe myself. I shall never see you again.

STONOR: How right *I* was to be afraid of that vein of fanaticism in you. (*Moves towards the door.*)

JEAN: Certainly you couldn't make a greater mistake than to go away now and think it any good ever to come back. (*He turns.*) Even if I came to feel different, I couldn't *do* anything different. I should know all this couldn't be forgotten. I should know that it would poison my life in the end. Yours too.

STONOR (*with suppressed fury*): She has made good use of her time! (*With a sudden thought.*) What has changed her? Has *she* been seeing visions too?

JEAN: What do you mean?

STONOR: Why is she intriguing to get hold of a man that, ten years ago, she flatly refused to see, or hold any communication with?

JEAN: 'Intriguing to get hold of?' She hasn't mentioned you!

STONOR: *What*! Then how in the name of Heaven do you know – that she wants – what you ask?

JEAN (*firmly*): There can't be any doubt about that.

STONOR (*with immense relief*): You absurd, ridiculous child! Then all this is just your own unaided invention. Well – I could thank God! (*Falls into the nearest chair and passes his handkerchief over his face.*)

JEAN (*perplexed, uneasy*): For what are you thanking God?

STONOR (*trying to think out his plan of action*): Suppose, (I'm not going to risk it) – but suppose – (*He looks up and at the sight of* JEAN'S *face a new tenderness comes into his own. He rises suddenly.*) Whether I deserve to suffer or not – it's quite certain *you* don't. Don't cry, dear one. It never was the real thing. I had to wait till I knew you before I understood.

JEAN (*lifts her eyes brimming*): Oh, is

that true? (*Checks her movement towards him.*) Loving you has made things clear to me I didn't dream of before. If I could think that because of me you were able to do this –

STONOR (*seizes her by the shoulders and says hoarsely*): Look here! Do you seriously ask me to give up the girl I love – to go and offer to marry a woman that even to think of –

JEAN: You cared for her once. You'll care about her again. She is beautiful and brilliant – everything. I've heard she could win any man she set herself to –

STONOR (*pushing JEAN from him*): She's bewitched you!

JEAN: Geoffrey, Geoffrey, you aren't going away like that. This isn't *the end*!

STONOR (*darkly – hesitating*): I suppose even if she refused me, you'd –

JEAN: She won't refuse you.

STONOR: She did once.

JEAN: She didn't refuse to *marry* you –

JEAN *is going to the door.*

STONOR (*catches her by the arm*): Wait! – a – (*Hunting for some means of gaining time.*) Lady John is waiting all this while for the car to go back with a message.

JEAN: *That's* not a matter of life and death –

STONOR: All the same – I'll go down and give the order.

JEAN (*stopping quite still on a sudden*): Very well. (*Sits.*) You'll come back if you're the man I pray you are. (*Breaks into a flood of silent tears, her elbows on the table, her face in her hands.*)

STONOR (*returns, bends over her, about to take her in his arms*): Dearest of all the world –

Door opens softly and VIDA LEVERING *appears. She is arrested at the sight of* STONOR, *and is in the act of drawing back when, upon the slight noise,* STONOR *looks round. His face darkens, he stands staring at her and then with a look of speechless anger goes silently out.* JEAN, *hearing him shut the door, drops her head on the table with a sob.* VIDA LEVERING *crosses slowly to her and* stands a moment silent at the girl's side.

MISS LEVERING: What is the matter?

JEAN (*lifting her head and drying her eyes*): I – I've been seeing Geoffrey.

MISS LEVERING (*with an attempt at lightness*): Is this the effect seeing Geoffrey has?

JEAN: You see, I know now (*as* MISS LEVERING *looks quite uncomprehending*) – how he (*drops her eyes*) – how he spoiled some one else's life.

MISS LEVERING (*quickly*): Who tells you that?

JEAN: Several people have told me.

MISS LEVERING: Well, you should be very careful how you believe what you hear.

JEAN (*passionately*): You *know* it's true.

MISS LEVERING: I know that it's possible to be mistaken.

JEAN: I see! You're trying to shield him –

MISS LEVERING: Why should I – what is it to me?

JEAN (*with tears*): Oh-h, how you must love him!

MISS LEVERING: Listen to me –

JEAN (*rising*): What's the use of your going on denying it? (MISS LEVERING, *about to break in, is silenced.*) Geoffrey doesn't.

JEAN, *struggling to command her feelings, goes to window.* VIDA LEVERING *relinquishes an impulse to follow, and sits left centre.* JEAN *comes slowly back with her eyes bent on the floor, does not lift them till she is quite near* VIDA. *Then the girl's self-absorbed face changes.*

Oh, don't look like that! I shall bring him back to you! (*Drops on her knees beside the other's chair.*)

MISS LEVERING: You would be impertinent (*softening*) if you weren't a romantic child. You can't bring him back.

JEAN: Yes, he –

MISS LEVERING: But there's something you *can* do –

JEAN: What?

MISS LEVERING: Bring him to the point where he recognises that he's in our debt.

JEAN: In *our* debt?

MISS LEVERING: In debt to women. He can't repay the one he robbed –

JEAN (*wincing and rising from her knees*): Yes, yes.

MISS LEVERING (*sternly*): No, he can't repay the dead. But there are the living. There are the thousands with hope still in their hearts and youth in their blood. Let him help *them*. Let him be a Friend to Women.

JEAN (*rising on a wave of enthusiasm*): Yes, yes – I understand. That too!

The door opens. As STONOR *enters with* LADY JOHN, *he makes a slight gesture towards the two as much as to say, 'You see.'*

JEAN (*catching sight of him*): Thank you!

LADY JOHN (*in a clear, commonplace tone to* JEAN): Well, you rather gave us the slip. Vida, I believe Mr Stonor wants to see you for a few minutes (*glances at watch*) – but I'd like a word with you first, as I must get back. (*To* STONOR.) Do you think the car – your man said something about re-charging.

STONOR (*hastily*): Oh, did he? I'll see about it.

As STONOR *is going out he encounters the* BUTLER. *Exit* STONOR.

BUTLER: Mr Trent has called, Miss, to take Miss Levering to the meeting.

JEAN: Bring Mr Trent into my sitting room. I'll tell him – you can't go tonight.

Exeunt BUTLER *centre*, JEAN *left*.

LADY JOHN (*hurriedly*): I know, my dear, *you're* not aware of what that impulsive girl wants to insist on.

MISS LEVERING: Yes, I am aware of it.

LADY JOHN: But it isn't with your sanction, surely, that she goes on making this extraordinary demand.

MISS LEVERING (*slowly*): I didn't sanction it at first, but I've been thinking it over.

LADY JOHN: Then all I can say is I am greatly disappointed in you. You threw this man over years ago for reasons – whatever they were – that seemed to you good and sufficient. And now you come between him and a younger woman – just to play Nemesis, so far as I can make out!

MISS LEVERING: Is that what he says?

LADY JOHN: He says nothing that isn't fair and considerate.

MISS LEVERING: I can see he's changed.

LADY JOHN: And you're unchanged – is that it?

MISS LEVERING: I've changed even more than he.

LADY JOHN: But (*pity and annoyance blended in her tone*) – you care about him still, Vida?

MISS LEVERING: No.

LADY JOHN: I see. It's just that you wish to marry somebody –

MISS LEVERING: Oh, Lady John, there are no men listening.

LADY JOHN (*surprised*): No, I didn't suppose there were.

MISS LEVERING: Then why keep up that old pretence?

LADY JOHN: What pre–

MISS LEVERING: That to marry *at all costs* is every woman's dearest ambition till the grave closes over her. You and I *know* it isn't true.

LADY JOHN: Well, but – Oh! it was just the unexpected sight of him bringing it back – *That* was what fired you this afternoon! (*With an honest attempt at sympathetic understanding.*) Of course. The memory of a thing like that can never die – can never even be dimmed – *for the woman*.

MISS LEVERING: I mean her to think so.

LADY JOHN (*bewildered*): Jean!

MISS LEVERING *nods*.

LADY JOHN: And it *isn't so*?

MISS LEVERING: You don't seriously believe a woman with anything else to think about, comes to the end of ten years still *absorbed* in a memory of that sort?

LADY JOHN (*astonished*): You've got over it, then!

MISS LEVERING: If the newspapers didn't remind me I shouldn't remember once a twelvemonth that there was ever such a person as Geoffrey Stonor in the world.

LADY JOHN (*with unconscious rapture*): Oh, I'm *so* glad!

MISS LEVERING (*smiles grimly*): Yes, I'm glad too.

LADY JOHN: And if Geoffrey Stonor offered you – what's called 'reparation' – you'd refuse it?

MISS LEVERING (*smiles a little contemptuously*): Geoffrey Stonor! For me he's simply one of the far back links in a chain of evidence. It's certain I think a hundred times of other women's present unhappiness, to once that I remember that old unhappiness of mine that's past. I think of the nail and chain makers of Cradley Heath. The sweated girls of the slums. I think of the army of ill-used women whose very existence I mustn't mention –

LADY JOHN (*interrupting hurriedly*): Then why in Heaven's name do you let poor Jean imagine –

MISS LEVERING (*bending forward*): Look – I'll trust you, Lady John. I don't suffer from that old wrong as Jean thinks I do, but I shall coin her sympathy into gold for a greater cause than mine.

LADY JOHN: I don't understand you.

MISS LEVERING: Jean isn't old enough to be able to care as much about a principle as about a person. But if my half-forgotten pain can turn her generosity into the common treasury –

LADY JOHN: What do you propose she shall do, poor child?

MISS LEVERING: Use her hold over Geoffrey Stonor to make him help us!

LADY JOHN: Help you?

MISS LEVERING: The man who served

one woman – God knows how many more – very ill, shall serve hundreds of thousands well. Geoffrey Stonor shall make it harder for his son, harder still for his grandson, to treat any woman as he treated me.

LADY JOHN: How will he do that?

MISS LEVERING: By putting an end to the helplessness of women.

LADY JOHN (*ironically*): You must think he has a great deal of power –

MISS LEVERING: Power? Yes, men have too much over penniless and frightened women.

LADY JOHN (*impatiently*): What nonsense! You talk as though the women hadn't their share of human nature. *We* aren't made of ice any more than the men.

MISS LEVERING: No, but all the same we have more self-control.

LADY JOHN: Than men?

MISS LEVERING: You know we have.

LADY JOHN (*shrewdly*): I know we mustn't admit it.

MISS LEVERING: For fear they'd call us fishes!

LADY JOHN (*evasively*): They talk of our lack of self-control – but it's the last thing they *want* women to have.

MISS LEVERING: Oh, we know what they want us to have. So we make shift to have it. If we don't, we go without hope – sometimes we go without bread.

LADY JOHN (*shocked*): Vida – do you mean to say that you –

MISS LEVERING: I mean to say that men's vanity won't let them see it, but the thing's largely a question of economics.

LADY JOHN (*shocked*): You *never* loved him, then!

MISS LEVERING: Oh yes, I loved him – *once*. It was my helplessness turned the best thing life can bring, into a curse for both of us.

LADY JOHN: I don't understand you –

MISS LEVERING: Oh, being 'understood!' – that's too much to expect. When people come to know I've joined the Union –

LADY JOHN: But you won't –

MISS LEVERING: – who is there who will resist the temptation to say, 'Poor Vida Levering! What a pity she hasn't got a husband and a baby to keep her quiet'? The few who know about me, they'll be equally sure that it's not the larger view of life I've gained – my own poor little story is responsible for my new departure. (*Leans forward and looks into* LADY JOHN'S *face.*) My best friend, she will be surest of all, that it's a private sense of loss, or, lower yet, a grudge –! But I tell you the only difference between me and thousands of women with husbands and babies is that I'm free to say what I think. *They aren't.*

LADY JOHN (*rising and looking at her watch*): I must get back – my poor ill-used guests.

MISS LEVERING (*rising*): I won't ring. I think you'll find Mr Stonor downstairs waiting for you.

LADY JOHN (*embarrassed*): Oh – a – he will have left word about the car in any case.

MISS LEVERING *has opened the door.* ALLEN TRENT *is in the act of saying goodbye to* JEAN *in the hall.*

MISS LEVERING: Well, Mr Trent, I didn't expect to see you this evening.

TRENT (*comes and stands in the doorway*): Why not? Have I ever failed?

MISS LEVERING: Lady John, this is one of our allies. He is good enough to squire me through the rabble from time to time.

LADY JOHN: Well, I think it's very handsome of you, after what she said today about men. (*Shakes hands.*)

TRENT: I've no great opinion of most men myself. I might add – or of most women.

LADY JOHN: Oh! Well, at any rate I shall go away relieved to think that Miss Levering's plain speaking hasn't alienated *all* masculine regard.

TRENT: Why should it?

LADY JOHN: That's right, Mr Trent! Don't believe all she says in the heat of propaganda.

TRENT: I do believe all she says. But I'm not cast down.

LADY JOHN (*smiling*): Not when she says –

TRENT (*interrupting*): Was there never a misogynist of my sex who ended by deciding to make an exception?

LADY JOHN (*smiling significantly*): Oh, if *that's* what you build on!

TRENT: Well, why shouldn't a man-hater on your side prove equally open to reason?

MISS LEVERING: That part of the question doesn't concern me. I've come to a place where I realise that the first battles of this new campaign must be fought by women alone. The only effective help men could give – amendment of the law – they refuse. The rest is nothing.

LADY JOHN: Don't be ungrateful, Vida. Here's Mr Trent ready to face criticism in publicly championing you.

MISS LEVERING: It's an illusion that I as an individual need Mr Trent. I am quite safe in the crowd. Please don't wait for me, and don't come for me again.

TRENT (*flushes*): Of course if you'd rather –

MISS LEVERING: And that reminds me. I was asked to thank you and to tell you, too, that they – the women of the Union – they won't need your chairmanship any more – though that, I beg you to believe, has nothing to with any feeling of mine.

TRENT (*hurt*): Of course, I know there must be other men ready – better known men –

MISS LEVERING: It isn't that. It's simply that they find a man can't keep a rowdy meeting in order as well as a woman.

He stares.

LADY JOHN: You aren't serious?

MISS LEVERING (*to* TRENT): Haven't you noticed that all their worst disturbances come when men are in charge?

TRENT: Well – a – (*laughs a little ruefully as he moves to the door.*) I hadn't connected the two ideas. Goodbye.

MISS LEVERING: Goodbye.

JEAN *takes him downstairs, right centre.*

LADY JOHN (*as* TRENT *disappears*): That nice boy's in love with you.

MISS LEVERING *simply looks at her.*

Goodbye. (*They shake hands.*) I wish you hadn't been so unkind to that nice boy!

MISS LEVERING: Do you?

LADY JOHN: Yes, for then I would be more certain of your telling Geoffrey Stonor that intelligent women don't nurse their wrongs and lie in wait to punish them.

MISS LEVERING: You are *not* certain?

LADY JOHN (*goes close up to* VIDA): Are you?

VIDA *stands with her eyes on the ground, silent, motionless.* LADY JOHN, *with a nervous glance at her watch and a gesture of extreme perturbation, goes hurriedly out.* VIDA *shuts the door. She comes slowly back, sits down and covers her face with her hands. She rises and begins to walk up and down, obviously trying to master her agitation. Enter* GEOFFREY STONOR.

MISS LEVERING: Well, have they primed you? Have you got your lesson (*with a little broken laugh*) by heart at last?

STONOR (*looking at her from immeasurable distance*): I am not sure I understand you. (*Pause.*) However unpropitious your mood may be – I shall discharge my errand. (*Pause. Her silence irritates him.*) I have promised to offer you what I believe is called 'amends.'

MISS LEVERING (*quickly*): You've come to realise, then – after all these years – that you owed me something?

STONOR (*on the brink of protest, checks himself*): I am not here to deny it.

MISS LEVERING (*fiercely*): Pay, then – pay.

STONOR (*a moment's dread as he looks*

at her, his lips set. Then stonily): I have promised that, if you exact it, I will.

MISS LEVERING: Ah! If I insist you'll 'make it all good'! (*Quite low.*) Then don't you know you must pay me in kind?

STONOR: What do you mean.

MISS LEVERING: Give me back what you took from me: my old faith. Give me that.

STONOR: Oh, if you mean to make phrases – (*A gesture of scant patience.*)

MISS LEVERING (*going closer*): Or give me back mere kindness – or even tolerance. Oh, I don't mean *your* tolerance! Give me back the power to think fairly of my brothers – not as mockers – thieves.

STONOR: I have not mocked you. And I have asked you –

MISS LEVERING: Something you knew I should refuse! Or (*her eyes blaze*) did you dare to be afraid I wouldn't?

STONOR: I suppose, if we set our teeth, we could –

MISS LEVERING: I couldn't – not even if I set my teeth. And you wouldn't dream of asking me, if you thought there was the smallest chance.

STONOR: I can do no more than make you an offer of such reparation as is in my power. If you don't accept it – (*He turns with an air of 'That's done.'*)

MISS LEVERING: Accept it? No! . . . Go away and live in debt! Pay and pay and pay – and find yourself still in debt! – for a thing you'll never be able to give me back. (*Lower.*) And when you come to die, say to yourself, "I paid all creditors but one."

STONOR: I'm rather tired, you know, of this talk of debt. If I hear that you persist in it I shall have to –

MISS LEVERING: What? (*She faces him.*)

STONOR: No. I'll keep to my resolution. (*Turning to the door.*)

MISS LEVERING (*intercepting him*): What resolution?

STONOR: I came here, under considerable pressure, to speak of the future – not to re-open the past.

MISS LEVERING: The Future and the Past are one.

STONOR: You talk as if that old madness was mine alone. It is the woman's way.

MISS LEVERING: I know. And it's not fair. Men suffer as well as we by the woman's starting wrong. We are taught to think the man a sort of demigod. If he tells her: 'go down into Hell' – down into Hell she goes.

STONOR: Make no mistake. Not the woman alone. *They go down together.*

MISS LEVERING: Yes, they go down together, but the man comes up alone. As a rule. It is more convenient so – for him. And for the Other Woman.

The eyes of both go to JEAN'S *door.*

STONOR (*angrily*): My conscience is clear. I know – and so do you – that most men in my position wouldn't have troubled themselves. I gave myself endless trouble.

MISS LEVERING (*with wondering eyes*): So you've gone about all these years feeling that you'd discharged every obligation.

STONOR: Not only that. I stood by you with a fidelity that was nothing short of Quixotic. If, woman like, you *must* recall the Past – I insist on your recalling it correctly.

MISS LEVERING (*very low*): You think I don't recall it correctly?

STONOR: Not when you make – other people believe that I deserted you. (*With gathering wrath.*) It's a curious enough charge when you stop to consider – (*Checks himself, and with a gesture of impatience sweeps the whole thing out of his way.*)

MISS LEVERING: Well, when we *do* – just for five minutes out of ten years – when we do stop to consider –

STONOR: We remember it was *you* who did the deserting! Since you had to rake the story up, you might have had the fairness to tell the facts.

MISS LEVERING: You think 'the facts' would have excused you! (*She sits.*)

STONOR: No doubt you've forgotten

them, since Lady John tells me you wouldn't remember my existence once a year if the newspapers didn't –

MISS LEVERING: Ah, you minded that!

STONOR (*with manly spirit*): I minded your giving false impressions. (*She is about to speak, he advances on her.*) Do you deny that you returned my letters unopened?

MISS LEVERING (*quietly*): No.

STONOR: Do you deny that you refused to see me – and that, when I persisted, you vanished?

MISS LEVERING: I don't deny any of those things.

STONOR: Why, I had no trace of you for years!

MISS LEVERING: I suppose not.

STONOR: Very well, then. What *could* I do?

MISS LEVERING: Nothing. It was too late to do anything.

STONOR: It wasn't too late! You knew – since you 'read the papers' – that my father died that same year. There was no longer any barrier between us.

MISS LEVERING: Oh yes, there was a barrier.

STONOR: Of your own making, then.

MISS LEVERING: I had my guilty share in it – but the barrier (*her voice trembles*) – the barrier was your invention.

STONOR: It was no 'invention'. If you had ever known my father –

MISS LEVERING: Oh, the echoes! The echoes! How often you used to say, if I 'knew your father!' But you said, too (*lower*) – you called the greatest barrier by another name.

STONOR: What name?

MISS LEVERING (*very low*): The child that was to come.

STONOR (*hastily*): That was before my father died. While I still hoped to get his consent.

MISS LEVERING (*nods*): How the thought of that all-powerful personage used to terrorise me! What chance had a little unborn child against 'the last of the great feudal lords', as you called him.

STONOR: You *know* the child would have stood between you and me!

MISS LEVERING: I know the child *did* stand between you and me!

STONOR (*with vague uneasiness*): It *did* stand –

MISS LEVERING: Happy mothers teach their children. Mine had to teach me.

STONOR: You talk as if –

MISS LEVERING: – teach me that a woman may do a thing for love's sake that shall kill love.

(*A silence.*)

STONOR (*fearing and putting from him fuller comprehension, rises with an air of finality*). You certainly made it plain you had no love left for me.

MISS LEVERING: I had need of it all for the child.

STONOR (*stares – comes closer, speaks hurriedly and very low*): Do you mean then that, after all – it lived?

MISS LEVERING: No; I mean that it was sacrificed. But it showed me no barrier is so impassable as the one a little child can raise.

STONOR (*a light dawning*): Was that why you . . . was *that* why?

MISS LEVERING (*nods, speechless a moment*): Day and night there it was! – between my thought of you and me. (*He sits again, staring at her.*) When I was most unhappy I would wake, thinking I heard it cry. It was my own crying I heard, but I seemed to have it in my arms. I suppose I was mad. I used to lie there in that lonely farmhouse pretending to hush it. It was so I hushed myself.

STONOR: I never knew –

MISS LEVERING: I didn't blame you. You couldn't risk being with me.

STONOR: You agreed that for both our sakes –

MISS LEVERING: Yes, you had to be very circumspect. You were so well known. Your autocratic father – your brilliant political future –

STONOR: Be fair. *Our* future – as I saw it then.

MISS LEVERING: Yes, it all hung on concealment. It must have looked quite simple to you. You didn't know that the ghost of a child that had never seen the light, the frail thing you meant to sweep aside and forget – *have* swept aside and forgotten – you didn't know it was strong enough to push you out of my life, (*Lower with an added intensity.*) It can do more. (*Leans over him and whispers.*) It can push that girl out. (STONOR'S *face changes.*) It can do more still.

STONOR: Are you threatening me?

MISS LEVERING: No, I am preparing you.

STONOR: For what?

MISS LEVERING: For the work that must be done. Either with *your help* –or *that girl's*.

STONOR *lifts his eyes a moment.*

One of two things. Either her life, and all she has, given to this new service – or a Ransom, if I give her up to you.

STONOR: I see. A price. Well – ?

MISS LEVERING (*looks searchingly in his face, hesitates and shakes her head*). Even if I could trust you to pay – no, it would be a poor bargain to give her up for anything you could do.

STONOR (*rising*): In spite of your assumption – she may not be your tool.

MISS LEVERING: You are horribly afraid she is! But you are wrong. Don't think it's merely I that have got hold of Jean Dumbarton.

STONOR (*angrily*): Who else?

MISS LEVERING: The New Spirit that's abroad.

STONOR *turns away with an exclamation and begins to pace, sentinel-like, up and down before* JEAN'S *door.*

How else should that inexperienced girl have felt the new loyalty and responded as she did?

STONOR (*under his breath*): 'New' indeed – however little loyal.

MISS LEVERING: Loyal above all. But no newer than electricity was when it first lit up the world. It had been there since the world began – waiting to do away with the dark. *So has the thing you're fighting.*

STONOR (*his voice held down to its lowest register*): The thing I'm fighting is nothing more than one person's hold on a highly sensitive imagination. I consented to this interview with the hope – (*A gesture of impotence.*) It only remains for me to show her your true motive is revenge.

MISS LEVERING: Once say that to her and you are lost!

STONOR *motionless; his look is the look of a man who sees happiness slipping away.*

I know what it is that men fear. It even seems as if it must be through fear that your enlightenment will come. That is why I see a value in Jean Dumbarton far beyond her fortune.

STONOR *lifts his eyes dully and fixes them on* VIDA'S *face.*

More than any girl I know – if I keep her from you – that gentle, inflexible creature could rouse in men the old half-superstitious fear –

STONOR: 'Fear?' I believe you are mad.

MISS LEVERING: 'Mad.' 'Unsexed.' These are the words of today. In the Middle Ages men cried out 'Witch!' and burnt her – the woman who served no man's bed or board.

STONOR: You want to make that poor child believe –

MISS LEVERING: She sees for herself we've come to a place where we find there's a value men see in them. You teach us not to look to you for some of the things we need most. If women must be freed by women, we have need of such as – (*Her eyes go to* JEAN'S *door.*) – who knows? She may be the new Joan of Arc.

STONOR (*aghast*): That *she* should be the sacrifice!

MISS LEVERING: You have taught us to look very calmly on the sacrifice of women. Men tell us in every tongue it's 'a necessary evil'.

STONOR *stands rooted, staring at the ground.*

One girl's happiness – against a thing nobler than happiness for thousands – who can hesitate? – *Not Jean.*

STONOR: Good God! Can't you see that this crazed campaign you'd start her on – even if it's successful, it can only be so through the help of men? What excuse shall you make your own soul for not going straight to the goal?

MISS LEVERING: You think we wouldn't be glad to go straight to the goal?

STONOR: I do. I see you'd much rather punish me and see her revel in a morbid self-sacrifice.

MISS LEVERING: You say I want to punish you only because, like most men, you won't take the trouble to understand what we do want – or how determined we are to have it. You can't kill this new spirit among women. (*Going nearer.*) And you couldn't make a greater mistake than to think it finds a home only in the exceptional, or the unhappy. It's so strange, Geoffrey, to see a man like you as much deluded as the Hyde Park loafers who say to Ernestine Blunt, 'Who's hurt *your* feelings?' Why not realise (*Going quite close to him.*) this is a thing that goes deeper than personal experience? And yet (*Lowering her voice and glancing at the door.*) if you take only the narrowest personal view, a good deal depends on what you and I agree upon in the next five minutes.

STONOR (*bringing her farther away from the door*): You recommend my realising the larger issues. But in your ambition to attach that girl to the chariot wheels of 'Progress,' you quite ignore the fact that people fitter for such work – the men you look to enlist in the end – are ready waiting to give the thing a chance.

MISS LEVERING: Men are ready! What men?

STONOR (*avoiding her eyes, picking his words*): Women have themselves to blame that the question has grown so delicate that responsible people shrink – for the moment – from being implicated in it.

MISS LEVERING: We have seen the 'shrinking'.

STONOR: Without quoting any one else, I might point out that the New Antagonism seems to have blinded you to the small fact that I, for one, am not an opponent.

MISS LEVERING: The phrase *has* a familiar ring. We have heard it from four hundred and twenty others.

STONOR: I spoke, if I may say so, of some one who would count. Some one who can carry his party along with him – or risk a seat in the Cabinet.

MISS LEVERING (*quickly*): Did you mean you are ready to do that?

STONOR: An hour ago I was.

MISS LEVERING: Ah! . . . an hour ago.

STONOR: Exactly. You don't understand men. They can be led. They can't be driven. Ten minutes before you came into the room I was ready to say I would throw in my political lot with this Reform.

MISS LEVERING: And now . . . ?

STONOR: Now you block my way by an attempt at coercion. By forcing my hand you give my adherence an air of bargain-driving for a personal end. Exactly the mistake of the ignorant agitators of your 'Union,' as you call it. You have a great deal to learn. This movement will go forward, not because of the agitation, but in spite of it. There are men in Parliament who would have been actively serving the Reform today . . . as actively as so vast a constitutional change –

MISS LEVERING (*smiles faintly*): And they haven't done it because –

STONOR: Because it would have put a premium on breaches of decent behaviour. (*He takes a crumpled piece of paper out of his pocket.*) Look here!

MISS LEVERING (*flushes with excitement as she reads the telegram*): This is very good. I see only one objection.

STONOR: Objection!

MISS LEVERING: You haven't sent it.

STONOR: *That* is your fault.

MISS LEVERING: When did you write this?

STONOR: Just before you came in – when – (*He glances at the door.*)

MISS LEVERING: Ah! It must have pleased Jean – that message. (*Offers him back the paper.*)

STONOR *astonished at her yielding it up so lightly, and remembering* JEAN *had not so much as read it. He throws himself heavily into a chair and drops his head in his hands.*

I could drive a hard-and-fast bargain with you, but I think I won't. If *both* love and ambition urge you on, perhaps – (*She gazes at the slack, hopeless figure with its sudden look of age – goes over silently and stands by his side.*) After all, life hasn't been quite fair to you –

He raises his heavy eyes.

You fall out of one ardent woman's dreams into another's.

STONOR: You may as well tell me – do you mean to – ?

MISS LEVERING: To keep you and her apart? No.

STONOR (*for the first time tears come into his eyes. After a moment he holds out his hand*): What can I do for you?

MISS LEVERING *shakes her head – speechless.*

For the real you. Not the Reformer, or the would-be politician – for the woman I so unwillingly hurt. (*As she turns away, struggling with her feelings, he lays a detaining hand on her arm.*) You may not believe it, but now that I understand, there is almost nothing I wouldn't do to right that old wrong.

MISS LEVERING: There's nothing to be done. You can never give me back my child.

STONOR (*at the anguish in* VIDA'S *face his own has changed*): Will that ghost give you no rest?

MISS LEVERING: Yes, oh, yes. I see life is nobler than I knew. There is work to do.

STONOR (*stopping her as she goes towards the folding doors*): Why should you think that it's only you, these ten years have taught something to? Why not give even a man credit for a willingness to learn something of life, and for being sorry – profoundly sorry – for the pain his instruction has cost others? You seem to think I've taken it all quite lightly. That's not fair. All my life, ever since you disappeared, the thought of you has hurt. I would give anything I possess to know you – were happy again.

MISS LEVERING: Oh, happiness!

STONOR (*significantly*): Why shouldn't you find it still.

MISS LEVERING (*stares an instant*): I see! She couldn't help telling about Allen Trent – Lady John couldn't.

STONOR: You're one of the people the years have not taken from, but given more to. You are more than ever . . . You haven't lost your beauty.

MISS LEVERING: The gods saw it was so little effectual, it wasn't worth taking away. (*She stands looking out into the void.*) One woman's mishap? – what is that? A thing as trivial to the great world as it's sordid in most eyes. But the time has come when a woman may look about her, and say, 'What general significance has my secret pain? Does it "join on" to anything?' And I find it does. I'm no longer merely a woman who has stumbled on the way. I'm one (*She controls with difficulty the shake in her voice.*) who has got up bruised and bleeding, wiped the dust from her hands and the tears from her face, and said to herself not merely, 'Here's one luckless woman! but – here is a stone of stumbling to many. Let's see if it can't

be moved out of other women's way.' And she calls people to come and help. No mortal man, let alone a woman, *by herself*, can move that rock of offence. But (*With a sudden sombre flame of enthusiasm.*) if many help, Geoffrey, the thing can be done.

STONOR (*looks at her with wondering pity*): Lord! how you care!

MISS LEVERING (*touched by his moved face*): Don't be so sad. Shall I tell you a secret? Jean's ardent dreams needn't frighten you, if she has a child. *That* – from the beginning, it was not the strong arm – it was the weakest – the little, little arms that subdued the fiercest of us.

STONOR *puts out a pitying hand uncertainly towards her. She does not take it, but speaks with great gentleness.*

You will have other children, Geoffrey – for me there was to be only one. Well, well – (*She brushes her tears away.*) – since men alone have tried and failed to make a decent world for the little children to live in – it's as well some of us are childless. (*Quietly taking up her hat and cloak.*) Yes, *we* are the ones who have no excuse for standing aloof from the fight.

STONOR: Vida!

MISS LEVERING: What?

STONOR: You've forgotten something. (*As she looks back he is signing the message.*) *This.*

She goes out silently with the 'political dynamite' in her hand.

Curtain.

LADY GERALDINE'S SPEECH

LADY GERALDINE'S SPEECH
Beatrice Harraden

The author of many novels, Beatrice Harraden was persuaded to write for the women's suffrage theatre by Inez Bensusan, and her style was similar to that of many other play writers. Rather than simply denounce the 'Antis', who were notoriously ill-prepared (and, according to the suffrage women, who had such weak arguments) it was clear that a dramatisation of this state of affairs would be far more popular – and effective. So Lady Geraldine enters to make the point; she is an 'anti' who has to make a speech and who rushes to her old school friend, Dr Alice Romney – a supporter of the Women's Social and Political Union – for assistance. Dr Alice Romney does not initially want to help Lady Geraldine, but friendship prevails and she sits down to write a stirring anti-suffrage speech. While she is in the process of drafting it however, her talented and spirited women friends call, and entertain Lady Geraldine who is, of coursel, ultimately converted to the cause.

For Inez Bensusan however, the problem was not just to persuade Beatrice Harraden to write the play; once it was written there were problems about booking it, for so pronounced was its support for the Women's Social and Political Union that it was likely to offend members of the National Union of Women's Suffrage Societies if it were performed at one of their gatherings.

Dale Spender

Characters

DR ALICE ROMNEY, *a medical woman*
LADY GERALDINE BOLEYN, *Dr Alice Romney's school friend*
MISS GERTRUDE SILBERTHWAITE, *an eminent artist*
MISS NORA BAILLIE, *a professor of literature*
MISS HILDA CROWNINSHIELD, *a famous pianist*
MISS NELLIE GRANT, *a typist and shorthand writer*
JANE, *a maid*

Note on Performance

All you need for this one is a piano and a few chairs. It is a delightful one acter which could be performed as a curtain raiser or in tandem with another short play as a double bill. The characters should all be fun to play and what is a joy is to see so many women exulting in their own ability and intelligence. Few plays provide such a soirée of talent or a picture of women self-sufficient and happy as professionals. Not at all like the grey boiler-suited, grim faced, unfunny, feminists popular in our culture. Lady Geraldine, who has not 'gone into' the pros and cons as thoroughly as she should, is won over (and who wouldn't be) by this room full of frank, easy going, sensible heroines. There are some smashing audition speeches in it also.

Carole Hayman

Scene: DR ALICE ROMNEY'S
*Drawing-room in Nottingham Place. It is
her fortnightly Suffrage At-Home day.
She is seated at her writing desk near the
window. She is of middle stature, and has
a strong, capable face.*

Enter MAID *with card.*

MAID: A lady asks specially to see you. I
said you were engaged until three
o'clock. But she insisted.

DR ALICE (*looking at her card and
smiling*): Show her in, Jane.

Enter hurriedly, shown in by maid, the
LADY GERALDINE BOLEYN.

LADY GERALDINE: Oh, my dear, how
good of you to see me. I hope I am not
interrupting any operation. Not that I
suppose you do perform operations in
drawing-rooms! But I had to see you
instantly, whatever you were doing. I've
dashed up purposely from Eastbourne.
The fact is, Alice, I've got myself into a
most awful hole. You'll help me out,
won't you? You always have helped me
out of my difficulties. Nothing more
than you ought to have done,
considering how I used to come to your
rescue over your French compositions in
the dear old Cheltenham College days.
My word, you were bad at French,
weren't you?

DR ALICE: (*nodding*): Yes. And I'm not
much better now. Languages were
always a trial to me. I used to think you
were a perfect wonder at them.

LADY GERALDINE: So I was. So I am
still. Don't let there be any mistake
about that! Well now, to business. As I
told you, I've got myself into a most
fearful scrape. The worst in my life –
absolutely the worst.

DR ALICE: (*reproachfully*): Geraldine,
Geraldine, what on earth have you been
up to? Are you never going to learn
discretion?

LADY GERALDINE: Apparently never.
There's no doubt that I have committed
a terrible indiscretion. I've compromised
myself with – well, I hardly like to tell
you – with – the Women's National
Anti-Suffrage League.

DR ALICE (*brightening up*): Is that all?

LADY GERALDINE: Isn't it enough, in
all conscience? I'm at my wits' end. I
haven't slept for nights, for years. Look
how drawn my face is. If I'm not
careful, I shall begin to look clever. Yes,
I've got into the toils of the National
Anti-Suffrage League. I've been made
into a president or vice-president, or
honorary secretary, or supporter, or
something of the sort, and I have to take
the chair at a large meeting at the
Imperial Hall next week and make a
speech, and use all the anti-suffrage
arguments on this wretched sheet of
paper – oh, where is it? (*Looking for it
in her muff and satchel.*) Ah, here it is.
It's like a nightmare to me. Every time I
try to look at it, all the letters seem to
chase each other off the paper, and
there's only a blank left – like my brain.
If you won't help me, I shall perish. I
know I shall.

DR ALICE: But my dear Geraldine, I'm
a Suffragist, a Suffragette, a militant.
You've come to the wrong person.

LADY GERALDINE (*coaxingly*): I've
come to my old school chum. As if
being a Suffragist or an Anti-Suffragist
could make any difference to that
eternal fact.

DR ALICE (*laughing*): No, you're right!
Well, what do you want me to do?

LADY GERALDINE: I want you to
write my speech for me, and coach me
up in it. There! Don't look so
disagreeable. You're so handsome when
you're pleasant. And so hideous when
you're cross. Ah, that's better. Now,
here are some of the arguments. As I
told you, I tried to glance at them, but
failed. So I haven't really gone into
details. I haven't really gone into the
matter at all, between you and me. But
(*Suddenly recollecting herself.*) I felt
strongly, on general lines, that it was
impossible for me to take the
responsibility of being in favour of
Woman's Suffrage.

DR ALICE: How well you roll those
words out! Someone has made you learn
that sentence by heart. (*Repeats it.*) 'But
I felt strongly, on general lines, that it
was impossible for me to take the
responsibility of being in favour of

Woman's Suffrage.' I must say I wonder you dare take the still greater responsibility of being against it.

LADY GERALDINE (*waving her hand in dismissal of* DR ALICE'S *remark*): Come now, Alice. Do begin. We're wasting time. Allow me to conduct you to your desk. Here's paper. And here's your stylo. And here am I waiting on you as usual. Oh, you can make as much fun of me as you like, and lecture me as much as you like. I was always good-tempered, wasn't I? I don't mind what you say to me, as long as you help me with my speech.

DR ALICE: Why don't you go and get an Anti-Suffragist friend to do this for you?

LADY GERALDINE: My dear girl, don't be ridiculous. With a few notable exceptions, all the Anti-Suffragists have my sort of brains. How can we possibly help each other? Do begin. I'm losing patience with you.

DR ALICE: But you have heaps of splendid men amongst you. Go to them.

LADY GERALDINE: Certainly not! It's one thing to sing small about your sex, but quite another thing to sing small about yourself – except to a dear old school chum who used to be a regular old brick, but who evidently isn't one any longer. (*Plaintively.*) I never dreamed that you would fail me. What on earth shall I do? I shall make an awful fiasco, and disgrace myself and my Cause, and it will be your fault. You wouldn't wish to see me humiliated, would you? And surely you wouldn't wish my Cause to be disgraced. You've always said Causes saved one. Those have been your very words, Alice. Causes saved one, it did not matter what they were.

DR ALICE (*laughing*): Nothing could ever save you. You're spoilt through and through. Here, give me the precious arguments. Sit down by the fire, and don't chatter for a minute or two, and I'll see what I can do for you.

LADY GERALDINE (*taking up her skirt and dancing round a little*): A – ha! I knew she would come round. These grim people are always the easiest to deal with. Be sure and write

clearly, dear. I never could read your handwriting.

She dances into a chair and sits primly up, twiddling her fingers.

A pause.

DR ALICE: I think you might begin in this way: 'Ladies and gentlemen, I am here to-night to explain to you some of the weighty reasons which have decided me, after much anxious thought and study, to become a determined opponent of Woman's Suffrage.'

LADY GERALDINE: Excellent! Sounds as if I'd studied the question for untold centuries, doesn't it?

DR ALICE: Then I think you'd better touch at once on the 'unwomanliness' of the whole movement, and the danger to the home. And you might enlarge on the 'harem' theme.

LADY GERALDINE: The harem theme? What's that? I don't remember that on the list. Not that I remember anything.

DR ALICE: It is not called that. It's called, 'The immense direct influence now possessed by women.' To me, personally, a most degrading influence. After that, you might beat the Imperial Drum.

LADY GERALDINE: The Imperial –

The door opens. Enter, unannounced, MISS GERTRUDE SILBER-THWAITE, *an eminent artist. She is charmingly dressed, and has an engaging personality.*

SILBERTHWAITE: Ah, busy, I see, Dr Alice. I'm rather early. Shall I go away and come back in half-an-hour or so?

DR ALICE: No, no. Sit down by the fire with my friend – an old school friend. I'm throwing together a speech for her. She's a new hand. I don't mind you talking so long as you don't talk to me.

LADY GERALDINE *and* GERTRUDE SILBERTHWAITE, *who have already greeted, settle down together.*

SILBERTHWAITE: Dr Alice has a most enviable gift of concentration. She can study the most abstruse subject under any conditions whatsoever. So she is helping you with your first speech?

Well, you couldn't have anyone better to help you. She's so splendid at arranging the arguments in their most forceful fashion. Shall you be nervous?

LADY GERALDINE (*uneasily*): Yes.

SILBERTHWAITE: Ah, well, we all have to go through that. But it's worth while for the sake of the Cause, isn't it?

LADY GERALDINE (*doubtfully*): Yes.

SILBERTHWAITE: I'm just painting Dr Alice's portrait. A difficult face. So handsome when she's pleasant! And so ugly when she's disagreeable.

LADY GERALDINE (*delighted*): That's exactly what I say. My very words a few minutes ago! Then you are an artist – a portrait painter? May I ask your name? I'm so interested in pictures.

SILBERTHWAITE: Silberthwaite.

LADY GERALDINE (*enraptured*): Gertrude Silberthwaite! You don't mean it. I am proud and delighted to see you. I've always wanted to meet you. But one never comes across you anywhere. I always heard you were a recluse.

SILBERTHWAITE (*smiling*): I'm not by nature a society-bird. And moreover I haven't much spare time – none, in fact. But the Suffrage Movement has brought all us professional women out of our libraries and studios and all our other hiding places. We had to take our share in it, or else be ashamed of ourselves. I really do think it is a wonderful movement, don't you? And quite apart from anything to do with the vote itself, it is so splendid coming in intimate contact with a lot of fine women all following different professions or businesses. That's one of our advantages over the Anti-Suffragists, isn't it? They have no means of understanding personally the inner meaning of the whole Movement. I'm sorry for them, aren't you?

LADY GERALDINE (*fervently*): Yes, for some of them.

SILBERTHWAITE: Do you know I'm planning to paint a Suffrage Picture for next year's Academy, a group of representative Suffragist Women. Ellen Terry for the Drama, Mrs Garrett Anderson for Medicine, Mrs Ayrton for Science, Miss Elizabeth Robins for literature, Christabel Pankhurst for Politics, and –

Enter MISS NORA BAILLIE *a Professor of Literature and a brilliant lecturer. She is particularly fresh-looking, and has a fine enthusiastic face, with eyes far apart.*

BAILLIE (*gaily*): What, Dr Alice, busy, making out prescriptions? Ah no, I see you haven't the prescription look on your face! A letter to the Prime Minister perhaps! A love letter to the Home Secretary! A valentine to the Governor of Holloway! Who can tell? Anything may happen in these days.

SILBERTHWAITE (*laughing and beckoning to* BAILLIE): Don't talk to her, Miss Baillie. She's concocting a speech. Come and talk to us instead. You do look in splendid form this afternoon. What have you been doing?

BAILLIE: I've just given the best Chaucer lecture I've ever given in my life. And the class was magnificent. Heavens, what a difference it makes when you know you have your class with you!

LADY GERALDINE: Chaucer! How interesting! I haven't heard his name mentioned since I was at school. Do tell me something about him!

BAILLIE (*quoting with animation*): 'His stature was not very tall. Leane he was, his legs were small, Hosed within a stock of red. A buttoned bonnet on his head, His beard was white, trimmed round. His countenance blithe and merry found.' I wonder whether Chaucer would have conceded us the vote. I have my doubts. But I have no doubt about Shakespeare. None. I can't conceive it possible that he who gave us Portia, Hermione, Cordelia, Rosalind, Beatrice, Imogen, and all his other splendid women of brain, education and initiative, would have withheld us grudgingly the rights of full citizenship. I intend to die in the belief that he would have been on our side. I'm sure he's on the platform at all Suffrage Meetings calling out inaudibly: 'Votes for Women!' (*Turning to* LADY GERALDINE). Don't you agree with me?

LADY GERALDINE (*shyly*): I've never

thought of it.

SILBERTHWAITE: Nor have I. But I daresay she's right.

BAILLIE: Of course I'm right! What a pity the Prime Minister hasn't Shakespeare's mind! There's no denying he hasn't, is there? (*To* LADY GERALDINE).

LADY GERALDINE (*pensively*): I suppose there isn't.

SILBERTHWAITE (*gaily*): You appear to be in some doubt.

LADY GERALDINE (*laughing*): Oh no, not about that! But I was just wondering –

Enter MISS HILDA CROWNINSHIELD, *a famous pianist.*

SILBERTHWAITE: Ah, here's Hilda Crowninshield. Hurrah!

CROWNINSHIELD (*greeting them all*): Here I am. Just back from a concert at Manchester. Good afternoon, Dr Alice. Busy, I see. (*Turning to* SILBERTHWAITE.) What is she doing? Shall I disturb her if I try the piano?

BAILLIE: Oh! dear no. She's only writing a speech. As long as you don't talk to her, you may introduce the whole of the Queen's Hall Orchestra into this room, and she won't turn a hair.

CROWNINSHIELD: Good. I want to run through the two little Brahms pieces I promised to play this afternoon. If the piano is very much out of tune, and there are more than five or six notes broken, I shall have to choose some other things, that's all!

She sits down at the piano. LADY GERALDINE, *who has been exceedingly stirred by her arrival, goes up to her.*

LADY GERALDINE (*excitedly*): Miss Crowninshield, I must speak to you. I cannot tell you what your playing means to me. I'd rather hear you than anyone in the world! I don't know what you do to me. When I hear you play, I feel myself capable of everything great and good.

CROWNINSHIELD (*greatly pleased,*

and touching her gently on the hand): Thank you. Then you must be passionately fond of music?

LADY GERALDINE: Passionately. It is the language I understand.

CROWNINSHIELD (*beginning to touch the notes*): Ah, not so bad! And I declare Dr Alice has had it tuned! I never expected such luck. Yes, I can play one or two of Brahms's Intermezzi, and perhaps a Chopin Waltz. Perhaps even a bit of Grieg. (*She addresses herself to* LADY GERALDINE) Yes?

LADY GERALDINE (*delighted*): Yes, yes! How good of you to come and play at Dr Alice's.

CROWNINSHIELD: Good? Why, I love playing to my Suffrage comrades. I'd do anything for them! Play the trombone, if they wanted it fearfully!

She begins Brahms's First Intermezzo. After she has been playing for a little while, enter NELLIE GRANT, *a typist and shorthand writer. She carries, slung over her shoulder, a bag with one remaining copy of* VOTES FOR WOMEN. *She looks extremely fatigued.* HILDA CROWNINSHIELD *glances up and leaves off playing and joins the others.*

CROWNINSHIELD: Why, my dear child, you look worn out. Thoroughly at the end of yourself. Let's ring for tea for her immediately. (*They ring for tea.*)

NELLIE GRANT: Tired, but very proud, Miss Crowninshield. I've had a most successful day. Sold all my Votes for Women except one solitary copy, and had some useful little talks with lots of people. One man bought six copies. He said he had been an Anti until yesterday, when he went to an Anti meeting and that converted him! (*Laughter.*)

CROWNINSHIELD: Bravo. (*Runs to the piano and plays a few bars of the waltz from 'The Merry Widow.' They laugh, clap, and dance a little.*)

BAILLIE: I really do think the Antis are our best friends.

LADY GERALDINE: Why? I don't quite understand. I should have thought they were very formidable foes.

SILBERTHWAITE: Oh dear no! You needn't have any fears about that. You see, with a few exceptions, they can't speak – they haven't had the practice – they haven't learnt how to hold an audience.

LADY GERALDINE: But when they have learnt, what then?

BAILLIE: Even then they can't be formidable. Remember for your comfort, that they haven't got an irresistible champion as we have.

LADY GERALDINE (*entirely mystified*): An irresistible champion?

CROWNINSHIELD: She means the Spirit of the Age.

LADY GERALDINE (*smiling blankly*): The Spirit of the Age?

BAILLIE: And lots of them haven't 'gone into it'! I know they haven't. One of them brought me the Anti-Suffrage Petition to sign, and told me quite frankly, when I advanced some arguments in favour of Woman's Suffrage, that she had not 'gone into it,' but that she wanted to get as many signatures as quickly as possible for that petition which was sent in yesterday, you know – seven miles long or seven feet high – I forget which! They may get signatures – whole villages of signatures – but they can't really hope to influence people if they haven't taken the trouble to influence themselves, can they?

LADY GERALDINE (*uncomfortably*): No.

SILBERTHWAITE: Don't give them one anxious thought. They'll soon 'fold their tents, like the Arabs, and as silently steal away'!

CROWNINSHIELD (*who is still at the piano, improvises and sings softly*): 'The night shall be filled with music, and the cares which beset the day, Shall fold their tents, like the Arabs, and as silently steal away.'

Tea is brought in.

LADY GERALDINE (*who has been slowly gathering herself together for a declaration of faith*): I have something to tell you all. You've been taking it for granted that I'm a Suffragist. Well, I'm not. I'm an Anti-Suffragist.

SILBERTHWAITE: Great heavens! How delightful! I've been longing to meet one face to face. No one brought me the Anti-Suffrage Petition.

BAILLIE: Do tell us your name. Who are you?

LADY GERALDINE: Geraldine Boleyn.

BAILLIE (*turning to the others*): Why, of course! Lady Geraldine Boleyn. She's going to take the chair on the 15th at the Imperial Hall. Surely I'm not mistaken.

LADY GERALDINE (*frankly*): Yes, that's quite right. And as I couldn't manage my speech, I came to my old school friend in my distress. I know it sounds absurd, but it's true.

DR ALICE (*looking up for the first time from her desk*): Idiot! Why did you give yourself away? I could shake you.

LADY GERALDINE: Alice, I simply couldn't have held out for a moment longer. I couldn't have gone on pretending by my silence that I was one of them.

DR ALICE (*getting up from her desk, and turning fiercely to her comrades*): You mustn't betray her. I wouldn't have her betrayed for worlds. She's very dear to me. She has always been wonderfully good to me, though she has been a great nuisance at times and has given me a lot of trouble, and has always made the most unreasonable demands on me – and – well – I've liked it. She's my oldest and dearest school friend, and we plotted all sorts of mischief together in the happy old days. And if that isn't a sacred bond, then nothing is. Nearly all the pleasures I had in my holidays came through her – I should never have known all the sweet pleasures of the country but for her – joys which abide with one for ever, when other things have passed out of one's life. I can't and won't have her humiliated. If I hadn't helped her over her speech, she would have probably made herself ridiculous – and I couldn't have stood that – I had to help her – and I shall always have to help her – if she becomes an anarchist and takes the chair at an anarchist meeting I shall have to write her speech for that too. I . . . (*She breaks off suddenly.*) Promise me you won't give her away.

ALL FOUR TOGETHER: Of course. Our word of honour.

They all stretch out their hands to LADY GERALDINE, *and make a charming group round her.*

BAILLIE (*gaily*): There's nothing, however, in our oath to prevent us from laughing a little, is there? Oh, and to think I shan't be able to go and heckle you! I can't heckle Dr Alice's old school friend. And I'd bought a ticket surreptitiously and with the utmost difficulty!

SILBERTHWAITE: As I told you, I've never seen a real Anti-Suffragist before. Do let me paint your portrait! Side face would be best, I think. I'm not quite sure, though. No, it must be full face. Yes, full face.

NELLIE GRANT: Do tell me if it's true that there's going to be a 'No Votes for Women' paper, with a Union Jack on the cover. I *shall* be jealous.

CROWNINSHIELD (*taking* LADY GERALDINE'S *arm*): Don't you dare tease her any more! Votes or no votes, she and I speak the same language, don't we?

DR ALICE: Well, now for the speech, Geraldine. I've quite enjoyed this little job. I'm rather pleased with it. I think I've brought in all the points. Degradation of Womanhood. Degradation and disintegration of entire Empire. Dominant female vote in all matters concerning the Army and Navy, our relations with foreign Powers, with our Colonies, and with India. Physical force argument. Women have to safeguard the past and the future, and it is the men's work to look after the present. I don't myself know what that means, but it sounds well. Absolute denial that the vote will improve the economic position of women. Indirect influence of women quite sufficient. Emphatic, nay passionate, insistence on your own brainlessness – that is very important. A few passing allusions to us Suffragists as obscure vulgarians. I think you might almost call us uneducated. Yes, uneducated and obscure vulgarians. That also sounds well. And as there's so little to say, it must sound well, my dear girl, or else the Cause perishes. Ah, yes,

and you mustn't forget to refer to yourselves as 'so-called traitresses to the sex, so-called survivals of the Dark Ages,' because that will elicit respectful sympathy. And be sure and mention that you have joined the Territorial Nursing Corps. I forget its name, but that's near enough. Have you joined it, by the way?

LADY GERALDINE (*who is standing all this splendidly*): No.

DR ALICE: Then do so at once, because that's a piece of subtle cleverness. You disclaim physical force, and yet are preparing indirectly to defend your country. There now, haven't I been a brick? Haven't I wiped out for ever the obligation of those French compositions?

LADY GERALDINE (*with spirit but good temper*): No, that obligation could never be wiped out. And besides, this service doesn't count. Do you know what I'm going to do with this speech? Look.

She throws it into the fire.

DR ALICE: Well, of all the ungrateful, aristocratic little wretches –

LADY GERALDINE (*with increased spirit and charm, turning to the others*): Do you know what I'm going to do next? I'm going home to think.

DR ALICE: Impossible! You've never done such a thing in your life!

BAILLIE: Shame, Dr Alice! It's never too late to mend – I mean to think!

LADY GERALDINE (*smiling at her*): I should love to come to one of your lectures. May I?

BAILLIE: Of course you may.

LADY GERALDINE (*to* GERTRUDE SILBERTHWAITE): And will you really paint my portrait?

SILBERTHWAITE: Of course I will. Full face. And when you're thinking!

LADY GERALDINE (*to* HILDA CROWNINSHIELD): The same language, votes or no votes?

CROWNINSHIELD: Yes, yes.

LADY GERALDINE (*to* NELLIE GRANT): Will you let me have your last remaining copy of your paper?

A CHAT WITH MRS CHICKY
&
MISS APPLEYARD'S AWAKENING

A CHAT WITH MRS CHICKY
(First performed at the Rehearsal Theatre, London, on 20th February, 1912.)
MISS APPLEYARD'S AWAKENING
Evelyn Glover

Evelyn Glover wrote quite a few pieces for the women's suffrage theatre; an entertaining monologue *Showin' Samyel*, the duologue *A Chat with Mrs Chicky* and the play *Miss Appleyard's Awakening*, among them. She was interested in dramatising the arguments of working-class women in particular, partly because one criticism that was levelled at the women's movement was that only middle-class women would benefit from sexual equality and the vote.

The character in *Showin' Samyel* (not included here) is a char-lady whose husband is against votes for women, and who thinks women should be a silent influence in the home. So she agrees with him. She shows him. She sits at home being a silent influence and Samuel of course, soon capitulates.

Mrs Chicky is also a char who finds herself confronted by Mrs Holbrook, (her employer's sister) who is seeking signatures for her anti-suffrage petition. Mrs Holbrook doesn't want to take Mrs Chicky from her work, so she proceeds to hold forth on the virtues of women's place in the home; much of the humour comes from the irony of Mrs Holbrook's statements about protected and revered womanhood as Mrs Chicky cleans around her. As Mrs Holbrook recounts the joys of motherhood, Mrs Chicky reminds her that married women cannot be the guardians of their children; as Mrs Holbrook goes off into the glories of man and woman being one, Mrs Chicky points out that that 'one' is the man – which is why Mrs Chicky is considered French –because her husband was. As Mrs Holbrook insists that it takes superior physical and mental qualities to be able to vote, Mrs Chicky lists the characteristics of some of the men she knows who can vote. And the case is settled in favour of Mrs Chicky, the working-class woman who has a lot to gain from sex equality.

Not surprisingly this was one of the most popular plays in the League's repertoire. *Miss Appleyard's Awakening*, although not quite so popular, contained a similar twist in the plot. As so often happens, even today, the women who advocate that women's place is in the home are caught in the contradiction of having to go outside their homes to put their case, and Evelyn Glover was quick to exploit the flaw in the anti-suffrage movement. Women who were against women being in politics were becoming very 'political' as they entered the fray to stop women getting the vote. Unless of course they were like Mrs Crabtree, who believed that women should be interested in nothing, and helped to awaken Miss Appleyard to the error of her anti-suffrage ways.

Dale Spender

A CHAT WITH MRS CHICKY

Characters

MRS CHICKY, *a charwoman*
MRS HOLBROOK, *an Anti-Suffrage canvasser*

A Chat with Mrs Chicky was first performed at the Rehearsal Theatre, London, in 1912, with the following cast:

MRS CHICKY   Miss Inez Bensusan
MRS HOLBROOK   Miss Marianne Caldwell

Note on Performance

The stage directions here obligingly offer two ways of doing the play, one with and one without set. If you go for the former, and there is certainly a good class comment to be got out of Mrs Chicky's ceaseless labour and Mrs Holbrook's absolute lack of it, then a carpet, a chair, and Mrs Chicky's props should be enough for this comedy of misunderstanding. The class confrontation, with the working-class woman coming out on top is a popular theme in these plays. Mrs Chicky is the salt of the earth, Mrs Holbrook the drone who wastes it. Chicky is poor and uneducated, Holbrook, comfortable and privileged; yet it is Chicky who, with pragmatic common sense, triumphs in every argument. She has a far superior grip on reality and understanding of what affects womens' lives to a dozen dozy Holbrooks, whose heads are so full of 'beautiful ideas' that they can't see what's under their noses. As a northern friend of mine would say, 'she doesn't know her A— from endive'. The play ends with an impassioned defence of suffrage (another good audition) by Mrs Chicky as she goes off to service the rest of the family.

Carole Hayman

Scene: *A Room in the house of* MRS HOLBROOK'S *brother. Window on left with desk and writing chair in front of it. Door left centre. Fireplace right with armchair (on castors) drawn towards it, facing audience. Bookshelf right centre. Table up centre. One small chair on top of another left of desk. Fender drawn away from hearth. Broom leaning against the wall. Pail of water, flannel, dustpan and brush, hearthbox with hearthcloth, scouring-stone, blacking brushes, old gloves, etc., up near door. Desk, table, bookshelf and armchair covered with dust sheets.*

N.B.– Although the effect of this duologue is much enhanced by the setting, it can quite well be played without it on small platforms, etc. Where this is desired, MRS HOLBROOK *should be discovered on rising of curtain, seated at a table with paper and pencil. She says,* 'Come in!' *in answer to a knock at the door, and* MRS CHICKY *appears, saying,* 'Sarah said you wanted to speak to me, M.' MRS HOLBROOK *answers:* 'So I do, Mrs Hicky. Sit down,' *and the duologue proceeds as written, except that instead of asking* MRS CHICKY *to go on with her work,* MRS HOLBROOK *says* 'I won't keep you from your work more than a few moments.' *Subsequent chance references to the 'turning-out' would, of course be omitted.*

On rising of the curtain MRS CHICKY, *with sleeves rolled up, skirts pinned high, etc., is discovered scattering tea-leaves from a jar over the carpet. She stops short as* MRS HOLBROOK, *in outdoor things, bustles into the room.*

MRS HOLBROOK: Oh, you're here, Mrs Hicky! I just want to –

MRS CHICKY: (*briefly*): Chicky.

MRS HOLBROOK: What do you say? Oh, Chicky – yes, of course. You're not the same charwoman my brother employed last time I came to see him, are you?

MRS CHICKY: I couldn't say.

MRS HOLBROOK: Ah, but I remember. I've such a memory for faces. She was short and stout, and –

MRS CHICKY (*interrupting*): If you're alludin' to Martha Buggins, 'M., she 'ad a cock-eye.

MRS HOLBROOK: Oh, poor woman, yes. She *had* a slight squint.

MRS CHICKY: 'Ope I may never see a severe one, then!

MRS HOLBROOK (*ignoring remark*): My brother said I might have a little chat with you, Mrs Chicky.

MRS CHICKY (*setting jar on table, pulling down sleeves, and looking round at general disorder*): Shall I come into the 'all, 'M.?

MRS HOLBROOK: No, no! I haven't come to keep you from your work. Please go on with it just as if I wasn't here – I shan't interfere with you. (*Laughs pleasantly.*) You and I are the sort of women who like to stick to our work and not interfere with other people's, aren't we?

MRS CHICKY: I'll answer for meself.

MRS HOLBROOK: It's a pity everybody can't say as much. (*Looks round for somewhere to sit down.* MRS CHICKY *takes up small chair, puts it centre and dusts it with apron.*) Ah, thank you! (*Sits down.*) Now please go on with whatever you're doing. We can talk just as well while you're working.

MRS CHICKY (*takes up broom leaning against wall*): Thank you, 'M.

MRS HOLBROOK (*as* MRS CHICKY *begins to sweep round the room*): That s right. Well, I'm trying to collect opinions wherever I go on a subject that a handful of women are making a great fuss about just now. I wonder if you know what I mean by Women's Suffrage?

MRS CHICKY (*looks thoughtfully at* MRS HOLBROOK, *then shakes her head and goes on sweeping*): No, 'M.

MRS HOLBROOK: All the better! *You* haven't got time to trouble your head about politics, have you?

MRS CHICKY (*sweeping tea-leaves and dust almost into* MRS HOLBROOK): I don't interfere with what don't interfere with me!

MRS HOLBROOK (*gathering skirts*

round her and putting feet on chair-rail.): Splendid! Well, the fact is, Mrs Hicky –

MRS CHICKY: Chicky!

MRS HOLBROOK: Chicky – I beg your pardon. The fact is that a few women who haven't got anything else to do have some ridiculous idea that they ought to have votes, and do men's work instead of their own and interfere with the government of the country, and if you and I and millions of other women who know better don't stop them at once we shall simply have England going to rack and ruin!

MRS CHICKY (*pauses, leans on broom, and asks as if seeking light*): Then I 'ave got to trouble me 'ead about pollytics after all?

MRS HOLBROOK: Oh no! Let me put it a little differently! If you don't want a thing you certainly oughtn't to be made to have it, ought you?

MRS CHICKY (*giggling as she goes on sweeping*): That's what John Joseph says when 'e sees me with 'is lickrice powder. 'E's my third, is John Joseph.

MRS HOLBROOK (*coughing as dust rises, but evidently determined not to show irritation*): And a credit to you, I'm sure. Well, what we want to do is to show everybody that by far the greater number of women *don't* want votes, and I'm doing my part by asking a hundred women, taken as far as possible from every station in life, and putting down their replies so that I can send the result to a newspaper.

MRS CHICKY: An' 'ow might you be gettin' on, 'M.?

MRS HOLBROOK: Oh – er – of course one can't quite tell till one's got to the end. But when once we show in figures that most women are *against* having the vote, of course nobody can go on saying anything in favour of it.

MRS CHICKY: Well I 'ope you won't be disappointed 'M., I'm shore. But some people are that obstinate you can't make 'em see nothin'.

MRS HOLBROOK: Oh those kind of people needn't be considered at all.

MRS CHICKY: No 'M. (*Stops sweeping*

again.) Why if you took one o' them lists of yours, down our Court to find out 'ow many wanted to wash theirselves every day I could tell you before 'and which side you'd 'ave a big balance on, an' yet I dessay you'd find some folks pig-'eaded enough to go on sayin' as they all orter use soap and water.

MRS HOLBROOK (*looks sharply at MRS CHICKY whose face remains impassive*): Please don't let me stop your work, Mrs Chicky. I don't think we need go into the question of your neighbours' cleanliness this afternoon. I merely want to know if I may put you down on my list as being against votes for women?

MRS CHICKY (*still pausing*): Well o' course 'M., if I was to set out to explain to you –

MRS HOLBROOK (*patiently*): I don't want *you* to explain anything to *me*, Mrs Chicky. I'm here to explain things to *you* this morning. (MRS CHICKY *still hesitates.*) You'd like to hear something more from me about it before you say yes, perhaps?

MRS CHICKY: I should, 'M.

MRS HOLBROOK: I thought so. Well, I can make the whole thing clear to you in a few minutes. Yes, please go on. (MRS CHICKY *begins to sweep again.*) You see *we* think that women have their own special work to do in their homes, and of course some of them have a Council vote already about things they can understand, like lighting streets and making roads.

MRS CHICKY (*encouragingly*): Yes 'M. (*For the next few minutes she takes* MRS HOLBROOK'S *chair as the goal towards which her tea leaves, etc. are to be swept, till she has finally collected little heaps all around it.*)

MRS HOLBROOK: Well isn't it better for them to leave the Army and Navy and wars with other countries to the men who know all about them? If women had the brains to understand the things men settle in Parliament it might be different, but they haven't. They're clever in another way. You can't combine politics and domestic matters. You – (*Turns first one way and then the other in chair to follow* MRS CHICKY *who is sweeping behind her.*) you see what I mean, don't you?

MRS CHICKY (*pausing again*): You mean as 'ome's one sphere an' Parlyment's another, an they didn't orter by mixed up?

MRS HOLBROOK (*much pleased*): Exactly!

MRS CHICKY (*reflectively*): It just shows you oughtn't to believe 'alf you 'ear! (*Crosses left as she sweeps again.*)

MRS HOLBROOK (*smiling*): What nonsense have you been hearing?

MRS CHICKY (*pausing*): Why I remember Marier Jackson down our Court tellin' me – oh it's some time back now – when 'er baby got pewmonier from sleeping in a banana box, as she didn't never take it to bed with 'er because Parlyment 'ad made a lor about it. I'll give it 'er proper for 'avin' me on like that! (*Sweeps vigorously again.*)

MRS HOLBROOK (*hurriedly*): Oh but I think she was quite right, Mrs Chicky. At least I know there has been some Act passed by Parliament in connection with poor children getting smothered in that way.

MRS CHICKY (*Pausing in surprise*): You don't say, 'M! Why you'd a' most think it was a-mixin' itself up with the 'ome if you didn't know different, wouldn't you?

MRS HOLBROOK (*hotly*): It's a splendid thing that such a law *has* been passed by men!

MRS CHICKY: Oh yes 'M., an' I'm not sayin' that pewmonier an' the Docter's certif'kit aint a sight more respectable than overlayin' an' the Crowner. I 'ope the dust don't worry you 'M.? (*As* MRS HOLBROOK *coughs again.*) Of course I like to see a woman 'ave a voice in settlin' what's best for children meself, but I know some ladies thinks diff'rent. (*Sweeps gradually right, crossing behind* MRS HOLBROOK.)

MRS HOLBROOK: You don't understand, Mrs Chicky! Nobody could feel more strongly than I do that the care of children is a woman's work above everything.

MRS CHICKY: She may care till she's black in the face, but she won't do much good if she's got the lor against 'er!

MRS HOLBROOK: My dear Mrs Chicky, you talk like an ignorant woman! How *could* the law be against her caring for her children?

MRS CHICKY (*a little huffily*): Ho, it's not for me to set my opinion against yours' 'M., bein', as you say, an ignerant woman. An' of course she's got the care of 'em right enough if she aint got 'er marriage-lines. It's on'y if she's kep' respectable as she can be 'ampered somethin' crool!

MRS HOLBROOK: You seem to have got some extraordinary ideas in your head!

MRS CHICKY: Yus I 'ave. The lor's put 'em there, wot's more.

MRS HOLBROOK: Now my good woman just tell me your difficulties and let me explain them away!

MRS CHICKY (*pauses again and delivers speech very clearly*): Difficulties? Well I guess many a married woman finds it a bit difficult not bein' 'er own child's parent – goin' by the lor, that is. It's a bit difficult for 'er as the lor don't give 'er no voice in 'er child's schoolin' nor religin' nor vaccinatin' nor such like, in the or'nary way. It's a bit difficult for 'er as 'er 'usband can pretty nigh starve 'er an' it if 'e's the mind, but she's got to go the lenth of leavin' 'im before she can get a maint'nance order, an' it's often none too easy to get *that* carried out. It's a bit –

MRS HOLBROOK (*interrupting*): But where have you read all this? I'm quite sure it's nonsense!

MRS CHICKY (*with a laugh*): Read it? Bless your 'eart, 'M., women like us don't 'ave to *read* about the lor like you ladies! We're too busy knockin' up against it, as you might say. I don't serpose any o' *your* lady friends comes before the Magistrit onst in a lifetime, but it's diff'rent with mine, though I've kep' clear so far meself, thanks be! (*Begins to poke broom vigorously under* MRS HOLBROOK'S *chair which is surrounded by a ridge of tea-leaves.*) Don't you move 'M.! I can sweep under you quite comfortable.

MRS HOLBROOK (*hastily*): No, no, thank you! (*Gets up and steps gingerly over tea-leaves to armchair right and sits down.*) But even if you're right, those difficulties would only arise where a husband and wife weren't doing their duty by living happily together.

MRS CHICKY (*setting broom aside and picking up dust-pan and small brush*): Well, the lor aint made for turtle-doves! (*Goes down on knees and begins to sweep leaves into pan.*)

MRS HOLBROOK: Of course not. But we were talking about votes, weren't we? All this has nothing to do with them.

MRS CHICKY: Votes wouldn't give women a bit of a voice in drorin' up the lors about their own affairs, then?

MRS HOLBROOK: Oh my dear Mrs Hicky –

MRS CHICKY: Chicky!

MRS HOLBROOK: – er – Chicky, if the women of England had a voice even in such a roundabout way as that in making laws, what would the homes of England be like?

MRS CHICKY: Maybe you're right 'M. 'Twouldn't never do for those as know most about 'omes to 'ave anythin' to do with fixin' rules for 'em.

MRS HOLBROOK (*testily*): You don't understand what I mean. Fancy giving any woman such a terrible responsibility!

MRS CHICKY: Yes 'M. You can understand some of 'em wantin' to shirk it, can't you? (*Goes on hurriedly as MRS HOLBROOK looks annoyed.*) But after all, there's many would say I 'adn't much call to trouble my 'ead about England! (*Gets up slowly.*)

MRS HOLBROOK (*Rising indignantly*): Anybody who would say such a thing to an Englishwoman ought to be ashamed of themselves!

MRS CHICKY: Yes 'M. But I aint an Englishwoman.

MRS HOLBROOK: You're not an Englishwoman?

MRS CHICKY (*serenely*): No 'M. (*Faces MRS HOLBROOK with dustpan in one hand and brush in the other.*) I'm French.

MRS HOLBROOK (*in bewilderment*): French?

MRS CHICKY: Yes 'M. My name's Chicky.

MRS HOLBROOK (*Puzzled*): How do you spell it?

MRS CHICKY: Well my 'usband 'e used to spell it C-h-i-q-u-e-with-a-mark.

MRS HOLBROOK (*crossing left*): Oh, Chiqué!

MRS CHICKY: Yes 'M. 'E did call it like that onst, but the men in the fact'ry always called 'im 'Chicky' and some'ow we got to writin' it like the poultry, too. 'E was French right enough though, Gawd rest 'im! Talk the langwige beautiful, 'e could!

MRS HOLBROOK: But that doesn't make *you* French!

MRS CHICKY: Yes 'M. 'E did call it like more's the pity. I don't serpose they'd give me one o' these 'ere votes if I wanted one. They won't let me 'ave one for the Council. 'E's been dead this four year, 'as my 'usband, but 'e never nateralised 'isself, you see.

MRS HOLBROOK: But why haven't you got a Council vote?

MRS CHICKY (*wearily*): Cos I'm French, as I'm tellin' you.

MRS HOLBROOK: But you're *not*! (*Crosses right.*)

MRS CHICKY: Oh yes 'M., the gentleman what come round to arsk Annie Mills to vote for 'im – she's the room below ours – 'e explained it to me. 'E said a wife's what 'er 'usband is – she don't count sep'rit.

MRS HOLBROOK: But you're a *widow*!

MRS CHICKY: 'E said that didn't make no diff'rence. I 'ave to be what Chicky was. (*Puts brush and pan aside and gets hearthbox.*)

MRS HOLBROOK (*moves down towards fireplace*): That *does* seem rather peculiar, certainly.

MRS CHICKY: Yes 'M. (*Comes down right with hearthbox.*) I don't *feel* French!

MRS HOLBROOK (*hurriedly*): Of course not – of course not. (*Pauses, leaning elbow on mantlepiece as* MRS CHICKY *shakes out hearthcloth, spreads it and kneels down to grate.*) Of course if one thinks a moment one sees the beautiful idea at the back of it. A husband and wife are one, you know.

MRS CHICKY (*docilely*): Yes 'M. Which one? (*Puts on dirty kid gloves and begins to black grate.*)

MRS HOLBROOK (*confusedly*): Oh – er – just one. (*Sits down.*) Let's go back to what we were talking about. I was trying to make you see, wasn't I, that all these ideas of women doing men's work are ridiculous.

MRS CHICKY: Well that's as plain to me as (*looks round*) you 'M., sittin' in that chair. I've no patience with the way you'll 'ear some folk settin' women against men as if they were oppersite sides in a battle!

MRS HOLBROOK (*much pleased, leaning forward*): I felt sure you were a sensible woman!

MRS CHICKY: Yes 'M., thank you 'M. There was a lady at my door it'll be a fortnight come Monday, an' me up to my elbers in soap-suds, talkin' a lot o' that nonsense, but she went off quicker'n she'd come, I can tell you!

MRS HOLBROOK (*leaning more forward excitedly*): I'm very glad to hear it!

MRS CHICKY: Yes 'M. 'Woman's spere this, an' Man's spere that,' I says. 'Goin' on for all the world as if one 'ad got four legs an' the other two! The Lord 'E started 'em fair when 'E cremated 'em' I says 'an' '*E* didn't lay down no rules about speres, nor make no diff'rence in their jobs. An' I guess thos 'oo go tryin' to parcel 'em off sep'rit' I says ' 'ave more'n one muddle to answer for!'

MRS HOLBROOK: I – I don't quite –

MRS CHICKY (*glorying in recollection of her own eloquence, waves blacking-brush to emphasise it and hits* MRS HOLBROOK *who starts back in annoyance*): 'Besides' I says – oh, beg pardon 'M., I'm shore! – 'besides' I says 'women are doin' men's work, an' men

women's, as you call it, all over the shop, an' if you want their speres to be diff'rent at this time o day' I says 'you've got to do more undoin' than'll larst your time an' mine.' She'd got a paper with 'er as she wanted me to put my name to, but I told her straight as I couldn't 'ave no truck with such silliness. (*Gets up and crosses left to fetch pail of water.*)

MRS HOLBROOK (*much perturbed*): But Mrs Chicky, you probably misunderstood her entirely. I – I more than suspect she was *against* votes for women!

MRS CHICKY: She was against common-sense, whatever she was. (*Carries pail across right and sets it down near hearth.*)

MRS HOLBROOK: And you know it's all nonsense to say women can do men's work. Women can't fight.

MRS CHICKY (*significantly, rolling sleeves higher*): Try 'em!

MRS HOLBROOK (*coldly*): I was alluding to fighting for their country.

MRS CHICKY: Lor bless you, 'M., I guess you an' me wouldn't be so far be'ind the men in that, neether, if it comes to the point! (*Kneels down, wrings out flannel in water and proceeds to wash over hearthstone.*) I'm the last in the world to belittle soldierin' – I'm proud to 'ave two brothers in that line meself – but the way some folks talk about men fightin' you'd think as there wasn't a man in England as didn't stand up to be shot at onst a week! It's a good job they don't 'ave the bearin' of the childring, or they'd be that set up at riskin' their lives so constant there'd be no 'oldin' of 'em in!

MRS HOLBROOK: You get so confused, Mrs Chiqué –

MRS CHICKY: Chicky!

MRS HOLBROOK: What I mean is that if women were soldiers and sailors there'd be something at once for them to have a vote *for*.

MRS CHICKY: Do soldiers 'ave the vote, then? Well I might 'ave knowed! They will 'ave their joke, will George an' Albert! If you'd 'eard 'em larst Election goin' on like bears with sore 'eads because they 'adn't a vote same as most o' their pals you'd never 'ave serspected it was just a do the 'ole time!

MRS HOLBROOK: You mean your brothers? Oh but it's quite likely that they hadn't.

MRS CHICKY: 'Ow's that, 'M.?

MRS HOLBROOK: Well you see to get a vote a man has to be a householder and pay rates and taxes, or a lodger, and stay in the same place a year and – oh, various things that most soldiers and sailors can't do.

MRS CHICKY: Oh then the vote *'asn't* got nothin' to do with fightin' for your country, after all?

MRS HOLBROOK (*testily*): I never met a woman more difficult to explain things to! Can't you see that the right to vote really depends on physical force – strength, you know – and that women haven't got that? (MRS CHICKY *finding* MRS HOLBROOK *in her way gets up and pushes her, chair and all, a foot or so centre with perfect ease.*)

MRS CHICKY (*returning right and kneeling down to hearth again*): Thank you 'M. – I couldn't quite get to this 'ere corner. Strenth, is it? There's a parrylised man down our Court what's wheeled to the poll regler. I pushed 'im there meself larst Election, wishin' to oblige.

MRS HOLBROOK: Yes, yes, but you mustn't take everything I say too strictly.

MRS CHICKY: I'm not doin'. (*Dips scouring-stone into water and begins to scour hearth.*)

MRS HOLBROOK: What I want you to see is the broad principle of the thing. A woman's place is in her home, you know.

MRS CHICKY (*sitting back on her heels*): Am I to understand as your brother's not requirin' of me no more?

MRS HOLBROOK: Oh really, Mrs Chiqué – Chicky, then! – (*As* MRS CHICKY *begins to correct her.*) please don't go on narrowing everything I say down to particular cases! Of course I don't mean that you ought to stop going out charing!

MRS CHICKY: Bad job for *my* 'ome if I did!

MRS HOLBROOK (*with brilliant inspiration*): Yes, but don't you see how it all works back to what I said at first? You'd never have time for voting *and* charing, would you?

MRS CHICKY: Well I should say it took me a quarter of a 'our to wheel Tom Welford to the poll an' it was on my way to my work. 'E was took back by motor because 'e'd said 'e wouldn't vote unless. (*Smooths hearthstone over with wet flannel.*)

MRS HOLBROOK: Ah, but it's not just the voting! Look how this Mr Welby had probably *studied* the question, and how he – (MRS CHICKY *emits strangled sounds.*) what's the matter?

MRS CHICKY: On'y – on'y you'll eggscuse me larfin' 'M., but Tom Welford can't read. 'E couldn't do no studyin'. My Josephine runs in now an' again to read 'im the football news – they say 'e was a rare player in 'is young days, pore feller – but 'e don't care to listen to nothin' else. (*The hearth finished, she puts fender back into place and tidies up.*)

MRS HOLBROOK: Very kind of her I'm sure. Well, to go back to what we were talking about –

MRS CHICKY: Yes 'M., we don't seem to be gettin' much forrader, do we? (*Carries hearth box and pail up left.*)

MRS HOLBROOK: But I don't think there's any need for us to argue when in your heart you agree with all I've said. I only wanted to be satisfied that I could put you down as being against votes for women.

MRS CHICKY: An' are you satisfied?

MRS HOLBROOK: Quite. There are hundreds of sensible hard-working women like you who merely want to have the thing simply explained to them and they see its dangers at once. (*Rises and crosses left.*) I don't think I've anything more to ask you Mrs Chicky, thank you.

MRS CHICKY (*coming down centre*): Then can I arsk *you* somethin' 'M.?

MRS HOLBROOK (*a little surprised*): Certainly.

MRS CHICKY: Speakin' straight as one lady to another, an' no offence meant or taken?

MRS HOLBROOK: Certainly.

MRS CHICKY: Well it's this. What are you worritin' about 'em for?

MRS HOLBROOK: About whom?

MRS CHICKY: Why this little 'andful of women you've been a-tellin' me about. What 'arm can they do?

MRS HOLBROOK: Oh they've grown – I don't say they haven't grown. They've such a dangerous way of getting hold of people. You see *they* promise excitement and bands and processions – *we* can only offer dull things like looking after one's children and caring for one's home. (*Crosses right again.*)

MRS CHICKY (*sharply, as she removes dust-sheet from table*): I've never found lookin' after *my* childring dull, though (*Looking meaningly at* MRS HOLBROOK.) I know it's what *some* ladies calls it! (*Fold dust-sheet and places same on table.*)

MRS HOLBROOK: You will keep misunderstanding me! I say that the women who want votes think looking after children dull. I believe they'd like to make all women fond of politics instead of children!

MRS CHICKY (*uncovering desk and folding its dust-sheet*): Will they *make* you vote, then, whether you've the mind or not? (*Places dust-sheet on table.*)

MRS HOLBROOK (*dramatically, as she crosses left.*) Never! (*After a little pause.*) I'm not saying that some of us might not think it right to use a vote if it was forced upon us, so that we might counteract all the harm the other women would be doing.

MRS CHICKY (*proceeding to uncover bookshelf and place its dust-sheet on table*): Would they all vote the same way, then?

MRS HOLBROOK: Oh women always herd together!

MRS CHICKY (*with puzzled expression, as she uncovers armchair*): But if you an' your lady friends was all votin' the other way, it don't look as if women *would* be 'erdin' together?

MRS HOLBROOK (*cornered, crossing right*): I – I – oh it's no use trying to explain!

MRS CHICKY (*folding last dust-sheet and putting it on table*): Seems to me this 'ere vote's mighty difficult to understand!

MRS HOLBROOK (*triumphantly*): *Too* difficult – for a woman!

MRS CHICKY (*with apparent relief*): Oh then *you* don't understand it, neether?

MRS HOLBROOK (*with annoyed little laugh*): My good Mrs Chicky, all that *I* don't understand is why any woman should be so ridiculous as to want it!

MRS CHICKY (*quickly*): You don't?

MRS HOLBROOK: I certainly don't!

MRS CHICKY (*Comes down centre, gazes at* MRS HOLBROOK *for a moment, and then speaks as if on a sudden thought*): Now I wonder if it would 'elp you if you saw it writ?

MRS HOLBROOK (*puzzled*): If I saw what written?

MRS CHICKY (*raises her skirt, dives into under-pocket with difficulty, and finally produces red handkerchief knotted at corner, keeping up running comments the while*): It must be 'ere somewhere. I don' know I'm shore why it didn't come to me sooner as I'd got it on me. I know I put it in me 'andkercher to keep it away from 'Eneryett cos she was wantin' to suck it all the time the lady was a-talkin' –she's my fourth, is 'Eneryett. Never give it a thought till this minit, I didn't. 'Ere it is! Funny 'ow if you onst put a thing in your 'andercher it can go there for days! (*She undoes knot in handkerchief with her teeth,* MRS HOLBROOK *watching her in bewilderment, and discloses small crumpled handbill which she smooths out and from which she proceeds to read.*) 'WHY WOMEN WANT THE VOTE' – that's on top – 'A FEW PLAIN REASINGS IN PLAIN WORDS' – I could 'ave give 'em a few more if they'd 'ave arsked me, but these is put very distink – very distink indeed they are. Praps you'd like to –

MRS HOLBROOK (*splutters interruption in horrified amazement.*) You – you – you're a *Suffragist*?

MRS CHICKY (*looking up from paper with something approaching grin*): What do *you* think?

MRS HOLBROOK (*furiously, flopping into chair*): You told me you knew nothing about Women's Suffrage!

MRS CHICKY (*sweetly*): Oh no 'M. You arsk me if I knew what you meant by it, an' I says no. (*Goes on hurriedly as* MRS HOLBROOK *gives angry exclamation.*) I was a-startin' to tell you as I knew what I meant meself right enough, but you stopped me. You said you was 'ere to explain things to *me*!

MRS HOLBROOK (*crosses left speaking hotly*): D'you suppose I'd ever have wasted my time over you if I'd known? We – we don't want to talk to people who are against us!

MRS CHICKY: I'm sorry, 'M, I'm shore. You see (*Tapping handbill.*) this lot's so diff'rent. Seems to revel in talkin' to them as don't agree with 'em, they do!

MRS HOLBROOK (*looking at paper as if it were poisonous*): May I ask where you got that?

MRS CHICKY: I bring it away from a meetin' larst Tuesday. Praps you'd like to borrer it, 'M.?

MRS HOLBROOK (*waving it hastily away*): Oh, if you're going to be taken in by all you hear at meetings –

MRS CHICKY (*interrupting quickly*): Taken in? No 'M., no one don't do no takin' in when Elizer Chicky's about, thankin' you kindly! Why we've 'ad two ladies down our street tryin' to stuff us with argyments that my own cat wouldn't 'ave swallered, an' 'e aint pernickety. 'We've h'always got on very well without women 'avin' the vote' says one. 'Yus' I calls back, '*you* may 'ave, but what price us?'

MRS HOLBROOK (*coldly*): Mere selfishness never did anybody any good yet!

MRS CHICKY (*apologetically*): Well 'M. I didn't like to call out that for fear she'd think I just wanted to sauce 'er.

MRS HOLBROOK (*losing control*): Stupid woman!

MRS CHICKY: So I thought 'M. But praps she was a bit 'ard of 'earin', for she just says over again, 'We've always got on very well without women 'avin the vote'. 'Splendid!' I calls back, 'with some of us makin' blouses at one an' a penny a dozen an' ackcherly managin' to earn six shillins a week for a fourteen hours day! We all keeps our kerridges!'

MRS HOLBROOK: But my good woman – (*Crosses right.*)

MRS CHICKY (*unheedingly*): 'Ho' says she, 'there's a lady in the ordyance what makes the mistake of thinkin' the vote's a-goin' to raise womens' wages!' 'No' I says, very prompt, 'the lady 'oo's makin' a mistake aint in the ordyance' I says 'but there's a woman there' I says 'oo's got the sense to see that if 'er sex 'as got a vote what's useful to the men they're more likely to listen to 'er than if it 'adn't!'

MRS HOLBROOK: But my good woman –

MRS CHICKY (*interrupting earnestly*): Look 'ere 'M., I arsk you before an' I arsk you again – what are you doin' it for?

MRS HOLBROOK: Doing what?

MRS CHICKY: Carryin' on this 'ere 'obby of yours – cerlectin' names?

MRS HOLBROOK: Why, I want to help to stop this movement! (*Crosses left.*)

MRS CHICKY: You might as well try to stop a leak in a saucepan with sealin'-wax!

MRS HOLBROOK: But my good woman –

MRS CHICKY: Yus you might! You take it from me 'M. The first time I 'eard a lady at a street corner sayin' as women orter 'ave votes, I listens for a bit 'an I says 'I'm on this job' I says. I says 'She knows. She's talkin' gorspel. She aint sat in no drorin'-room an' *read* about us' I says. 'She knows.' (MRS HOLBROOK *tries to interrupt with little indignant exclamations all through this speech, but* MRS CHICKY *once fairly started, refuses to be baulked.*) She didn't waste no time tellin' women out workin' to keep body an' soul together as they orter be queens of their 'omes! She didn't go talkin' about a man's 'ome for all the world as if 'e orter knock at the door an' arsk 'is wife's leave every time 'e wanted to get inside it! (MRS HOLBROOK *crosses right.*) She didn't waste no time tellin' women 'oo'd sent their lads off to fight with their own 'earts breakin' for all their lips were smilin', as women 'adn't no feelins for their country an' didn't understand nothin' about war! She didn't waste no time tellin' sweated women drove on the streets – women 'oo's 'usbands give 'em a drib 'ere an' a drab there when they're sober, an' the childring goin' 'alf-naked – women 'oo's 'usbands take up with another woman, an' 'I'm afraid the lor can't 'elp you my good woman' says 'Is Wushup, in nine cases outer ten – women 'oo get drove to despair with facin' their trouble alone while the man 'oo's brought 'em to it gets off scot free – women 'oo'll take on their 'usband's job when 'e's ill, to keep the 'ome goin', an' get eight or ten shillins docked off for the same amount of work cos they aint men – she didn't waste no time, I say, jorin' to women like that about the splendid way their int'rests are pertected already! She *knew.* (MRS HOLBROOK *crosses left.*) Oh I'm not sayin' this 'ere vote's goin' to set everythin' right, but I do say as anythin' that's done without it'll be just patchin' an' nothin' more! It's goin' to make women *count!* It'll make 'em *'ave* to be reckoned with! I've nothin' against the men. (*Draws hand across eyes.*) I'd the best 'ushand as ever stepped! I believe same as you do that the men want to do what's best for us, but – *you 'ave to be a woman yourself to know where things 'urt women!* It's Gawd's truth, that is, an' I say Gawd bless the ladies 'oo are 'elpin' us by stickin' out for it!

MRS HOLBROOK (*with satirical little smile*): Well, I'm afraid *you* would be wasting less time scrubbing your floors than as an orator, Mrs Chicky.

SERVANT'S VOICE (*heard off*): Mrs Chicky! Mrs Chicky! You're wanted! (MRS CHICKY *hesitates.*)

MRS HOLBROOK: Oh pray go! Of course you won't understand my attitude, but nothing that you or anybody else could tell me would make me alter my mind!

MRS CHICKY (*picking up hearthbox and dust-sheets*): Oh yes 'M., I've 'eard of that before. (*Pauses at door.*) You see 'M. my 'usband lived in France till just before we was married, an' *'e kep' MULES!*

Exit. MRS HOLBROOK *drops on to chair and stares after her in open-mouthed amazement.*

Curtain.

MISS APPLEYARD'S AWAKENING

Characters

MISS APPLEYARD
MRS CRABTREE, *her visitor*
MORTON, *her parlourmaid*

Scene

Small chamber set
Window, centre
Door upper right end
Writing table and chair, down right
Sofa, left; bell in wall, down left below sofa

Note on Performance

A play in which the ASS (whoops those initials) is seen to score another own goal.
When Mrs Crabtree of the Anti-Suffrage Society calls upon Miss Appleyard, she should
be preaching to the converted. Instead, the more the nonsense of the anti-suffrage
arguments dawns on Miss Appleyard, the more she realises she has been contradicting
herself in believing them. Mrs Crabtree is typical of the anti-suffrage woman,
shortsighted and clinging desperately to the only territory women can call their own, that
of home and children. She has not done her research and admits confusion about her
own cause, nevertheless she sets herself up as an authority on the subject. Miss
Appleyard is a sensible if rather ignorant young woman, when the truth becomes clear
she takes a stand. We are left with the impression that she will soon be a Suffragette,
her servant however is ahead of her. She and cook have already seen the benefits of
having a say in their future. Yet again the mistress is taught a lesson by the maid.
    A very simple setting is all that is needed. A couple of chairs a writing desk and a
general air of comfort. Miss Appleyard should be practically dressed and Mrs Crabtree
overtly feminine.

Carole Hayman

Scene: *A Drawing-room.*
Time: *During an Election.*

MORTON *is discovered arranging blind, tidying up room, etc.*

Enter MISS APPLEYARD *in outdoor things.*

MISS APPLEYARD: Oh, Morton, I must have some tea now – I really can't wait till half-past four. I don't think there's anything in the world so tiring as canvassing! (*Sits at table.*)

MORTON: I hope you got a proper lunch 'm?

MISS APPLEYARD (*drawing off gloves*): No, it wasn't at all proper – two stale sandwiches at Owen's – but I couldn't get home. The dinner hour was the best time for catching some of the men. Fancy, Morton. I've got three fresh promises for Mr Sharp!

MORTON: How splendid, 'm! Were you up by the factory?

MISS APPLEYARD: Yes, in Dale Street and Quebec Street. I begin to think half the idiots in Mudford must have settled there judging from the intelligence of some of the voters I've been arguing with this morning!

MORTON: Won't you go and lie down a bit, 'm? You look tired out.

MISS APPLEYARD: Oh no, I shall be all right when I've had some tea. I should have been home earlier only I simply couldn't get through the crowd in Nevil Square where one of those dreadful Suffragists was speaking. I really could shake the whole lot of them!

MORTON (*evidently interested*): I suppose she was talking about votes for women, 'm?

MISS APPLEYARD: Oh yes, I suppose so – I didn't really listen. I heard something about some bill they wanted to get passed. The less women have to do with bills the better, to my mind – Parliamentary *and* other kinds.

MORTON (*as if wishing to hear more*): I daresay she'd plenty to say, 'm?

MISS APPLEYARD (*suppressing a yawn*): I daresay she had, Morton. I wish I'd been near enough to tell her to go back and look after her home and leave Parliament to manage its own affairs! (*Pauses a moment, then speaks as if on a sudden recollection.*) Oh by the way, Morton, if you and Cook would like to go to Mr Sharp's meeting at the Town Hall tonight I think the house might be shut up for a couple of hours. I can take my key in case I get back first.

MORTON: Thank you, 'm, we should very much.

MISS APPLEYARD: Well tell Cook, then. You could manage to get off by half-past seven, couldn't you, as I'm having dinner earlier? She'll have no washing up to speak of.

MORTON: Oh yes, 'm.

MISS APPLEYARD: Don't leave it later because the place is going to be crowded. (*Looks at her hands.*) I'm too dirty to eat – those factory chimneys were simply raining blacks! I'll be ready in two minutes! (*Crosses left and exit.*)

Exit MORTON *and returns with tea cloth, putting it on table, right and humming 'March of the Women'. While she is doing this a bell rings outside. She ignores it, and rings again.*

MORTON: All right – all right! Somebody else has got things to do as well as you!

Exit, to reappear almost immediately and usher in a visitor.

MORTON (*about to leave room*): What name shall I say, please?

MRS CRABTREE (*crosses to right on entrance*): Miss Appleyard wouldn't know my name. Just say that a lady from the Anti-Suffrage Society would be much obliged if she could speak to her.

MORTON: Thank you, 'm. (*Crossing to door left.*)

MRS CRABTREE (*sitting down right*): I won't keep her more than a moment or two. Oh – er – (MORTON *stops.*) I shall be asking her to allow you and your fellow-servants to sign a petition I've got with me. How many of you are there?

MORTON (*evidently surprised*): Two, 'm.

MRS CRABTREE (*disappointedly*): Not more? Still, two names are something.

MORTON (*hesitatingly*): What is the petition about 'm?

MRS CRABTREE (*as though she thought the question unnecessary.*) About? – Oh it would take rather long to explain. But *you* don't want women to sit in Parliament and leave their homes to go to rack and ruin, do you?

MORTON: Oh no, 'm.

MRS CRABTREE: And you don't want every woman in England to have a vote so that they can swamp the men and govern the country themselves?

MORTON: That's never what the Suffragists want, is it 'm?

MRS CRABTREE: Oh they'll all *tell* you they don't, but of course they do really. When a woman leaves her own duties to take up a man's she soon loses her sense of truth and everything else.

MORTON: Really, 'm?

MRS CRABTREE: Why this very petition you were asking about is against a set of women who pretend that they don't think their sex ought to meddle with politics and yet they're working themselves in this Election as hard as they can!

MORTON: Oh that doesn't seem right 'm does it?

MRS CRABTREE: Right? It's very wicked and deceitful, of course but that's just an example of the sort of thing that happens when a woman interferes with – (*She stops short as* MISS APPLEYARD *enters the room and looks round inquiringly.*)

MORTON: A lady to see you, 'm.

Exit.

MRS CRABTREE (*rising*): Good afternoon, Miss Appleyard, hope I'm not disturbing you? I'm afraid you're just going out?

MISS APPLEYARD: No, I've just come in. Please sit down.

MRS CRABTREE (*seating herself again*): I won't detain you more than a few minutes. My name is Crabtree – Mrs Crabtree. I've come as a delegate

from the Mudford ASS – I understand that you belong to it?

MISS APPLEYARD (*puzzled*): The ASS (*Sitting on sofa.*)

MRS CRABTREE: The Anti-Suffrage Society.

MISS APPLEYARD (*laughing*): Oh, I beg your pardon. I didn't recognise those rather unfortunate initials for the moment. Yes, I've been a member for nearly a year, I think. A friend of mine gave me no peace till I said she might send in my name.

MRS CRABTREE: We have one or two noble proselytizers! They stop at nothing!

MISS APPLEYARD: Oh, I'd no real objection – I've always steadily declined to listen to anything on the subject of Women's Suffrage.

MRS CRABTREE: I wish there were more like you! I've really come to ask if you would be good enough to sign a petition that some of us are getting up?

MISS APPLEYARD: Oh certainly. I never refuse my name to any Anti-Suffrage Petition. I should think I've signed four this last month.

MRS CRABTREE (*looking at her admiringly*): How splendid of you! And yet Suffragists say we don't work for our cause!

MISS APPLEYARD: Oh but Suffragists will say anything! I suppose you've read the accounts of the disgraceful disturbances in Liverpool last night?

MRS CRABTREE (*indifferently*): No. Were there any? I can't say that I trouble my head much about that sort of thing.

MISS APPLEYARD (*astonished*): But don't you think it's abominable?

MRS CRABTREE: There are worse things in connection with the Suffrage movement than disturbances.

MISS APPLEYARD: Worse?

MRS CRABTREE (*impressively*): Very much worse.

MISS APPLEYARD: But what *could* be worse?

MRS CRABTREE: Oh my dear Miss

Appleyard, if a woman's in a policeman's arms – of course it's very deplorable, but at least you know where she *is*!

MISS APPLEYARD: Certainly – but –

MRS CRABTREE (*interrupting*): And if she's shouting in the market-place like the female I saw addressing crowds in Nevil Square just now – at all events she's fighting you in the open!

MISS APPLEYARD (*puzzled*): Of course.

MRS CRABTREE: Even if she's never done anything for her side but join a Suffrage Society – well, you do know she's against you.

MISS APPLEYARD: Certainly, but I'm afraid I don't quite see what you mean to imply.

MRS CRABTREE (*drawing her chair closer to* MISS APPLEYARD *and lowering her voice*): What should you say to traitors within the camp?

MISS APPLEYARD (*in bewilderment*): Traitors within the camp?

MRS CRABTREE: Traitors within the camp, Miss Appleyard. Women who join *Anti*-Suffrage Societies and under the cloak of such a membership go about propagating the very ideas they pretend to abhor!

MISS APPLEYARD (*incredulously*): You can't possibly be serious!

MRS CRABTREE (*triumphantly*): I thought I should startle you. My firm belief is that they're in the pay of the Suffragists.

MISS APPLEYARD: But how perfectly disgraceful! I hadn't the slightest idea that such a thing existed! Surely it can be stopped?

MRS CRABTREE: We hope so – we believe so. That is the object of the petition I'm asking you to sign. (*Draws paper from long envelope.*) We want some pronouncement from headquarters in London that will make treachery of this kind impossible.

MISS APPLEYARD: That's an excellent idea. I'll sign it with pleasure.

MRS CRABTREE: Thank you very much. And I hope you'll allow your servants to do the same?

MISS APPLEYARD (*a little astonished*): My servants?

MRS CRABTREE: Well it swells a list of signatures so beautifully – especially if a large staff is kept. Lady Carter's signed to the boot-boy!

MISS APPLEYARD: I'm afraid I don't keep a boot-boy and I have only two servants. I've really never asked them their views on the Suffrage.

MRS CRABTREE: Their views? I didn't ask my servants their views. I merely sent the petition to the kitchen for signatures. Nobody will think we're in earnest if we don't get plenty.

MISS APPLEYARD: Well to be quite frank with you, one rather hesitates – I mean it might be a little difficult for a servant to refuse her mistress, mightn't it?

MRS CRABTREE: Refuse? (*She is apparently about to go on, then looks at* MISS APPLEYARD *again and checks herself.*) Oh, of course I don't press the point for a moment, Miss Appleyard. We shall be only too pleased if you will give us your own signature.

MISS APPLEYARD: May I have the petition? (*Takes paper from* MRS CRABTREE *and goes to writing table, where she sits down, picks up a pen and examines it.*) I always write particularly badly when I inscribe my name on a public document. Do you want full Christian names? I'm afraid I've got four.

MRS CRABTREE: They would look imposing.

MISS APPLEYARD (*putting a new nib in penholder and talking rather absently*): As you say, treachery within the camp must be put down at any cost. One can hardly believe that women would stoop to it!

MRS CRABTREE: I'm surprised at nothing in connection with the Suffrage.

MISS APPLEYARD: I wonder if you're right in thinking that the Suffragists are responsible?

MRS CRABTREE: I'm convinced of it.

MISS APPLEYARD (*still manipulating penholder*): Of course the quickest way to stop anything so flagrant would be to show it up in the papers. (*Draws petition towards her.*) If you'll give me a few particulars I don't in the least mind writing a letter to the *Spectator*.

MRS CRABTREE: Oh that would be splendid! There's every excuse for a woman to come out into the open in an exceptional case like this. Besides you could use a *nom to plume*.

MISS APPLEYARD (*rather surprised*): I haven't the slightest objection to signing my name to any letter I write.

MRS CRABTREE (*hurriedly*): Just as you like, of course. A name often does work wonders. I've got twenty-three to my petition already.

MISS APPLEYARD (*smiling*): I'd better complete your second dozen before we discuss the matter further. (*Turns to petition again.*) After all, though one must make a stand against it, conduct of this sort is bound to defeat its own ends. Every decent-minded woman will turn from it in disgust.

MRS CRABTREE (*gloomily*): How many decent-minded women will there be left in England if this Suffrage movement goes on?

MISS APPLEYARD (*laughing*): Oh come, Mrs Crabtree, we're not all going to bow the knee to Baal! I can't think that the Suffrage has made any open headway in Mudford and you must get this petition sent in in time to prevent any secret proselytizing.

MRS CRABTREE (*sighing significantly*): Prevent? I wish we *were* in time for that!

MISS APPLEYARD (*sitting back in chair*): You surely can't mean that there are any of these atrocious women among *us*?

MRS CRABTREE: I do, Miss Appleyard. I have only too good reason to believe that we are warming a viper in our bosoms!

MISS APPLEYARD: Tell me her name! Don't hesitate to mention a name in a case like this!

MRS CRABTREE: I don't know it yet unfortunately. I'm waiting to discover it

before I denounce her openly.

MISS APPLEYARD: Nothing would give me greater pleasure than to help you?

MRS CRABTREE: I wonder if you could! Do you know anything of the streets behind the factory? (*Rises, and comes to writing table.*)

MISS APPLEYARD: What Dale Street and Quebec Street do you mean?

MRS CRABTREE: Yes – with the little red houses where so many of the hands live.

MISS APPLEYARD (*excitedly*): You don't mean to say she's dared to go there?

MRS CRABTREE *looks round, draws a little closer, and lowers her voice.*

MRS CRABTREE: Miss Appleyard, I've just been told on excellent authority that a member of our own Anti-Suffrage Society was seen canvassing in Quebec Street and Dale Street this very morning!

There is a moment of absolute silence. MISS APPLEYARD'S *pen falls to the ground and she gazes at* MRS CRABTREE *as if petrified.* MRS CRABTREE *picks up pen, and gives it back to* MISS APPLEYARD. MISS APPLEYARD *pulls herself together and ejaculates faintly.*

MISS APPLEYARD: C-canvassing?

MRS CRABTREE: Dear Miss Appleyard, you evidently haven't grasped the brazen tactics of these women. They pretend to be Anti-Suffragists and they *canvass*!

MISS APPLEYARD (*much embarrassed*): But surely I – they –

MRS CRABTREE (*excitedly*): They subscribe – openly – to the tenet that woman is incapable of forming a political opinion, and they not only form one for themselves, but they go about trying to influence those of *men*!

MISS APPLEYARD: Yes, but you surely –

MRS CRABTREE (*working herself up and ignoring any interruption*): They assert – with us – that woman's place is the home and spend long hours away from their own in the arena of politics!

MISS APPLEYARD: But do you seriously mean that an Anti-Suff –

MRS CRABTREE (*striking table with her hand*): They profess to leave imperial matters to men with one hand and force their way into meetings at which such matters are discussed with the other!

MISS APPLEYARD: But is it possible that –

MRS CRABTREE (*still more heatedly*): They proclaim that political activity tends to break up the harmony of the home and go straight out and address envelopes in Committee rooms by the hour! The insidiousness of it! Of course the ignorant women to whom they talk are drawn into politics in spite of themselves and the way is paved for the Suffragist who works openly! It's a far more dangerous crusade than the militant one, in my opinion, because it wears the guise of an angel of light!

MISS APPLEYARD (*faintly as* MRS CRABTREE *pauses for breath*): I see what you mean, of course. But perhaps it hasn't occurred to them that they're doing – doing all you say!

MRS CRABTREE (*with a snort*): Don't tell me!

MISS APPLEYARD: Don't you think they might never have looked at it in that light?

MRS CRABTREE (*a little impatiently*): Oh my dear Miss Appleyard, one either is or isn't in favour of a thing. You can't do it in practice and denounce it in print, you know!

MISS APPLEYARD: I – I never thought of that. Of course it *is* inconsistent.

MRS CRABTREE: It's worse than inconsistent, to my mind. Personally I strongly disapprove of the way in which I'm sorry to say some of even the leaders of our party try to defend the municipal vote for women. I prefer to be honest and deplore the mistake which granted it to them.

MISS APPLEYARD: You don't think women should have the municipal vote?

MRS CRABTREE: Of course I don't! What is it but a smaller edition of the Parliamentary one? There's merely a

difference of degree. The qualities that unfit a woman for one naturally unfit her for the other.

MISS APPLEYARD: What qualities do you mean, exactly?

MRS CRABTREE: Why, Lord Cromer has told us. Hasty generalisation – vague and undisciplined sympathies – extreme sentimentality – I can't remember all he said, but it was in the papers. He said they were characteristic of a majority of the female sex.

MISS APPLEYARD (*grimly*): Oh, did he?

MRS CRABTREE: Yes – at a meeting for men only, in Manchester.

MISS APPLEYARD: Perhaps it's as well that women weren't admitted.

MRS CRABTREE: Well, I believe there were a few women on the platform, but I agree with you. I'm not at all in favour of women attending public meetings as a rule, though I *have* made an exception myself to hear Lord Cromer.

MISS APPLEYARD: Really?

MRS CRABTREE: He's such a marvellous grasp of this subject. There's Lord Curzon, too – of course you know his fifteen reasons against Women's Suffrage?

MISS APPLEYARD: No, I'm afraid I don't.

MRS CRABTREE: Oh, I must send them to you! I'm always meaning to learn them by heart. I know the first – (*shuts her eyes and repeats as from a lesson book*) – 'Political activity will tend to take away woman from her proper sphere and highest duty, which is maternity.'

MISS APPLEYARD: But we can't *all* be mothers.

MRS CRABTREE: Oh, he recognises that! Only no doubt he considers married woman particularly because, as he says in a later reason, they, if any, are best qualified to exercise the vote.

MISS APPLEYARD: But I thought he said it would interfere with maternity?

MRS CRABTREE: So he did.

MISS APPLEYARD: Then how can he

say that married women are best qualified to exercise it?

MRS CRABTREE: I don't altogether follow that myself, I admit. I'm content to leave it to a superior brain to my own.

MISS APPLEYARD (*after a pause*): And even in the case of mothers – of course I've never been in favour of their having votes, but supposing they *had* – *would* they be constantly engaged in political activity? Fathers aren't!

MRS CRABTREE: Men are political by nature – women are not. If women got votes they would have so much to learn that they'd never have time for anything else. (*Goes on as* MISS APPLEYARD *is evidently about to demur but thinks better of it.*) But you must read the reasons for yourself – that is if you think it advisable to go into the subject. They set forward so plainly the awful dangers of adding a host of unbalanced judgments to a logical male electorate.

MISS APPLEYARD (*dryly*): I happened to be talking to one of the logical male electorate this morning. He's my chimney-sweep. He informed me that he was going to vote for Mr Holland because his own wife is a Dutchwoman.

MRS CRABTREE: Really? Which is Mr Holland?

MISS APPLEYARD (*curiously*): Do you mean to say you didn't know that he was the Labour Candidate?

MRS CRABTREE (*indifferently*): Oh, I must have seen the placards and heard people talking, of course. But I naturally don't take any interest in politics. I don't consider them to be a woman's concern.

MISS APPLEYARD: What *do* you consider to be a woman's concern?

MRS CRABTREE (*impressively*): Her HOME! (*Crosses left and sits on sofa.*)

MISS APPLEYARD: But – do excuse me – you're putting things in rather a new light to me. Don't vague sympathies and sentimentality and – what else did Lord Cromer say? – hasty generalisation? – matter in the home?

MRS CRABTREE (*a little taken aback*): Oh – er – well – of course it would be

better *without* them, but as Lord Cromer says, most women *are* like that. I mustn't trespass longer on your time, Miss Appleyard. If I may have your signature I won't detain you any more.

MISS APPLEYARD (*taking up petition*): I haven't really looked at the text of this – I'd only surmised it from what you told me. (*Scans paper in silence, then looks up.*) I see that it's a request to headquarters that some rule may be framed which shall debar any member of an Anti-Suffrage Society from canvassing.

MRS CRABTREE: We thought it better to confine ourselves to the canvassing to start with. Later we hope to attack more of these abominable tactics. (*A bell is heard outside.*)

MISS APPLEYARD (*folding up paper deliberately and handing it back*): Well, Mrs Crabtree, I may as well tell you quite frankly that you won't attack them through me. (*Rises.*)

MRS CRABTREE (*in astonishment*): Miss Appleyard – I don't understand you!

MISS APPLEYARD: I can't sign that paper.

MRS CRABTREE: May I ask why not? (*There is a tap at the door.*)

MISS APPLEYARD: Come in! (*Enter* MORTON.)

MORTON: Excuse me disturbing you a moment, please 'm.

MISS APPLEYARD: What is it, Morton? (*To* MRS CRABTREE.) Excuse me, Mrs Crabtree!

MRS CRABTREE *bows, and crosses over to right.*

MORTON (*at door –* MISS APPLEYARD *goes up to her*): – Miss Allbutt's called, 'm, and she won't come in, but she says could you kindly send word if it's ten or half-past that she's to go canvassing with you tomorrow.

There is a gasp from MRS CRABTREE *who stares at* MISS APPLEYARD *in absolute horror.* MISS APPLEYARD *after a moment's pause turns to* MORTON.

MISS APPLEYARD (*firmly*): Say ten o'clock, please.

MORTON: Yes 'm.

Exit.

MISS APPLEYARD: I beg your pardon, Mrs Crabtree. You were asking –

MRS CRABTREE (*very excitedly*): I am answered, Miss Appleyard – I am answered! Little did I think when I denounced the women among us who are secretly undermining our influence that they had so far worked upon your feelings as to persuade you to join them!

MISS APPLEYARD: I really don't understand you. Nobody has worked on my feelings. I offered to help with canvassing this time as I did at the last Election. I was just going to tell you so when my maid came in.

MRS CRABTREE (*agitatedly*): Then – then is it possible that *you* are the woman who was canvassing in Dale Street and Quebec Street this morning?

MISS APPLEYARD (*quietly*): It's more than possible – it's a fact.

MRS CRABTREE: This – this is beyond everything! You consider yourself capable of forming a political opinion?

MISS APPLEYARD: Well – shall we say at least as capable as the gentleman whose going to vote for Mr Holland because his own wife's a Dutchwoman!

MRS CRABTREE (*almost in a scream*): You don't think that woman's place is the home?

MISS APPLEYARD: Place – certainly. Prison – no. You might as well say that a man's place is his office and blame him for coming home in an evening or taking an interest in his wife's duties or his children's lessons!

MRS CRABTREE (*solemnly and loudly*): Man is Man and Woman is Woman!

MISS APPLEYARD (*with a twinkle in her eye*): Oh I'm quite prepared to concede that.

MRS CRABTREE: And conceding it, you actually think that a woman ought to meddle with politics?

MISS APPLEYARD: Meddle? How can

any intelligent woman help taking an interest in the affairs of her country?

MRS CRABTREE: *Her* country? It's the country of the men who fight for it!

MISS APPLEYARD: You mean that only soldiers and sailors should be politicians?

MRS CRABTREE: This is ridiculous! It is only too easy to see what influences have been at work!

MISS APPLEYARD (*coldly*): Would you kindly explain what you mean?

MRS CRABTREE: I mean that your line of reasoning is taken straight from the publications of the Suffrage Societies!

MISS APPLEYARD: The publications of the Suffrage Societies? I've never even seen any!

MRS CRABTREE: I cannot, of course, dispute your word. But Suffragists think that a woman should take what they call an intelligent interest in the affairs of her country! Suffragists maintain that a woman doesn't unsex herself by political activity. Suffragists declare that the average women is as capable of forming an opinion in these matters as hundreds of the men voters of today!

MISS APPLEYARD (*defiantly*): And so do I!

MRS CRABTREE: Then, Miss Appleyard, all I can ask is, what are you doing among *us*?

There is a silence. MISS APPLEYARD, after a moment's pause, turns down left below sofa, and is evidently nonplussed. MRS CRABTREE prepares to leave and continues speaking.

I am glad that you see the absurdity of your position for yourself. It would be a waste of time to argue further with you today, but I shall never rest until you are back within the true fold. (*Slowly and solemnly.*) I want every woman to be a perfect woman!

MISS APPLEYARD (*nettled*): It seems to me that you want every woman to be a perfect fool!

MRS CRABTREE (*after an indignant glance*): Good afternoon, Miss Appleyard.

MISS APPLEYARD (*rings bell*): Good afternoon, Mrs Crabtree!

They bow stiffly. Exit MRS CRABTREE *with head in air.* MISS APPLEYARD *stands in a listening attitude until an outer door bangs; then goes up to the door.*

MISS APPLEYARD (*calls*): Morton!

MORTON: I'm just bringing your tea 'm. (MORTON *enters with tea things on a tray, and puts on table, right.*)

MISS APPLEYARD (*coming down to table, right, and sitting*): Morton, some papers came by post this morning – printed papers from a Suffrage Society. I put them in the waste-paper basket. I suppose they'll have been thrown away by now?

MORTON: No 'm, they've not. Cook and me have got them in the kitchen.

MISS APPLEYARD: I'd rather like to have a look at them.

MORTON: I'll bring them, 'm. (*Hesitating.*) If you'll excuse my saying so, 'm. Cook and me think there's a deal of sound common sense in this Suffrage business.

MISS APPLEYARD (*slowly*): D'you know, Morton, I'm beginning to think it's quite possible that you may be right!

Curtain.

A WOMAN'S INFLUENCE

A WOMAN'S INFLUENCE
Gertrude Jennings

Gertrude Jennings was another woman Inez Bensusan enlisted to help with writing suffrage plays. This play is slightly less amusing and more biting than some of the others, and one of its most salient features is its portrayal of men as fools. *A Woman's Influence* combines the class and sex issues as men who cannot be reasoned with are taken on as a bet by Aline Perry, who is certain that she can get them to do anything by the use of 'a woman's influence'. Through flattery (and flirting) she gets Herbert Lawrence on her side, only to discover that if women have equality – and equal pay –her profits will decrease. So she quickly withdraws. Revealing to her husband that he has been 'tricked', Margaret Lawrence manages to carry him along the path of reason – but the question remains as to why she should bother.

Dale Spender

Characters

HERBERT LAWRENCE
MARGARET, *his wife*
MISS THICKET, *her secretary and friend*
ALINE PERRY, *a widow*
MARY BALL, *a factory hand.*

Note on Performance

This play is fascinating as it deals with the still ongoing debate on how to 'manage' men. Do you play the game as laid down, be 'feminine', sexy, dumb, attempting to exert power through devious emotional holds and throwing in a few squeezes or a fit of tears? Or do you insist upon being treated as an equal, a creature with powers of intelligence and reason, as able and responsible as any man?

Aline Perry is a real man's woman, idle, heartless and deeply selfish, depending on her wiles to get her way. Margaret is a sensible and good woman who scorns foolish tricks and has too much self-respect to stoop to them. Her misfortune is to be married to a man who, though beneath her in every possible way, still has the power to call himself head of the household. Weak-minded though he is, she loves him, and like many women excuses his silliness and supports his behaviour. How irritating it must have been for the suffragettes to be dependent upon halfwits to help them win their cause!

When Herbert realises he's been fooled he gets annoyed and turns the tables on Aline, but one can't help feeling that wounded pride has more to do with his conversion than Margaret's glowing plea for womankind. The play ends on a vision, beloved of Suffragettes, of men and women going hand in hand to equality.

It is wittily written but has a rather serious tone. Margaret is a formidable woman, kind, intelligent and moral. Herbert probably finds her terrifying. Care should be taken not to make her too 'righteous'. Aline should be a lot of fun to play, kittenish and charming on the outside but with a brain as sharp as a carving knife; lucky for Herbert he finds out in time. Herbert is also an enjoyable part; the kind of man who likes his grilled chop on the table and his shirt ironed and buttoned on to him before he says good morning. The set needs only a comfortable chair and a few middle-class decorations.

Carole Hayman

Scene: *Room in Mrs Lawrence's house.*

Enter HERBERT LAWRENCE, *followed by* MARGARET: HERBERT *is a good looking, youngish man;* MARGARET *a grave, beautiful woman of twenty-seven or twenty-eight.*

HERBERT (*in loud, cheerful tones at top speed, giving* MARGARET *no chance of replying*): Come along, my dear, come along, if you want to speak to me. I'm off to the Club, you know, want to see old Bob Thurlow just back from the South Pole, great sport. Must hear the news – Well, what do you want? Don't keep me, I'd like to shake old Bob by the hand, give him my congratulations and all that sort of thing, don't you know. Good fellow, Bob, one of the best; never gasses about himself or what he's done, goes straight at a thing, never satisfied till he's pulled it off. Get on with what you want to say, Margaret, I want to be in at the start, takes me five minutes to get to the Club, due there at three. The boys will steal a march on me if I don't. What is it, what is it?

MARGARET: Herbert, I want you to speak to Mr Reed for me.

HERBERT: What about? No use my speaking to Reed unless I know what I'm going to say. Reed's alright enough, but –

MARGARET: Herbert, do listen to me. Something *must* be done for these poor women at Hill Rise Factory. The sweating that goes on there is a disgrace to this town, and I can do nothing to prevent it.

HERBERT (*jovially*): Ah, that's just it – Nothing can be done, nothing can be done. Don't worry your pretty little head – it'll all come out in the wash.

MARGARET: But, Herbert, something *can* be done, and ought to be done. Mr Reed, as member here, ought to know the condition of the people, he ought to remedy it.

HERBERT: Well, duckey, tell me another time. I'm busy now, dear old Bob, you know – I'm just off.

MARGARET: But, Herbert, you are

always just off. Do promise to see Mr Reed for me, just for a minute – do.

HERBERT: Why not see him yourself, old girl. You know I don't take much interest in all these things – rather chuck the poor beggars a cheque and have done with it. I'll do that any day, Margaret. But then, you've plenty of your own.

MARGARET: It isn't only money, Herbert, that they want, it's their whole social condition that's wrong.

HERBERT: Well, you tell Reed about it yourself, there's a dear – he's not a bad sort, rather an ass, perhaps.

MARGARET: Mr Reed won't listen to me.

HERBERT: Won't listen? There, there, just think of that – won't listen! well, well.

MARGARET: He thinks women ought not to meddle in politics.

HERBERT: Well, dear old girl, you know I rather agree with him! Anyway pretty women like you. Always get what you want, you know; ask me, I'll do it; ask your husbands! Much better than fussing about votes for yourselves. What are votes? Sweet womanly influence worth much more.

MISS THICKET (*outside*): All right, I'll go in.

HERBERT: Bless me, it's Thicket! Two to one not fair! I'm off. How do, Miss Thicket. Goodbye. (*Exit as* MISS THICKET *whom he nearly knocks over comes in.* MISS THICKET *is a pleasant, comely young woman, with very neat hair and a decided manner.*)

MISS THICKET: Any good?

MARGARET: No.

MISS THICKET: Thought as much. Any news from Reed?

MARGARET: Yes.

MISS THICKET: Any good?

MARGARET: No.

MISS THICKET: Thought as much.

MARGARET: I'll show you the letter, here. You've brought the Report?

MISS THICKET: Oh yes, it's taken

much longer than I thought. Mary Ball is bringing a list of names; the women working outside the factory are very difficult to trace; they weren't over anxious at the factory to give me any information about them.

MARGARET (*drily*): No, I daresay not. Where are the figures?

MISS THICKET: Here.

MARGARET: I see. About what we thought. The wages average six shillings a week all round.

MISS THICKET: Yes, about that, and most of these women have five or six children. That's piece work, of course. The factory isn't officially supposed to know anything about it, but they wink at it all the same.

MARGARET: I wonder what people who talk about women preserving the sanctity of the home would think of that!

MISS THICKET: So do I. Sanctity comes rather expensive when you've only got six shillings a week.

MARGARET: It's heartrending. But what can we do? Temporary help is so little use. If only we had the power to bring the matter before Parliament.

MISS THICKET: Has our promising member said nothing?

MARGARET: You may well call him our *promising* member. He certainly doesn't perform. He has written politely refusing to give me an interview.

MISS THICKET: Impertinence! If you'd ask him to tea he'd have come like a shot. But because he knows you want to speak to him on a grave social question, no.

MARGARET: Can you wonder? Why should he consider a creature who in political life doesn't exist.

MISS THICKET: Ridiculous nonsense, that it is. Here are you an intelligent, well-read, thoughtful woman taking a deep interest in the good of the country. You have plenty of money which you've earned by your pen, you pay taxes, you contribute to the State, yet you can't get your voice heard at all. Look at me! I'm not as rich, but I'm just as clever – and just as helpless!

MARGARET: If only Herbert would take the thing up.

MISS THICKET: But he won't! Herbert takes no interest in reform. How often does he even trouble to vote?

MARGARET: Never, unless he's badgered into it.

MISS THICKET: There, you see? You've got the money and the brains, he's got the vote. Seems to me an unfair division.

MARGARET: Really, Carrie!

MISS THICKET: Oh, I daresay I'm rude, but then I'm truthful. Politically, your husband *has* nothing, *does* nothing, and *is* nothing. I know he's very charming, a thoroughly nice fellow and a good sort, and all that sort of thing, but why *he* should represent your interests I don't know.

MARGARET: Mrs Perry says I ought to blandish him (her own words) into helping my poor starving workers.

MISS THICKET: Mrs Perry's a snake! How you can have that woman to stay here beats me.

MARGARET: She is very lonely and has no settled home to go to, no children to care for.

MISS THICKET: Good thing too! She's no woman to bring up children! I tell you this, Margaret, there'd be much less wickedness in the world if all women brought up their children as you do.

MARGARET: It's not to *my* credit, Carrie, it's simply that I've lived in a time when women have become thinking creatures and not mere puppets. Oh, if men only realised how the future of the race lies in our hands! Would they still like the fluffy ruffles of life, the flirt or the fool? So attractive during the engagement – so useless as a wife, worse than useless as a mother!

MISS THICKET: What do men care? As long as it's some pretty round faced minx with curly hair, what does the future matter? They jaw about divine motherhood and do their best to drag it down.

MARGARET: I think you're wrong, Carrie. It used to be so, I know, but men understand us better now, and respect us much more. It's the result of civilisation. The test of man's refinement is his attitude towards woman. Does a savage respect woman? Of course not.

MISS THICKET: Well, what does Reed say?

MARGARET (*reading*): Dear Mrs Lawrence, I am sorry to hear there is so much misery amongst the women in the Hill Rise Factories. No doubt the matter will be gone into before long.' Before long! 'I cannot see my way clear to doing anything just at present.'

MISS THICKET: Pig!

MARGARET: Are you really a suffragette? If you knew how very little savour there was in Parliamentary life you wouldn't thirst for it.'

MISS THICKET: He thirsted for it right enough. Besides, whose talking about Parliamentary life?

MARGARET: 'I hope to come in and see your husband soon. There are so many matters I want to discuss with him. Yours sincerely, R.R. Reed.' He'll discuss things with the voter, not with me.

MISS THICKET: And meanwhile, this awful sweating business has got to go on unchecked. Oh, Margaret, it's heartbreaking!

Enter MRS PERRY.

MRS PERRY (*a pretty babyish little woman of thirty-five, with a drawling voice; she is very well dressed*): What's heartbreaking? Do tell me. It sounds too interesting.

MISS THICKET: It wouldn't interest you, Mrs Perry.

MRS PERRY: Dear Miss Thicket! So nice to see you. And you haven't changed a bit. It was only yesterday I said to Margaret: 'As Miss Thicket was in the beginning, so she is in the middle, and so she will be to the end.'

MISS THICKET: How very sweet of you.

MRS PERRY: Not at all. It's just how I feel. Oh dear, what a lot of papers. My darling Margaret, what are they all about?

MARGARET: They're chiefly reports on the sweating system. I'm interested in these mills, and I'm trying to get the women's condition improved.

MRS PERRY: Oh, Margaret, how good of you to take up such funny, dull subjects. Don't you find it terribly ageing?

MISS THICKET: She doesn't look as if she did.

MRS PERRY: No, she's very precious! Still, I think all these things ought to be done by men, don't you?

MARGARET: No, Aline, men with the best will in the world can't understand the subject as we do.

MISS THICKET: I should like to see a man's face when he's suddenly confronted with the details of some of our cases. This one, for instance – (*Pokes paper into* MRS PERRY'S *face.*) see that – and that?

MRS PERRY: Ah yes, very sad – but really, they oughtn't to have children, ought they? I mean, if they will work?

MARGARET: *Will* work, Aline? What are these poor women to do unless they work? This one, Annie Matthews, has been deserted by her husband. She brings up and supports her children, by making shirts at 1d. an hour. Liza Green works inside the factory, standing for eight hours, though her baby is only a week old. Mary Ball, wage earner for the household, husband drinks – she does one man's work for the Factory at Hill Rise, but because she's a woman she only gets half wage.

MRS PERRY: Dear me! Too bad, isn't it? But it's no use trying to do anything for them, dear. These people are so ungrateful. Why, I gave the charwoman a fur jacket once, and I found out afterwards she'd pawned it.

MISS THICKET: To buy food, I expect.

MRS PERRY: Dear Miss Thicket, you're so strenuous. But, Margaret, if you really want to agitate or legislate or whatever it's called, why don't you take my advice and coax your husband into helping you? Mr Reed would listen to him.

MARGARET: Herbert doesn't care about these things, nor does Mr Reed for that matter.

MRS PERRY: My dear! *Make* them care. You can surely do that!

MARGARET: They are not so easily influenced.

MRS PERRY: I expect you don't know how to set about it.

MISS THICKET: You can't expect her methods to be quite the same as yours.

MARGARET: Carrie.

MRS PERRY: Never mind, dear, I like it. After thirty, a woman does so appreciate a little flattery.

MISS THICKET: Flattery! That's just it, you *would* think it flattery. (*Fumes.*)

MRS PERRY: All these things, dear Margaret, are so easy to get from men. A woman's influence –

MISS THICKET: Isn't always for good!

MRS PERRY: Dear Miss Thicket, I'm sure yours would be. Such a waste, isn't it, to think it will never be exercised. Can't I speak to your husband, Margaret?

MARGARET: I hardly think, Aline –

MRS PERRY: Oh, do let me try, just for fun. Sometimes a word from a stranger will be listened to when the poor wife preaches in vain.

MARGARET: It's very kind of you, but – (*Bell rings.*)

MISS THICKET: That's Mary Ball, I expect.

MARGARET: I'll go and see, she is very shy. (*Exit.*)

MRS PERRY: A dear soul, isn't she, and so quaint.

MISS THICKET: Quaint?

MRS PERRY: Yes, about this Woman Movement and Votes, and all that sort of thing. I'm sure I'm perfectly satisfied. I find nothing in life to grumble at. I don't want a vote.

MISS THICKET: No, you wouldn't, why should you?

MRS PERRY: Exactly! Why should I?

Enter MARGARET *followed by* MARY BALL, *a thin, pale, shabby woman, with the flatness of voice and manner of one used to privation and unhappiness.*

MARGARET: Come in Mary, don't be afraid, here is a friend of yours, and this – is a friend of mine, Mrs Perry. Sit down and tell me how things are going.

MARY: Much as usual, thank you, Mum.

MARGARET: How is the baby?

MARY: He's rather poorly still, thank you, Mum. He seems 'ardly to 'ave any strength, so to speak.

MISS THICKET: How is it you're away from the Works so early, Mary?

MARY: They turned me off, Miss.

MARGARET: Turned you off?

MARY: Yes, Mum. On account of Baby it was. I wouldn't leave 'im alone, and there wasn't anybody to mind 'im, so they turned me away. I shall have to do outside work now, Miss.

MISS THICKET: What are you paid for that, Mary?

MARY: A penny an hour, Miss; that's if I work sharp but if I take my eyes off time's lost, and my sight isn't what it was. Still, the summer's coming, Miss, and that means longer time for working, so one mustn't grumble.

MARGARET: Is there much trouble down your way just now?

MARY: Well, Mum, there's always trouble, so I 'eard and I don't suppose ours is worse than others. But we 'eard a bit about these 'ere votes for women, and some of us was thinking if that came along it might do us a bit of good.

MRS PERRY: Oh no, my good woman, that wouldn't help you. What use has it been to the men?

MARY: Asking your pardon, my lady, but we think different. We don't get much time for reading our way, but we do 'ave a look at what's going on, and my father's often told me how many things have been put right for working men since they 'ad a chance of saying what they wanted. No one gives the women a chance, my lady.

MRS PERRY: You should get your husband to speak for you. (*A silence.*)

MARGARET: Mr Ball is unfortunately not quite responsible.

MARY: He's most kind, I'm sure, only for the drink, my lady. He's never raised 'is 'and to me. But as ter givin' 'is vote – I don't 'ardly know –

MARGARET: He does vote, I suppose?

MARY: Oh yes, Mum, but he never knowed which way. Here's the list you asked me for, Mum. I could get more names if I 'ad the time – these is just the neighbours that 'ave signed. Some sez the Vote's no use to 'em because their 'usbands pay the rent, so I sez – if you don't want it yourself give it to them as does, I sez.

MARGARET: Quite right, Mary. You see, Aline, thirty-five names in Mary Ball's own little circle. Isn't that a proof that working women are beginning to take the vote seriously?

MRS PERRY: Oh, poor dears, of course they want it! But I'm sure I could do more for them in five minutes with Mr Reed or even Mr Lawrence than a hundred votes!

MARY: Then in 'evin's name, my lady, I wish you'd do it. But, asking yer pardon, I don't suppose you know just what your saying, or what it all means to us. It's a pretty rough life down there, and its a rough lot that live it. But we ain't beasts though we've bin treated like 'em. I'm not saying anything against the men – they're as God made 'em – but there are some things no man can understand the way of. I don't know if you're a mother of children, my lady, if you are you'll know what I'm saying's right; it's not men as can help us any more, it's women – it's ourselves, and that's the truth. (A pause.)

MRS PERRY: Really, you quite overwhelm me.

MARY: I ask your pardons – I – I forgot myself. I oughtn't to have spoke, but these things – they burn inside us like fire till it seems they must out. I'm sorry, Mum.

MARGARET: Oh, Mary, I'm glad you've spoken, you bear too much in silence.

MISS THICKET: It falls on deaf ears half the time. (Glaring at MRS PERRY, who is quite complacent.)

MARGARET: Come, Mary, I want to see you get some tea, and I've got plans for you. You mustn't worry, you and the children will be cared for till the day comes when you can speak for yourselves.

MARY: Thank you kindly, Mum, but I'm sore ashamed to 'ave said anything. I felt sort of carried away – Good day, Miss, Good day, Milady.

MARGARET: Come. (MRS LAWRENCE and MARY exit.)

MISS THICKET: So you see, Mrs Perry, women do want the vote.

MRS PERRY: Dear Margaret oughtn't to encourage this discontent among the lower classes. It's so unnecessary. They're always making demands upon us.

MISS THICKET: Then let them demand something that'll improve their condition. Might as well, you know.

MRS PERRY: Well, you haven't convinced me in the least little bit, dear Miss Thicket. I still believe that my way of getting a thing is the best way, and I'll tell you what. Just for a joke, I'll bet you a sovereign that I'll get Mr Lawrence and through him Mr Reed, to take up this woman sweating business at Hill Rise, and at least ask a question in the House about it.

MISS THICKET: How are you going to do it?

MRS PERRY: Ah, that's my affair. Well, what do you say?

MISS THICKET: Oh, all right, it can do no harm. (Gathers up papers.)

MRS PERRY: If I succeed, it will rather shake your belief in Votes for Women won't it?

MISS THICKET: No more than, if you fail, it will shake your belief in yourself. Good day. (Exit left. MRS PERRY laughs. HERBERT'S voice heard off.)

HERBERT (off): How do again, Miss Thicket? Just off? Goodbye – Can I get you a cab?

MISS THICKET (off): No thanks. I want to say goodbye to Margaret.

HERBERT: Right, she's giving Mary somebody tea somewhere. – (Pause.)

Ah yes, I daresay.

MRS PERRY *listens to above, looks meaningly at the door, goes to glass, powders her nose, and puts her hair straight, makes a face at the door, sits by table, leans her head on her hands, pretends to cry, pause, no one comes, she rises – goes to door.*

(*Off.*) Where are you going to have tea, Marg, old girl? Boudoir? Right oh! You'll find me there.

MRS PERRY *claps her hands, runs to table, hides her face once more in sham tears.* HERBERT LAWRENCE *enters, whistling cheerily. He does not at once see* MRS PERRY, *when he does his expression changes to one of concern.*)

What's up, by Jove, anything wrong? Is it you, Mrs Perry?

MRS PERRY: Yes. (*Muffled sobs.*)

HERBERT: I say, don't do that! What's happened? I'll call Margaret. (*Backing.*)

MRS PERRY: No, no, dear Mr Lawrence, please don't.

HERBERT: Well, then Miss Thicket, she's only just gone, a woman knows what to say.

MRS PERRY: No, no, please –

HERBERT: Well I'll – I'll get out of the way – get out – you know –

MRS PERRY (*with a wail*): Oh, don't leave me here alone!

HERBERT: Well, what *am* I to do?

MRS PERRY: Nothing, it's all right, really, I shall be better in a moment. So stupid of me. We women are such foolish creatures, so different from you. How I envy your strength, your self-control.

HERBERT: Oh – ah. (*Flattered.*)

MRS PERRY: Do sit down and talk to me for a moment. I feel sure it would do me good. I'm afraid I'm an awful sight.

HERBERT: Not at all, you wouldn't be that.

MRS PERRY: Oh, it's so sweet of you. (*Gazes into his eyes.*)

HERBERT: Nonsense, you're top hole in looks, and so I've always said to Margaret.

MRS PERRY (*slightly chilled*): Margaret!

HERBERT: Yes, she quite agrees with me. But now, Mrs Perry, won't you tell me what's troubling you? (*Laughing.*) I know it can't be money as I'm your trustee!

MRS PERRY: Oh, no, it's not money, in fact, it's not my own troubles at all.

HERBERT: Not?

MRS PERRY: No, indeed, far, far otherwise.

HERBERT: Won't you tell me?

MRS PERRY (*leaning towards him*): May I?

HERBERT: *Do!*

MRS PERRY: Oh, Mr Lawrence, it's *these* poor women in the factories, the distress, the misery is awful. I can't do anything. But what the weak, faltering instinct of a woman discovers the strong hand of a man can put right. Dear Mr Lawrence, won't you help me?

HERBERT: In what way, Mrs Perry, what can I do? What can I do, you know?

MRS PERRY: Won't you go to Mr Reed and ask him to do something about this awful business? He would listen to you when he wouldn't pay any attention to poor me.

HERBERT: I'm quite sure that if you went to see him, Mrs Perry, he would do anything he could for you.

MRS PERRY: Ah no, I have heard that he is most unsympathetic, that he cares very little about other people's troubles, so different from *you*, dear, kind Mr Lawrence.

HERBERT: Oh, ah. I'm afraid I can't do very much, but what I can is at your service.

MRS PERRY: How *very* good you are! How absurd it is to talk about Votes for Women, when men are so gentle, so unselfish.

HERBERT: Now what do you think can be done, Mrs Perry? Eh?

MRS PERRY: Oh, I'm so ignorant, I hardly like to say, but I think perhaps Mr Reed ought to ask a question in the House about the underpayment of women workers. Why shouldn't he mention this factory as a case in point?

HERBERT: He couldn't do that, I'm afraid, but I dare say he could quote statistics. I'm no business man – I mean, these things are hard to explain to a lady, but if you start monkeying with wages, shares go down, and then there's a row with the shareholders, see, and no end of a fuss begins.

MRS PERRY: Oh, but surely shareholders oughtn't to mind if their shares *do* go down a little if it's to help the poor woman.

HERBERT: No, they *oughtn't*, of course, but they're not all like you, Mrs Perry, not all like you, that's the trouble, you see. Now, you wouldn't care a bit, I'll swear, if your shares weren't to pay 7 per cent for a year or two if the workers benefited.

MRS PERRY: Not at all, but, of course, *my* shares couldn't go down. They are in Consols, or something, aren't they?

HERBERT: Bless my soul, no, you wouldn't get 7 per cent in Consols. No, no, Mrs Perry, I promised your husband I'd look after your money for you, and I kept my word. It's invested in Hill Rise Securities.

MRS PERRY: What! (*Horrified.*)

HERBERT: Yes. Why, the factories are in Margaret's district, jolly investment I tell you. Not likely to go down either, unless anything happens to upset it.

MRS PERRY: Unless anything happens to upset it! (*She is stricken by the news.*)

HERBERT: But what's the matter?

MRS PERRY: It's nothing, really nothing.

HERBERT: Oh, *that's* right! Well, what shall I say to Reed? I'll see him tomorrow, if you like – he thinks a lot of what I say, nice fellow Reed, he'll get the whole thing going in less than no time.

MRS PERRY: Oh, will he?

HERBERT: Rather! Leave it all to me, go like a flash!

MRS PERRY: Mr Lawrence, I've thought out a little plan!

HERBERT: Oh! what might it be?

MRS PERRY: I think perhaps I'd better wait till I've worked it all out, then I'll tell you, and it shall be our little secret, and you'll help me with it, won't you?

HERBERT: Rather! You know I will – anything I can do – Trust me!

MRS PERRY: *Thank* you! I will let you know as soon as I have got it all fixed up. But meanwhile, dear Mr Lawrence, I want you to keep *absolute silence* over this matter – *not* to see Mr Reed or upset yourself over the question in any *way*. I can't explain why, but if you do it will absolutely *ruin* my little scheme. Will you promise?

HERBERT: Certainly, but what am I to do about Margaret?

MRS PERRY: Margaret?

HERBERT: Yes, she is always wanting me to go into it with her.

MRS PERRY: Well, tell her that you can't just now, will you?

HERBERT: She talks such a lot about it – never lets me get a word in.

MRS PERRY: Ah! but I am sure you can be firm when really necessary. Yes! I can tell that you are full of hidden strength.

HERBERT: Oh well, as to that, I'm master here, of course. (MARGARET *enters.*)

MRS PERRY: Of course, so you'll tell dear Margaret you can do nothing!

HERBERT: Very well.

MRS PERRY: And you'll keep my little secret? (*Edging nearer him.*)

HERBERT: I swear it. (*He kisses her hand.* MRS PERRY *sees* MARGARET, *draws her hand away and rises,* HERBERT *much embarrassed.*)

MRS PERRY: Ah, dearest Margaret, so you gave the poor creature her tea. What a ministering angel you are! Well, I must really tidy myself up a little before tea, I shan't be a moment. (*Exit.*)

Pause.

HERBERT: I know what you think, Margaret?

MARGARET: What *do* I think?

HERBERT: You – er – think I was – er – flirting with Mrs Perry.

MARGARET: Well, and why shouldn't you?

HERBERT: What?

MARGARET: My dear old boy, do you think I don't know Aline by now? Why, she behaves like that with every man she meets. Besides, do you suppose I don't know you?

HERBERT: How do you – mean?

MARGARET: Only that I've absolute confidence in you!

HERBERT: You're not angry then?

MARGARET: Not the least little bit in the world.

HERBERT: By jove, Margaret, you're the nicest, dearest, most sensible –

MARGARET: Oh, yes, yes, I know. The only thing I don't understand is why Aline was making such a mystery of it all.

HERBERT: Of all what?

MARGARET: Why, that she was asking you to help us.

HERBERT: You know that then?

MARGARET: Of course, why not?

HERBERT: Well she's got her *own* idea about it, you see, Margaret.

MARGARET: And you've promised not to do anything for Hill Rise yet awhile?

HERBERT: Yes. (*suddenly paying attention.*) What factory did you say, Margaret?

MARGARET: The Hill Rise, of course. That's the worse by far. Didn't you know?

HERBERT: No.

MARGARET: Herbert, dear. I've told you over and over again.

HERBERT: Yes, I know, but I wasn't paying much attention you know how it is, men have so much to think about, they can't always be listening, can they? So much chatter! But now you tell me that, I begin to realise that's why she changed all of a sudden and didn't want me to go to Reed. I see.

MARGARET: She changed and didn't want you to go to Reed?

HERBERT: No, because, don't you see, all her money's in Hill Rise and she only just found it out.

MARGARET: Oh, I see. So you'd promised to go to Reed before that?

HERBERT: We'll, er – you know what it is, old girl, when I saw her crying –

MARGARET: Crying?

HERBERT: Yes. For the poor women. It was awfully sweet of her.

MARGARET: Oh, Herbert? So this is what you mean by a woman's influence! This is how we are to wield our power, to arm fighters in our great cause to carry out our mighty enterprise! Any little flirt, or idle, heartless woman is to bend a man's will to do her bidding of the moment. What can be done with such weapons?

HERBERT: What *do* you mean, Margaret?

MARGARET: I mean that Mrs Perry was wheedling you into doing this for a joke, a bet.

HERBERT: A bet.

MARGARET: Yes, a bet with Miss Thicket. Then, of course, when she found it would damage her own interests she drew back and made you promise not to do anything.

HERBERT: By Jove! What makes you think so?

MARGARET: I don't think: I know.

HERBERT: 'Pon my word, it's too bad, and I shall tell her so.

MARGARET: She'd only laugh.

HERBERT: Laugh, indeed! It simply horrifies me. I don't think it's at all amusing.

MARGARET: No, Herbert, it isn't really amusing if one thinks of all the sin and misery that lie underneath it all, the helplessness of Woman using her one weapon, sometimes beautifully, sometimes merely frivolously (like today), sometimes with degradation, but always – always the same weapon. Ah, if you men would only give us *another* one, the use of our intelligence, so that we could realise that we are reasonable creatures, fit to be heard equally with man, not parasites. You love and respect me, I know; I want you to love and respect Woman for my sake, to give her that place in social life which is her right. She *is* worthy, she will be *more* worthy – help her then, and some day you will be proud of what you have done.

HERBERT: I wonder if you are right, Margaret. I begin to think there's something in what you say, and that I ought to help you after all.

MARGARET (*with deep thanksgiving*): Oh, my dear. (*Slight pause.*) But I don't want you to come just because I persuaded you, or to do anything against your better judgment. I want you to come because you see the cause is just.

HERBERT: I *do* see it. Yes, Margaret, I *will* help you; I can in a hundred ways, and the work will be ever so much easier if we do it together.

MARGARET: Ah, my dear! that's the key to the whole Woman's Movement. We can do so much more if we work together.

Curtain.

THE APPLE

THE APPLE
Inez Bensusan

Given the significant contribution that Inez Bensusan made to the women's theatre, it would be remiss not to include one of her own plays. It is not strictly about the vote but concentrates more on sex equality. Cyril, the son, is the apple, 'the apple of his father's eye', and the whole family revolves round him. Ann and Helen, the daughters, must make him the centre of their attention, wait on him, and give up their share of the family finances to procure Cyril's advancement in the world.

Helen has been 'propositioned' by her employer and wants to leave, to emigrate to Canada, but Cyril's needs must come first. And she is left to face the sexual harassment. If the play were written today, perhaps it would have a different, and happier ending.

Dale Spender

Characters

ANN PAYSON
HELEN PAYSON, *her sister*
CYRIL PAYSON, *their brother (the Apple)*
NIGEL DEAN

Note on Performance

I find this play very upsetting. Its theme is as topical as ever. Girls shall be sacrificed
for boys. In many families in many cultures girls are second class children. The
assumption is that boys will get the education, the property and the biggest plate of food,
the girl will get what's left over. The play examines this state of affairs with great
bitterness and comes to an unhappy conclusion. There is no way out for Helen, she must
even accept the unwelcome sexual attacks from her boss to save the wretched Apple.
Her honour is unimportant beside his success. It's very well written with crisp dialogue
and very clearly drawn characters. Both Helen and Ann are totally believable and Cyril
is a thoroughly nasty piece of work. The set is quite complicated in the description, but
could be simplified by having the kitchen and the hall in the wings. The furniture used
should be shabby and the costumes (except for Cyril's) similarly make-do-and-mend.
Helen should have a smartness and care about her that Ann does not, however. Since
she brings a wage packet into the house certain concessions would have to be made. She
must look nice to keep her job, Ann as a mere domestic slave, has no reason to own a
good frock. Cyril's costume should be as ostentatious as possible, no expense spared
where he is concerned.

Though the play is serious and often angry in content the dialogue is witty and skips
along. It should be played pacily and with the intimacy of people who know each others'
little weaknesses inside out. Helen's feelings are particularly complex, she loves her
family and feels the weight of filial duty even though she resents and resists her role. In
the end though, she is forced back into the traditional self sacrificing life of a woman
who has nowhere else to turn. Her sister, more conventional in her attitudes, thoroughly
approves the decision. Helen is left wishing hopelessly for '. . . a glimpse of life, a taste
of the joy of living, a few pence in my pocket, my rights as an individual . . .' It's a
battlecry for women everywhere.

Carole Hayman

Scene: *Useful room in suburban villa.*
The furniture is very worn, giving the
impression of poor gentlefolk trying to
make a brave show. Doors right and left.
Door right gives onto hall and through it
is seen, if possible, a staircase. Door left
gives into kitchen and, if possible, shows
interior with pots and pans, etc. Table left
with sewing machine. Sofa right. Mirror
over mantlepiece right. Armchair right
centre.
As curtain rises ANN *is discovered at*
table left working the sewing machine.
She is a slight short-sighted girl about
twenty-seven, but looks older, as though
all her life she had been overworked. She
wears a washed-out cotton frock and a
big apron. She is an alert, active, nervous
type. A noise as of opening and banging
of hall door heard, then enter HELEN
through door right. She is a tall, buxom
type, very handsome with a fine figure,
neatly dressed in tailor-made style, stiff
collar, little tie, short pleated skirt, plain
hat, simple but distinctly smart, the type
to be met with frequently in city offices,
but young with good colour and clear
complexion. ANN *looks up in surprise,*
then looks at clock and back again at
HELEN.

ANN: How awfully early you are Ellie, –
it's only half-past three.

HELEN *comes down to armchair and*
resolutely throws herself into it, begins
almost savagely to tear off her gloves.
She looks heated and excited.

I do hope you're not ill? What's the
matter? I'll make you a cup of tea.

HELEN *does not answer.*

You're sure you're quite well, dear?
(*Rises.*)

HELEN: Yes, there's nothing wrong with
me. Don't start fussing for goodness
sake. (*Takes off her hat, jabs the pins*
into the crown, and throws it across the
room on to the sofa.)

ANN: But, Ellie dear –

HELEN *holds her hands before her*
eyes.

There! I'm sure you're ill. (*Comes to*
her. HELEN *sits up quickly.*)

HELEN: Don't talk rubbish, I tell you.
I'm as strong as a bullock, worse luck!

ANN: Ell, what do you –

HELEN: I'm excited, bad-tempered, that's
all. I've been thinking hard on the way
home. Too much thinking is more than
my cheap brain can stand I suppose.

ANN: Then you've a headache? I was
sure of it. I *will* make you some tea.
(*Moves towards kitchen.*)

HELEN (*petulantly*): Oh, sit down, do!
I'll get my own tea when I want it. I
won't have you slaving for me. You're
worked to death as it is. Do sit down!

ANN: The kettle won't be a minute. –
(*Moves up.*)

HELEN (*jumps up, goes after* ANN,
seizes her by the shoulders and pushes
her into chair by table): What a blessed
nuisance you are Ann, always on the
hop, like a jumping bean. It's bad
enough the way the others make use of
you, but I'm hanged if I'll allow it.
(ANN *protests.*) What's this you're
making? (*Picks up material.*)

ANN: It's Norah's dress for the Lamond's
party. Isn't it sweet? (*Holds it up.*) The
bodice is such a dear, its going to be
crossed over like this (*showing her*) and
have lace and insertion and blue ribbons
run through. (HELEN *crosses to left of*
table.) Don't you like it?

HELEN: Why can't Norah make her own
things? She has more spare time than
you.

ANN: But the poor child is so tired after
her day's work. I wouldn't be a nursery
governess for anything.

HELEN (*bitterly*): She's not too tired to
go to a party anyway. (*Sits.*)

ANN: You don't grudge her that surely? I
never thought Mrs Prescott would spare
her, but she said if she got up at five
next morning she might go. Poor Norah!
she will be tired.

HELEN: You're giving it to her of course?
(ANN *nods.*) Where did you get the
money?

ANN: Whatever's come over you today,
Ell? I'm sure you're ill.

HELEN (*firmly*): Where did you get it?
Father didn't give it to you. (ANN

shakes her head.) Mother hasn't got it to give. You've pawned something again. What?

ANN (*uncomfortably*): It wasn't a bit of good to me. I didn't want it.

HELEN (*sternly*): What?

ANN: That little medallion thing. (*Quickly.*) I never wore it. It was no good to me.

HELEN: Ann! You're awfully fond of it. How dare you!

ANN: But the poor child – she had to wear something, and they pay her so badly where she is. She can't save a penny. I couldn't bear the thought that –

HELEN (*angrily*): Why didn't you ask father?

ANN (*surprised*): What an idea!

HELEN (*bringing her hand down violently on the table*): He ought to pay for Norah's clothes – not you or me. It's a sin, a disgrace, that a girl should have to – to pawn her trinkets, in order to go decently clad! Ugh! It makes me sick. (*Crosses to armchair.*)

ANN: You know Ellie, father would give it if he had it to give. It isn't that he's mean – you know if –

HELEN *sits.*

HELEN: I know that every penny that can be saved or squeezed out of the miserable family exchequer goes to support the Apple, instead of supporting us! And I consider it's high time the Apple was self-supporting. He's older than Norah or me – he's a man, a strong healthy male thing. What right has he to everything, while we girls are struggling to – to cover ourselves decently?

ANN: It isn't Cyril's fault, Ellie dear. You know there are things a man must have that girls can do without.

HELEN: Clubs, cigarettes, hansoms and so on? Oh yes. Because he's the son, the apple of his parents' eyes, everything has to be sacrificed for him – everything! His own sisters' comfort – more – their very chances in life!

ANN: I never heard you speak like this. Has anything happened?

HELEN: Yes. The worst has happened. I've awakened to a sense of the injustice of it all. I'm going to rebel. I'm going to fight for my rights, your rights, equal rights for us all.

ANN: But how? You know father can't afford to give us pocket money and things. You know what a struggle it has always been, dear.

HELEN: Oh, I'm not grumbling with father, he's acting according to his lights I suppose. It's the gospel of the generation that everything must be done for the boy – the son – he's the rare and precious individual in a country where there are more than a million superfluous women! (ANN *shakes her head mournfully; gets up and goes to the kitchen door.* HELEN *leans her elbows on her knees and takes her head in her hands. A slight pause.*) What a pity we don't live in China!

ANN (*pausing at door*): Whatever for? (*Goes through, leaving door open, gets kettle, and puts on stove or gas ring.*)

HELEN (*with bitter laugh*): Superfluous girl babies there are legally and comfortably done away with directly they're born.

ANN (*horrified; drops teapot lid*): Oh! how awful – how ghastly!

HELEN: It's far more merciful than letting them live to toil and moil and scrape and scratch along through the best years of their life as hundreds of us girls have to do.

ANN *looks compassionately at her a moment, then bustles about getting a cup and saucer, etc. A slight pause.* HELEN *turns round.*

Have your own way then. I'll submit. You won't have me here much longer so I may as well try to be decent for the time being. (*Crosses to table and sits at machine and commences work.*)

ANN (*at door*): I can't understand you, Ellie. You're so queer today. What are you talking about? Never mind that, Ellie, I'll get along with it all right. I do wish you'd lie down. You seem so unhappy somehow, I'm quite worried.

HELEN (*working machine almost viciously*): Don't you worry, I'm all right. In luck most likely – very much in luck. I thought it would come to it some time, but I didn't expect it quite so soon, not quite. But anyway since it had to come –

ANN *listens, quite at sea. She is seen inside the door cutting bread and butter.* HELEN *takes work out of machine, shakes and turns bodice over with critical eye.*

You can't get on properly with this until it's fitted – come here and try it on.

ANN: It will do when I go to bed, I always fix Norah's things in front of the glass our figures are so alike. Don't you bother.

HELEN: You can't possibly fix the back on yourself.

ANN: But Ellie, you know how tired you are –

HELEN: Not anything like the corpse you'll be, by bedtime.

ANN: But really –

HELEN (*turns*): Let me swallow that tea, and then see whose will is strongest.

ANN: I'll bring it to you. What a trial you are to be sure. (*Sighs goodnaturedly, brings cup in one hand, brown teapot in the other.* HELEN *puts work down and takes cup.*) I've put the milk in. Is this strong enough? (*Pouring.*)

HELEN: Fine. That's enough, thanks. (*Drinks. A pause.* ANN *gives her a plate of bread and butter on her lap.*) Awfully good. You *can* make tea, Ann – I'm glad I let you have your own way, for once. I feel better already – at least my temper does. Aren't you going to have a cup?

ANN: I'm not thirsty.

HELEN: Economy or honour?

ANN (*laughing*): Honour bright.

HELEN (*between her mouthfuls*): Off with your bodice then, I want to try this on.

ANN: I can do it quite well tonight, really.

HELEN (*firmly*): I'll rip it off you myself if you don't. It will take half the time my way – come one.

ANN (*protesting*): I do wish to Goodness that –

HELEN (*putting down the cup*): Now then – (*Rising.*)

ANN (*weakly*): You really are too awful.

HELEN (*centre*): Never mind – you won't have to put up with your bully of a sister much longer. Take it off.

ANN: But someone might come.

HELEN: No fear. Mother won't matter, and there's no danger of the Apple returning just yet. He's swaggering down Pall Mall or lounging in the Park if the office is too dull for him.

ANN: You've heaps of your own things to see to.

HELEN: Heaps. More than you think, considering the journey I'm going shortly.

ANN (*taking off blouse*): Whatever nonsense are you talking now?

HELEN (*helping her on with the other*): It's anything but nonsense. It's the solemn truth. I've been hinting at it for the last half hour, but you've taken no notice.

ANN (*turning*): Ellie! What do you mean.

HELEN: Keep still, or the pins will stick in you. (*Fitting and pinning.*) It means this. Today week I'm going to Canada.

ANN: Canada? (*Turns sharply and squeals.*)

HELEN: In the 'Cymric' with Mabel Arnott and her friends.

ANN: But how? why? what will you do there? where will you get the money? – Ellie –

HELEN (*firmly*): Keep still! Father will have to give me the money. He *must*. I mean to have a talk with him tonight. Nothing will change my determination. I mean to go. I'm sick of this life of scrape and screw – this narrow hemmed-in existence. I've had enough of it.

ANN: But suppose Father can't give you the money?

HELEN: There's no suppose in it. The bit of money Grandfather left for us has so far been used to further Cyril's interests *only*. We three girls haven't had a penny of it. Cyril must go to Oxford – Cyril must belong to a fashionable club

– Cyril must have a good tailor – he must keep up appearances – he must play the gentleman. Well, I don't grudge it to the Apple, but the time has come when *I* need help, consideration, money, and I mean to have it. (*All through this speech she has been fitting the bodice, pinning and adjusting in true dressmaker style.*)

ANN: When did you make up your mind to this? It's very sudden, isn't it?

HELEN: Very. This afternoon.

ANN: But why? How?

HELEN: I had a – I had words with Mr Dean. He annoyed me. I threw something at him – a ruler I think it was – I don't know exactly, anyway I put on my things, and walked out of the office there and then. I can't go back. I've got to do something. Canada's best. It's farthest away. (*Crosses to table.*)

ANN (*listening breathlessly*): You threw – a ruler – at Mr Dean? Mr –? Ellie! Nigel Dean, Father's *chief*! Oh, what will Father say?

HELEN (*pinning at shoulder*): I don't think Father's likely to hear about it.

ANN: Not? (*A pause.*) What was Mr Dean doing in your office anyway?

HELEN (*meaningly*): Ah! (*Fitting again.*)

ANN: How did he annoy you?

HELEN: He kissed me.

ANN (*shocked*): Ellie! (*Turns sharply and screams.*) Oh!

HELEN: I told you to keep still. (*Picks out pin.*)

ANN: What an awful man. How dare he!

HELEN (*smiling*): He's not awful at all. That's the worst of it. He's rather nice.

ANN (*aghast*): But he's nearly as old as Father.

HELEN: Says he's forty-five.

ANN: And he's married!

HELEN (*laughing ironically*): Poor Ann! It's easily seen you haven't been a typist in a city office. You're so unsophisticated. (*Leans her head down an instant on ANN'S shoulder.*) It's my own fault, I suppose. I'm cursed with some sort of

attraction for that kind of man.

ANN (*after a little pause*): Poor Ellie. It's awful to think that such a vile man should be father's chief. How could he treat you so! He always seemed such a friend of the family. (*HELEN looks at her steadily.*) Perhaps he didn't *mean* anything. Don't you think he might have, – well, – just felt sorry for you somehow? (*HELEN smiles.*) He's always been particularly nice to you, hasn't he?

HELEN: Always.

ANN: Perhaps he only called at the office to see how you were getting on. After all it was through him speaking for you that Mr Thatcher gave you the post. Wasn't it?

HELEN: Yes.

ANN (*cheering her*): Then it's not half as bad as you imagine, Ellie. I see it quite clearly. He called because he was interested in you, – he thought you looked overworked, – you are, you know. I've noticed it myself, and seeing the lines under you eyes, he felt sorry for you, – so sorry that –

HELEN (*interrupting with a burst of laughter*): That he offered me anything, anything I wanted in the whole world.

ANN: Really? Ah, he meant it kindly you see.

HELEN: He did (*with intensity*): He is very generous, very thoughtful, very understanding.

ANN: And so fond of father.

HELEN (*not heeding*): So concerned about my happiness . . . so anxious to lighten the burden . . . to make things easy –

HELEN *sinks down at table full of thought.*

ANN: He must be a real dear! A trump I call him. Don't you think so? (*HELEN does not answer. A pause.*) I hope you did not hurt him with the ruler? (*No answer.*) It was rather unkind of you, don't you think? (*No answer.*) (*Struggling to get out of bodice, but cannot.*) I must say I think you're rather foolish to go flying off to Canada just because Mr Dean gave you a *fatherly* kiss. I do really. At his age it's rather a compliment than anything else, – and to throw up your billet, and annoy Father by asking for money, and make Mother miserable, and upset us all by having to answer all sorts of questions about you, – all because, – (*Struggling.*) Unpin me, Ellie, I can't get out of the thing. (*Comes centre to* HELEN.)

HELEN *rouses herself and undoes pins.*

HELEN: One, two, three, four, five! I'm so sorry. Five years to wait for a husband. I ought to have been more considerate.

ANN (*taking it off finally*): I don't mind that. All I care about is to see you sensible and happy. (*Sees clock.*) Dear, dear, the time I've wasted! I must go and put the kettle on. And Cyril's dining out this evening and wants his shoes cleaned. And I've Mother's cap to do up, and all the – (*Knock heard.*) Who's that? Thought this would happen if I tried it on –

Knocking repeated. ANN *hurries into her things.*

HELEN (*rising wearily*): I'll go.

ANN: No, don't you bother. Just fasten me up. (*Double knock.*) Good gracious, how awful, dear, dear! Haven't you done? do be quick. Where's my belt? (*Bustles about.*)

HELEN *goes to the door right and as she opens it* CYRIL *comes in. He is a dapper conceited youth of twenty-three. The sort of superior bank clerk type. Very well dressed, rather overdressed in fact. His hair is shiny and sleek; he wears a large buttonhole, fawn doeskin gloves, smart socks and immaculate shoes.*

CYRIL: What are you girls thinking about? Father's been knocking for the last ten minutes. Says the lock's stuck – but that's rot – my key opened it right enough, when I came along.

HELEN *seats herself again at chair right of table.*

ANN: I'm so sorry, Cyril. It's my fault.

CYRIL: I'd advise you to take some tea in, to appease him. He's got his chief in there with him.

ANN: }
HELEN: } Nigel Dean?

CYRIL: Yes. There must be something good in the wind. The Governor's all over him.

ANN (*looking at* HELEN *but speaking to* CYRIL): But how strange of Mr Dean to come here. (*Goes into kitchen.*)

CYRIL *smooths his hair at the glass, straightens his tie, and when perfectly approving of his appearance, throws himself full length on the sofa.*

CYRIL: Oh well, I can't stand the man. Thinks a jolly sight too much of himself. Conceit's a thing I bar. (*Stretches himself, yawns.*)

HELEN *sits at table thinking.* ANN *busy in kitchen preparing tea. Clatter of cups, etc, heard.*

What a beastly noise you're making in there, Ann.

ANN: I'm so sorry. (*Nervously watching* HELEN.) I – I shan't be a minute now.

CYRIL (*knocking off* HELEN'S *hat which is in his way on the sofa*): What the deuce is this?

HELEN: My only hat when you're done with it.

CYRIL: Shouldn't leave your things kicking around. Must teach you girls a few things. Look at the mess this room's in. There's never a decent corner in the house I can ask anyone into.

HELEN (*who has rescued her hat and is restoring it*): Why ask then? I don't suppose anyone's dying for that honour.

CYRIL: That shows all you know.

HELEN: Your friends can't be over particular then.

CYRIL: Why not?

HELEN: Need you ask? Look at yourself.

CYRIL (*sitting up*): What's wrong with me?

HELEN: You've the manners of a potboy.

CYRIL (*enraged*): Manners of a – well I'm –

ANN *comes in with tray.*

ANN: Oh please don't quarrel. Can't you

see Ellie has a headache? – Cyril do let her alone.

CYRIL: Let her alone? I've done nothing. She's been saying the most brutal things I ever heard, – finding fault with my manners, as though hers were so perfect. (*Shrugging.*) Manners! Wants me to model myself on the young men she comes in contact with perhaps? Fifteenth rate fellows earning their paltry twenty-five bob a week, – manners indeed! A miserable typewriting girl to prate about manners, ha, ha! That's funny, damn funny!

HELEN (*flaring up*): Typewriting girl! You *would* turn up your nose, it's what one expects of you. You think it's degrading for a girl to work in an office, you and father with your high and mighty notions of woman's sphere, and all that bosh! You'd like me to be a cipher in the house like Mother or sit at home like Ann, wearing my fingers to the bone over the housework, slaving for your comfort, with never a sixpenny piece in my pocket but for what you, in your magnanimity choose to bestow. Yes, that's your idea of how a girl ought to live. But because I choose to earn a decent living you do nothing but sneer!

CYRIL *attempts to interrupt, but* HELEN *goes on heatedly.* ANN *meanwhile makes futile attempts to pacify both. She has the tray in her hands and goes from one to the other.*

ANN: He didn't mean to sneer, Ellie, did you Cyril? He only said –

HELEN: If you think it's degrading to be a typist, perhaps you'll find me something better to do? Something more to your aesthetic taste? Do you think it's fun to sit stewing in a city office for hours and hours, at the beck and call of small-minded, self-satisfied men like yourself? That's where the degradation comes in. The work's all right. I don't mind the work, but it's the fact of having to knuckle under to the very men I wouldn't even wipe my boots on in the ordinary course of things, that's degrading. It's men like you, that make office work degrading to girls like me.

CYRIL (*curious*): Serve you right if you don't like it. Who asked you to go to work? Whose fault is it if you are

treated like – like you deserve to be?

HELEN: Whose fault indeed? Yours! Everything's yours. You've been spoiled and pampered and given into, since the day you were born. Everything's been sacrificed for you, and for what? I wouldn't mind if you were worth it, but you're not, you're just a selfish conceited jackanapes, and that's all we've been sacrificed for!

ANN: Oh don't shout like this, – please don't! Father will hear you. Oh! (*Sees her efforts are futile, goes up, stops at door.*) Well, do stop till I open the door, please.

CYRIL: Sacrificed? What damn nonsense.

ANN: Cyril!

CYRIL: Well, it's enough to make a fellow swear to have a girl ragging him like this, though she is only a sister, I've done nothing. Why's she got her knife into me?

ANN: She doesn't mean it, she's out of sorts. Let her alone. If you'll only be quiet for a few minutes it will all come right. Ellie, I wish you'd go and lie down. Do like a dear.

HELEN: Oh shut up Ann.

A pause. CYRIL *goes back to the glass and tidies himself up.* ANN *waits a moment then goes to door right.* HELEN *looks up to see if* CYRIL *makes any attempt to open it, but he makes no movement.*

ANN: It would be so awful if Mr Dean had heard you.

HELEN *rises and opens door for* ANN, *with an expression of utter contempt for* CYRIL *on her face.*

Why did you bother, Ellie dear? thanks so much. Now promise me you won't –

HELEN: There's the gentleman for you! and no mistake. Manners if you like!

CYRIL: You'd like me to cavort round you all day like a circus horse perhaps?

HELEN: Don't flatter yourself. You've neither the brains nor the beauty of a circus horse.

ANN (*just going out*): Do wait till the door is shut, please!

Exit.

CYRIL *kicks the fireirons savagely. A pause.* HELEN *goes back to table, gives a deep sigh, and picks up work.* CYRIL *lights another cigar. Looks round at her once or twice, and is about to speak, but changes his mind each time. In reality he is a little afraid of her.* HELEN *puts down work and collects hat, gloves, etc., goes to door, looks out.* DEAN'S *voice heard off:* 'Ah yes, just so, just so –' HELEN *re-enters quickly and reseats herself. She has seen that the other door is open, so will not go upstairs. She goes back to armchair.* CYRIL *calms down, throws himself full length on sofa, smacks rather savagely at the cushions. He smokes away in silence a few minutes.*

ANN *re-enters.*

ANN: Ellie, Mr Dean's asking for you.

HELEN: Let him ask. I don't want to see him.

ANN: But Father told me to tell you –

HELEN: I'm not going, that's the long and short of it.

ANN (*changes the subject forcibly. Goes to* CYRIL *and pats his head*): It's been a tiring day, Cyril, hasn't it?

CYRIL: It's jolly hard luck on a fellow just when he's feeling particularly fit, to have a girl jump down his throat for nothing. It makes him feel a bit –

HELEN: Sick. Naturally.

CYRIL *starts up.* ANN *quiets him. He turns to her, ignoring* HELEN.

CYRIL: Thought I'd give you girls a treat by getting home early. I was feeling as fit as a fiddle. I had something to tell you, something interesting – and suddenly Helen goes for me like a bull at a gate.

HELEN: No. Like a terrier at a rat. You need well shaking.

CYRIL *is about to explode again but* ANN *restrains him.*

ANN: It's only her fun, Cyril. Don't take any notice. What is the something interesting you were going to tell us?

CYRIL: It will be a great surprise. (*Stops.*) Have you cleaned my shoes?

ANN: Yes, yes, go on.

CYRIL: Put the links in my dress shirt? I'm going out early.

ANN: I'll have everything ready for you dear. Now do tell me.

CYRIL (*condescendingly*): You're not at all a bad sort, Ann. I know you'll wish me luck anyway.

ANN *nods.*

Well, here goes. I'm thinking of getting married.

Both girls exclaim in surprise. They look at one another a moment, then ANN *shakes him by the hand.*

ANN: No? Really? How exciting. Who to?

HELEN: Poor girl!

CYRIL: What?

HELEN: No. My mistake. I meant rich girl, of course.

CYRIL: How did you guess?

HELEN: What has she done to deserve it?

ANN: Anyone we know?

CYRIL: No, no, – no third-rate suburban miss for me, thanks.

ANN: But what are you going to marry on?

HELEN: Her money, of course.

CYRIL (*furious*): I've stood enough of this, Helen, and I'm full up. If you can't keep a civil tongue in your head perhaps you'll hold it altogether, or I'll – (*Picks up something to throw at her.*)

HELEN: Temper! Temper! It's in the family, you see, Ann.

ANN: You really are awful, you two. Ellie, what is the matter?

HELEN (*roaring with laughter*): He takes himself in such deadly earnest.

ANN: Tell us all about it – when did it happen? The engagement, I mean.

CYRIL (*putting himself tidy at mirror*): Oh, it hasn't exactly happened yet. But it will pretty soon – perhaps this very evening.

HELEN: Remember the adage. Pride, etc. Look out for stray pieces of banana skin.

CYRIL (*contemptuously*): Vulgarian.

ANN: Do go on dear.

CYRIL: Not unless Helen shuts up.

HELEN: All right. I can't help it though, you're so funny. (*Crosses to table and sits right chair.*)

CYRIL (*continuing, very self-importantly*): It depends of course whether she'll have me, but I don't think there's much doubt about that. Only seeing the inequality of our pecuniary positions it is only fair that I shouldn't ask her until I'm able to offer her – well, something worth having.

HELEN: Yourself, for instance.

CYRIL (*ignoring her*): Any other course would be hardly honourable. Consequently I am going to buy a partnership –

ANN: You? How?

HELEN *turns round aghast.*

CYRIL: Oh, easily managed. I've had a talk with the Governor. It's all but settled.

HELEN: Is it?

CYRIL: There's that nest egg of grandfather's it's time it was put to some practical purpose.

HELEN: What's left of it.

CYRIL: There's really no need for me to discuss the matter with you girls at all. Father, as sole trustee, may spend it as he thinks fit, but I am inclined to let you know what is being done in the interest of all concerned.

HELEN: Just as well, considering it is ours as much as yours.

CYRIL: Quite so. Well, the important point is that my future should be considered.

HELEN: Naturally. Your future is the only thing that matters. Being a son. (*Quotes.*) 'Where the apple reddens never pry.' (*Laughs a little bitterly.*)

CYRIL: I don't understand.

HELEN: You wouldn't. Go on. Only there's no Eden to lose in this case. (*Sighs.*)

CYRIL: I'll need several hundred pounds. It's a great chance, a favour almost. But it's worth it. And with such good prospects my future father-in-law can't withhold his consent. Later on I can buy a still larger interest.

ANN: But I don't understand where the money is coming from?

CYRIL (*loftily*): Girls don't understand these things, it's done by mortgage. Father's estate, what he'll leave, by and by, do you see? And with the money already in hand –

HELEN (*rises. Blazing*): Part of that money is ours – it belongs to us girls, it belongs to me, and I'm going to have my share now, at once. (CYRIL *stares at her thunderstruck.*) Of course you're surprised, but you'll have to get used to it. I've thrown up my job, I'm going to Canada next week, and I want my share. Don't you dare talk to father until I've done with him, don't dare let him keep my share from me, or there'll be trouble, worse, much worse, a scandal, do you hear? (*Going to him.*) I want £100 before another week is out, so for once you and your prospects don't count, see? (*Crosses back to the table.*)

CYRIL: Are you going dotty?

ANN: No, no, it's true, Cyril. Ellie must have some money, you must help her to it.

CYRIL: Money? What does she want with money? What's all this bunkum – this talk about Canada.

HELEN: It's this. I'm going with the Arnotts next week. There are sure to be openings there, and there are none here. I'll find work to do, only I need money to start, for my passage for clothes, I must have it, I will!

CYRIL (*crosses to her. Sneering*): So my career is to be jeopardised by a wild cat scheme of yours? For your pleasure, your amusement? It's abominable. The most selfish thing I ever heard.

HELEN: Selfish? Because I'm trying to go straight? Trying to help myself, to fight my way? Selfish? And what are you?

CYRIL (*stamping about, his hands in his pockets. Cross back right*): It's confounded cheek, I think, for you to suggest such a thing. My chances are to be flung to the winds, I suppose, my whole future ruined on your account.

Very nice, I must say!

ANN (*coming centre*): Perhaps something can be arranged. It does seem such a pity that –

CYRIL (*walks about blazing with rage*): Just as everything was carefully planned out. Just as I had got over the worry, the difficulty, when not only my happiness, but hers, the girl I love –

ANN: Poor boy!

CYRIL (*continues*): Her happiness is to be ignored, by Jove! It's more than a fellow can stand.

HELEN: And what about my happiness? My future? My chances?

CYRIL: Girls don't want chances. They only want husbands. If you'd stay at home like a decent young woman, some decent man might want to marry you, but while you prefer –

HELEN: I don't want your decent husband. I want a little pleasure, a glimpse of life, a taste of the joy of living, a few pence in my pocket, my rights as an individual –

Voice off calling 'Ann, Ann!'

ANN (*running off*): Yes father, I'm coming.

Exit.

CYRIL: Rights as an individual! Bosh! Twaddle! What you really want is a good hiding, and bread and water for a week.

ANN (*anxiously*): It's for you, Ellie, Father wants you, that is –

HELEN: What for?

ANN: It's Mr Dean wants to speak to you about something.

HELEN (*tossing her head*): Let him want. I shan't come.

ANN: But father says – it's – it's important.

HELEN: I don't care what it is. Tell him I won't.

CYRIL: Shan't. Won't. Nice behaviour I must say. I'll have to teach you a little obedience, a little discipline, I can see. (*Going to door.*) See if I don't.

Exit.

ANN: Ellie! whatever can Mr Dean want with you? I wonder if he's told father?

HELEN: Not likely.

CYRIL (*opens door preceding* NIGEL DEAN): She's here, Sir. Will you come in. Helen, here's Mr Dean. Ann, take some shaving water up to my room. I'm just going to have a few minutes business talk with Father. (*Looking meaningly at* HELEN.)

ANN *shakes hands with* NIGEL, *goes into kitchen, looking nervously at* HELEN. CYRIL *chuckles at* HELEN'S *discomfiture. She remains at table left pretending to sew, but in reality trembling with excitement.* DEAN *is a tall, good looking man. He has a large patch of sticking plaster on his forehead. He stands right quite composedly, as though knowing himself master of the situation.*

Manners! Helen, offer Mr Dean a chair. He's come to give you a talking to, to oblige Father. Perhaps you'll listen to him. Aren't you going to offer him a seat?

HELEN *bites her lips to control herself.*

DEAN: Thanks. Don't trouble.

CYRIL: Must apologise for her, she doesn't know any better. Excuse me, won't you?

DEAN: Certainly, certainly.

Exit CYRIL *very pleased with himself. Exit* ANN *after* CYRIL *with shaving water.*

A pause. HELEN *does not look up. She controls her emotions with utmost difficulty.*

You're surprised to see me? (*She does not move.*) Come come, let's have it out. I've been talking to your father –

HELEN: Throwing dust in his eyes, you mean.

DEAN: If you like, yes. I've spoken about you –

HELEN (*looks up, sees plaster on his forehead, gives an exclamation of horror*): Oh! (*Tears start to her eyes.*) Your forehead.

DEAN: What's the matter? This? Oh, its

nothing. It doesn't even throb any more.

HELEN (*weakly*): I didn't mean to – to hurt – I'm sorry.

DEAN (*lightly*): Not at all. I deserved it. Don't let's talk about that. I want to put things right.

HELEN (*sullenly*): They're quite right as they are, thank you. I'm not going back to the office any more. I'm going abroad.

DEAN: Abroad? Where? When?

HELEN: That's my business. (*Sits.*)

DEAN: Pardon me. It's mine. (*Sits.*) Mr Thatcher gave you the post on my recommendation. I'm responsible for you, as it were. I've already made it all right with the head clerk about today, and you'll find no difficultues in the way when you return to the office in the morning.

HELEN (*struggling with her tears*): I'm not going back.

DEAN (*softening his tone*): Yes you are, Helen. (*Rising and going up to centre.*) You are. You must. I've spoken to your father about you, I've been reconciling him to the fact that work is good for you – that a girl like you needs occupation. (*During this comes above table.*)

HELEN: Occupation? It's freedom I want.

DEAN (*very low*): Freedom? You know what your answer was when I offered you that. (*She draws in her breath.*) You thought it brutal of me. So it was. But I'd like to give you a good time. No good looking girl ought to fight for a living. I've told you this over and over again. Do you suppose I don't understand? I'd like to take you abroad, anywhere you please, show you how to enjoy life, let you revel in pretty things, buy you new hats enough to turn your head, take you to dances, theatres,

HELEN: You've said all this before.

DEAN: I know. But I mean it. (*Comes down left of table.*) Well, you won't have it. Of course, quite right if you don't care for me enough. It's my misfortune that I'm married, but there you are. I'm not a villain in a melodrama. I'm a reasonable human being, I'm willing to give you what you want, and you won't take it. Can't be

helped. I won't worry you. I'll let you alone, that's all. (*He waits for her to speak. She keeps her head turned from him. He looks nervously towards the door once or twice, then continues.*) I've done the next best thing I can think of. I've been to your father –

HELEN: About – me?

DEAN: Among other things, yes. It appears he's in some difficulty over a sum of money for –

HELEN: The Apple?

DEAN (*smiles*): Well yes, the Apple? H'm, it's rather a case of another apple, don't you think? But I'm afraid I'm an indifferent Eve, and you're no Adam at all. (*She smiles in spite of herself.*) Ah! that's better. (*Sitting right of table.*) Now, let's make it up. I've promised to see your father through his difficulty – help him –

HELEN (*quickly*): With money? (*He nods, she stamps her foot.*) I won't have it. It's scandalous, it's vile of you. It's buying my silence. I won't keep it. I'll make a clean breast of everything, I'll tell Father the truth, and though I'll get all blame, at least he'll see you as you really are.

DEAN (*sits quite composedly*): Do just as you think best. I don't wish to come between you and that conscience of yours. It's a pretty conscience. I admire it. But remember what it will mean. Your Father will have to look out for another billet, his self-respect will force him to, and billets are not so easy to find at his time of life. Then again Cyril's chances won't be worth that! (*Snaps his fingers.*) he won't have a sixpence to scratch himself with, and the girl's father won't hear of the match – and as for all you girls – well, is the prospect attractive?

HELEN *watches him with quivering lips.*

HELEN (*under her breath*): I don't care, I don't care.

DEAN: Yes you do, Helen, and you know it. Now think what will happen if you're sensible. Cyril helped to a good match, which will set him on his feet commercially – and for yourself –

HELEN (*between her teeth*): Never mind about me.

DEAN: Oh, but I must. You're the crux of the whole concern. I'll keep out of the way till you've forgotten this little episode – unless you'll let me take you about a bit as usual – a luncheon, a theatre, now and again.

HELEN: Never, never!

DEAN: Nonsense. You'd never have had any pleasure at all if it hadn't been for me. You've said so again and again.

HELEN: That was different. I thought of you as a friend of the family, I liked you, I never dreamed –

DEAN: That I'd want to kiss you? I had no right, but I couldn't help it. It's your own fault, you're too good looking.

HELEN (*impatient*): I wish you'd go. I've quite made up my mind. (*She moves to centre.*)

DEAN: Not yet. (*Rises.*) Not for a minute or so. (*Going to HELEN centre.*) I want you to tell me something. (*She comes down.*) Was it the – the kiss you objected to – or the principle?

HELEN (*looking at him a moment taken aback*): How – how can you! (*Bursts into tears. Comes down to the armchair and sits.*)

DEAN (*coming to HELEN and placing his hands on her shoulders*): Hush, hush. That's all I want to know. (*Pause. He moves down left.*)

HELEN (*fights with herself, then begins in a low hysterical voice*): I – I always blamed girls – who – who had experiences like this. I've always been so scornful. We've talked things over, compared notes, hundreds of times. I've always rebelled so against the lot of the millions of office girls like myself, felt so sorry for their dull drab lives, the hopeless monotone of their existence. We women have such a few years to be young, hardly as many as can be counted on the fingers, we ought to enjoy those few years at any rate to the full, it's our right. We long for a little amusement, we snatch at a little fun when it offers, it's natural. A little admiration – even a little flirting helps to kill the tedium of the day – that's why I've let you take me about –trusting

you – never realising until – (*Pulls herself up with a jerk and raises her hand to her face.*)

DEAN (*listening with knitted brow, coming to HELEN and placing his hand on hers, half compassionate, half impatient*): You'll have forgotten all about it in a week.

HELEN: Never, never. (*Crosses to fireplace right.*) That's what a man can't understand. It means nothing to him. But with a girl, like me – it's – it's like losing something that's best in her. Something she can *never get back*.

DEAN (*shakes his head indulgently*): Come, come Helen, a kiss isn't worth the upheaval of a home, is it? (*She looks at him fixedly without speaking, he watches her.*) Think, think what it will mean to Cyril –

HELEN (*knitting her brows*): The Apple again!

ANN *enters anxiously, after obviously giving warning at the door.*

ANN: I do hope nothing has boiled over – please excuse me, won't you? (*Looks at HELEN then goes into the kitchen and closes the door.*)

DEAN (*coming up*): I must be getting along. What have you decided? (*HELEN crosses him and sits right of table. He holds out his hand. She does not take it.*) You aren't going to treat me like an enemy are you?

HELEN: Do you think you deserve to be a – a friend?

DEAN: Most certainly. Try me. (*She shakes her head.*) Ah well, you know best. (*Moving to the door.*) Goodbye. (*CYRIL opens the door just as he gets there.*) Ah, Cyril, I've administered the lecture your Father wished, and I must say I congratulate you on your sister. You should be proud of her, she has character *and* common sense, a rare combination – and that common sense of hers will be more helpful to you than you imagine. (*With meaning.*) Well, (*Turns.*) Goodbye again.

Exit CYRIL and returns at 'till tomorrow, Helen' with DEAN'S hat and stick.

Till tomorrow, Helen.

HELEN (*shakes her head quickly, but controls the impulse to contradict him. He waits a moment. Then she says almost inaudibly*): Goodbye.

CYRIL *holds door open.*

CYRIL: If you care to wait a moment – Ann will call a hansom.

DEAN: Thanks, I'll walk a bit.

DEAN *and* CYRIL *go out.*

ANN (*comes right of the table, whispering*): Well Ellie dear, what did he say? Who got the best of the argument?

HELEN (*tossing the dress over and turning the handle of the machine savagely*): Who do you think? The Apple of course!

ANN *stirs the contents of the saucepan with vigour expressive of her complete satisfaction.* HELEN *continues sewing with tears streaming down her cheeks.*

Curtain.

OTHER PLAYS

There were other plays which the League produced and which have not been reprinted here. Cicely Hamilton's *A Pageant of Great Women* was an immense success at suffrage gatherings as one after another a procession of great women (often played by great women) paraded across the stage and marked women's achievements. Gertrude Vaughan also contributed *The Woman with the Pack*; a sketch in four scenes and two tableaux, to the pageant-type theatre: Vera Wentworth added *An Allegory* to the repertoire of the League and struck a blow for experimental theatre. *The Better Half* was written by Alison Garland, and *The Reforming of Augustus*, written by Irene Rutherford McLeod, was produced in January 1910 at the Rehearsal Theatre, London. There are probably many more, but all these plays help to remind us that early in the twentieth century there was a thriving women's political theatre. We have a long way to go today if we are to reach such heights again.

Dale Spender